GANDHIAN SOCIAL WORK

Gandhian Social Work

Sarat C. Joshi

AKANSHA PUBLISHING HOUSE
NEW DELHI - 110 002 (INDIA)

AKANSHA PUBLISHING HOUSE
4649/21-B, Ansari Road
Daryaganj, New Delhi - 110 002
E-mail: ektabooks@yahoo.com
Phones: 011-23263193, 09435116718
visit us: www.akanshapublishinghouse.com

Gandhian Social Work

First Published, 2009

ISBN 978-81-8370-164-8

PRINTED IN INDIA

Published by Akansha Publishing House, New Delhi - 2 and Printed at Capital Offset Press, Delhi.

Contents

Preface

> "If we wish to be just judges of all things, let us first persuade ourselves of this: that there is not one of us without faults."
>
> —*Seneca*

Gandhiji and Gandhism need no introduction. Popularly regarded as 'Father of the Nation' in India, in fact, Gandhi belonged to entire mankind and not to India alone. His doctrines and views on society, education development, economy, dalits (Harijans), adivasis (tribals), women, children, polity and peace etc. may still prove guiding to the tumultous present day world. Concerns for conflict resolution, globalization of economy and need for democratism of quality life places Gandhi in a unique place. Currently we observe, a renewed interest in Mahatma Gandhi. Political leaders, social activists, environmentalists, educators, development economists, social scientists and even cinema makers besides a host of others are innovatively advocating and practicising Gandhian ideas to address the changing scenario of the world amicably.

His concept of Sarvodaya, moral approach to economics, doctrine of trusteeship, ideas on village and cottage industries, Khadi programme, social welfare etc. are still relevant, though some of his ideas are considered outdated, like we can not return to an ideal (utopian) village of Gandhi in the present age.

Since past few years many books have come on Gandhi besides a plethora of already available literature by different scholars from India and abroad.

So far as Gandhian Social work (better social service) is concerned, it is being taught to learners/trainees and included in the curriculum at various universities and schools of social work.

Here in this book we have collated the judiciously selected readings with particular emphasis on social work perspective. The valuable information is gathered under the following headings—Introduction; Social Work Perspective of Gandhian Philosophy; Gandhi on Dalits; Social Work Through Harijan Sevak Sangh; Gandhi and the Tribals; Gandhian Scheme of Education; Gandhian Thought on Social Problems; Gandhi on Women: Lesson for Social Workers; Gandhi and Village Economy; Glossary and bibliography are added features.

Definitely, this will serve the purpose of students pursuing their MSW, MPhil, PhD etc., academics, social activists, NGOs and voluntary organisations besides general readers.

In preparing this book we have consulted various works on Gandhi by many learned scholars of repute. I owe a deep sense of gratitude to all those for liberally borrowing their views. I am also grateful to my seniors and colleagues at NIPCCD for their guidance, moral support and assistance. I acknowledge my thankfulness to my family members, especially to my wife and children for their inspiration and also for providing congenial environment at home to pursue my research and literary activities. I am also thankful to my publisher for materializing this work in superb way.

Constructive criticism and comments are welcome from all quarters to enhance its utility and quality of information.

—Sarat C. Joshi

1

Introduction

India has had great legacy of social work since very ancient times. With the passage of time during different phases the nature and form of social work changed, somewhat. Broadly, this can be grouped in the following five periods.

1. Social Work during Community Living Era

The prevalence of the system of *Yajna, Havana* and *Dana* in the Ancient Indian Society clearly unravels that it was a society in which all the members used to participate in productive enterprise and fruits of their collective labour used to be distributed among them. *Yajna* was the sum total of activities of the community for the sustenance of its life and reproduction. It was a collective form of labour without any division. *Havana* was the distribution of the daily proceeds of collective labour among the individual members who used to consume them. *Dana* was the distribution of goods acquired in war among the people in the community at festive times. (R.R. Shastri, pp. 2-3)

2. Charity Era

In course of time the proceeds of war came to be accepted as the private property of the conqueror and distribution among people was not obligatory on his part; instead its distribution became a private affair dependent on his sweet-will. Undoubtedly, such a deed was considered to be virtuous. It has been rightly maintained by Raja Ram Shastri, "when private property and class-rule arose, *Dana* was converted from an instrument of social insurance to privilege of ruling class." During the period of Upnishads concepts of *'Ishtas'* and *'Apurtas'* become socially accepted. *Ishtas* were individual goods performed by philanthropic and economically well-off persons; and *Apurtas* were social goods in the form of wells, rest-houses *etc.* performed by the people for the general welfare of the public. The concept of individual charity as an instrument of repayment of various types of *Rinas* (debts) also became widely accepted during this period. During the period of Smritis, psychological help in the form of *'Tatwa Jnana'* and *'Atma Jnana'*, in addition to material assistance, was also made available to the people in order to improve their social functioning. Buddhists and Jains also continued the tradition of helping people in different manners.

With the advent of Mughal period when society was being ruled in accordance with the principles of Islam, concepts of *Zakat* and *Khairat* were socially accepted. Muslims in India have been giving two and-a-half per cent of their earnings compulsorily as alms to the poor and needy by way of *Zakat*. Similarly they have been giving alms to the indigents and destitutes by way of *Khairat* which has been voluntary. The practice of building mosques with attached schools has been quite prevalent in Muslim community in India. Many Muslim rulers has been deeply interested in the organisation of social services for the needy.

3. Religious Reform Period

During British colonial regime, the Charter Act of 1813 made provision for promotion of education and approved the work of the Christian missionaries. Emphasis laid on spreading the Western education, recognition of the dedicated and devoted service rendered by the Christian Missionaries and impact of christianity were significantly instrumental in bringing about a change in the outlook of Indians, especially towards the then prevalent social evils like *Sati* and social prohibition on widow remarriage. Though Serampore Missionaries in Bengal had started a crusade against the evil of *Sati*, it was Raja Rammohun Roy who gave a fillip to the movement and fervently continued it till 1929 when Lord Bentinck declared the practice of *Sati* as illegal, and persons participating in its observance as punishable in the criminal court.

Despite his devotion to the cause of abolition of *Sati*, Rammohun Roy was never in favour of proselytisation and social legislation as a means of eradicating social evils; instead he wanted this to be done through enlightened public opinion which he thought could be built up through education for the spread of which he established a number of educational institutions. He vehemently advocated the abolition of caste distinctions. He started the Atmiya Samaj in 1815 which later on in 1828 grew into *Brahmo Samaj* which advocated 'the one Brahm without a second'. Dwarkanath Tagore, Devendranath Tagore and Keshub Chander Sen as followers could successfully carry on the activities of the Brahmo Samaj. The direction of the Brahmo Samaj that 'no object, animate or inanimate, that has been or is or shall hereafter become or be recognised as an object of worship by any man or set of men, shall be reviled or slightingly or contemptuously spoken of, or alluded to, either in preaching or praying or in the hymns or other modes of worship that may be delivered or used' was followed by Prarthnaa Samaj which was established in Bombay by Dr. R. C. Bhandarkar and Justice M. G. Ranade. *Paramhans Sabha* was organised in Maharashtra in 1849 for bringing about caste reforms. Ishwar Chandra Vidyasagar was the first to launch a movement against the prohibition of widow remarriage by establishing that it was not in contravention to the preachings of Hindu scriptures, and it was a result of his incessant efforts, especially of an appeal made by him to the Government in 1855, that the Hindu Widow Remarriage Act was passed in 1856, despite the tooth and nail opposition of orthodox Hindus. In order to bring about an improvement in the condition of women, Ishwar Chandra Vidyasagar started a large scale programme of girls' education.

Similarly Justice Ranade, pursuing the cause of widow remarriage, formed Widow Marriage Association in 1861 which was aimed at promotion of widow remarriage. He also helped in the foundation of the *Sarvajanik Sabha* in 1870.

The Marriage Act providing for remarriage and inter-caste and inter-community marriages and laying stress on monogany and attainment of majority was passed in 1872. The Act aimed at validating marriages between persons of different castes and communities performed without observance of religions rites and rituals.

Dayanand Saraswati established *Arya Samaj* in 1875, which was against idolatory, caste and child marriage. It was in favour of widow remarriage and abolition of untouchability. It counteracted the work of proselytisation that was being vigorously undertaken by christian missionaries by permitting the readmission of converts from Hinduism. It led to the establishment of a chain of educational institutions in the country. As an Arya Samaji Lala Lajpat Rai started many types of social services and Swami Shradhanand undertook the work of the uplift of the depressed classes.

Sir Syed Ahmad Khan who had strong faith in English education founded the Anglo-Mohammedan College at Aligarh in 1875 which later on developed into renowned Aligarh Muslim University. He also founded the *Mohammedan Social Reformer* as a means of publishing his views.

Further, in 1882, *Arya Mahila Samaj* was organised by Pandia Ramabai, an Indian Christian missionary, with a view to improving the condition of women.

The Age of Consent Act was passed in 1891 at the instance of Bombay Parsi, Behramji M. Malabari. The Theosophical Society which was founded by Madame Blavatsky and Colonel Olcott in Madras did not play any significant role till 1893 when it was joined by Mrs. Annie Besant who actively involved herself in exposing the Hindu doctrines and defending the rites and rituals. She also established a Central Hindu College at Benaras.

Swami Vivekanand founded the Ramkrishna Mission in 1897 which has been rendering varied kinds of services which according to the Karm Yoga preached by Swami Vivekanand, enjoy the place of highest sanction. The Mission has been seriously pursuing 'service of the needy' as its motto. Swami Vivekanand was of the view that to serve the afflicted and brethren was an act of greater religiosity than praying in the temple. He advocated that steadfast devotion to the selfless service of the people was the most pious act.

4. Secular Reforms Era of Social Services

Secular reform movement gathered momentum in the 1880's though it had already started in Bombay in 1830's when professors of the Elphistone Institute, Bombay took much active interest in the spread of education through voluntary efforts. Under the leadership of Bal Gangadhar Shastri Jambhekar, first alumnus of the Institute, it organised classes for women, persuaded the orthodox Hindus to permit the proselytisation of converts and simplified marital rites and rituals. A literary and scientific society was founded by the students of the Institute in 1849, which acted as a torch-bearer and in course of time could organise several associations with which Shapurji Bengali and Dadabhai Naoroji were actively associated.

Inspired by the activities of these societies, Karsondas Mulji started the work of providing relief from licentious priesthood and widow remarriage. In order to bring about radical change in the outlook of orthodox Hindus, Mulji himself got married to a widow and thus demonstrated that he practised what he preached. Allen Octavian Hume perceived the need of the formation of an all-India platform for analysing the problems that were being faced by the workers engaged in the task of rendering social services to the people throughout the country in 1880. However, on the suggestion extended by Lord Dufferin, Hume agreed to include politics also within the scope of the activities of the organisation which he wanted to establish; and this resulted in the formation of the Indian National Congress, a socio-political organisation.

But since the Congress became dominated with political issues, with social affairs having been relegated to the background, in 1887 Justice M.G. Ranade organised the Indian Social Conference which used to hold its session along with that of the Congress.

The Conference was successful in creating enlightened public opinion in the country. However, it could not take proper cognisance of the local problems that were confronting the different parts of the country. After the death of Ranade, Chandrawarkar assumed its leadership. He widened the scope of the Conference by enlisting the participation of members of various castes having their association with different kinds of social service organisations; and thus a wide variety of subjects including solution of the communal problems, organisation of workers' education, formation of women's association and removal of caste disparities were brought within its scope.

In 1897, Sri Shankarn Nair made a demand of a strictly secular government from the Congress President. A women's session was held in 1904 at the instance of the Bombay group of social reformers and it was this seed which after a period of twenty three years grew into the All India Women's Conference. Gopal Krishna Gokhale who had deep interest in the work of social services, established the Servants of India Society in 1905. The Society laid stress on activities relating to multisided development of society, especially of the depressed classes. G.K. Deodhar, N.M. Joshi, V.S. Srinivasa Shastri and Pandit H. N. Kunzru were actively associated with the activities of the society. Considerably commendable work in the field of child welfare was done by the Bombay Presidency Infant Welfare Society under the leadership of Lady Cowasji Jahangir and Sir Mangal Das Mehta, and by the society for the Protection of Children in Western Asia under the direction of Sir Rustam and Lady Masani. The atmosphere that was created as a result of these works led to the enactment of the Children's Act in various states in nineteen twenties.

A miraculous event, Mahatma Gandhi appeared on the Indian public scene in 1920. Gandhiji was interested in the welfare of everyone and propounded the concept of '*Sarvodaya*' (welfare of all). Instead of the greatest good of the greatest number, he stressed on the 'greatest good of all' which inevitably includes the greatest good of the greatest number. He wanted *Ram Rajya*—a society where the values of love prevail and the conditions necessary for all-round development of the individual exist. He gave a constructive programme which was aimed at welfare of Harijans, welfare of aboriginals, rural welfare, welfare of women and children, welfare of the handicapped, educational reforms, national integration and prohibition.

He believed in the purity of both ends and means, insisted on putting the service above the self, and emphasised devotion and dedication to the cause of service emanating from the core of heart. And since, "the very genesis of the profession of social work implies a spirit of dedication," Gandhiji was a true social worker.

Mention must be made here of Har Bilas Sharda whose efforts culminated in 1929 into the enactment of the Sarda Act fixing the minimum age of marriage at 14 for girls and 18 for boys; of Pandit Madan Mohan Malviya and Seth Jamnalal Bajaj who got the temple entry thrown open for all castes; and of Narayan Guru of Travenncore who propounded the doctrine of 'one religion, one God', launched a vigorous campaign for the temple entry of untouchables and built up a net-work of temples and educational institutions.

5. Modern Period

As a remarkable phenomenon, history of organisation of formal training for workers engaged in the work of social welfare dates back to nineteen twenties when Social Service League, Bombay started, without any intention to prepare its trainee volunteers to take up any paid assignment, formal orientation training courses which consisted of lectures on selected subjects, agency visits and supervised field experience. However, the year 1936 marks a water-shed in the history of professional social work training in this country. There was a major departure in 1936 when with the intention of developing trained worker adequately equipped with knowledge and skills required for taking up various types of paid jobs in different fields of social welfare, the Trustees of the Sir Dorabji Tata Trust, under the advice of Dr. Clifford Manshardt of the American Marathi Mission, established Sir Dorabji Tata Graduate School of Social Work which was based on the pattern of schools of social work in the United States of America.

The school undoubtedly had certain distinctive characteristic features, especially in respect of social work intervention in industrial organisations with a view to ameliorating the appalling conditions of workers in this country. The School sponsored a series of lectures on "Some Social Services of the Government of Bombay" and it was as a result of the finalisation of major areas of Government responsibility that there was a change in the functions of the State which accepted that promotion of social welfare was its prime concern. This was the only institution providing professional training of social work till 1947 when the country became independent. After Independence, Kashi Vidyapith, Varanasi, and College of Social Service, Gujarat Vidyapith, Ahmedabad were established in 1947, followed by Delhi School of Social Work in 1948, and Department of Social Work, Lucknow University in 1949. Constitution of India was adopted in 1950 which clearly enunciated that the State shall strive to promote the welfare of people; provided for abolition of untouchability and all sorts of discrimination based on religion, race, caste, sex and place of birth, and guaranteed special protection to children, minorities, Scheduled Castes, Scheduled Tribes and other weaker sections.

Thus 1950 has been a watershed in the history of assumption of responsibility for social welfare by the state in this country. In 1951 started the era of planned development, which resulted in the creation of a large number of social welfare jobs. In 1953 was created the Central Social Welfare Board by the Government of India with a view to promoting and strengthening the voluntary efforts in the field of social welfare. Consequently, need of the trained manpower to handle various types of responsibilities in the field of social welfare became aggravated; and in order to cater to this need, the number of social work institutions providing professional training with the object of preparing trained social welfare manpower started swelling. Some of them are still providing Bachelor's degree; and some Certificate in social work as well as Bachelor's degree. Some of them are giving Post-Graduate Diploma. Most of them are conducting courses leading to Master's degree in Social Work. About 1/3rd of them are having Ph.D. courses. And many of them have made provision for the pursuit of research work leading to the highest research degree of D. Litt. in Social Work.

With an increase in the number of training institutions and trained professional social workers, professional organisations have also come up to evolve and maintain standards of professional service and to protect and promote the interest of their members. The idea of forming an association of trained social workers was mooted for the first time by late Dr. J.M. Kumarappa in 1951 at the time of the annual session of the Indian Conference of Social Work held at Jamshedpur; and thus the Indian Association of the Alumni of the Schools of Social Work was formed. It used to hold its separate meeting of trained social workers at the time of the annual meeting of the India Conference of Social Work.

It was not a very well-knit organisation; instead, it was an informal organisation and its members had very loose ties with it. In 1959-60, the Association was reactivised. In 1961 its constitution was revised and in September, 1962 it was registered and its chapters were opened in different parts of the country. It was affiliated to International Federation of Social Workers. In 1964, its name was changed to Indian Association of Trained Social Workers. The Association is pledged to promote and maintain the professional standard of social work and to safeguard the interests of trained social workers in this country. It organises seminars and symposia on a wide variety of subjects related to social welfare and also brings out a quarterly journal titled *Social Work Forum*. It is also taking up some action programmes, especially during emergencies. It has its branches at Mumbai,

Chandigarh, Coimbatore, Delhi, Dharwar, Hyderabad, Indore, Jamshedpur, Chennai, Nagpur, Trivandrum, Udaipur, Varanasi, Lucknow and Waltair.

The Association of Schools of Social Work in India was established in 1960 to act as a non-official organisation in the field of social work education.

The Association is concerned with

(i) laying down and maintaining proper standards in professional social work education and promoting the profession on scientific lines;

(ii) providing opportunity to faculty members to meet and exchange their ideas;

(iii) arranging seminars and refresher courses for faculty members;

(iv) encouraging and co-ordinating researches and promoting publication of literature on different subjects relating to social work;

(v) disseminating information pertaining to social work education and

(vi) working as a national forum on all matters concerning social work education.

It has been organising seminars and workshops relating to social work theory and practice; offering consultancy services and providing information of developments in the field of social work education throughout the world. It has its affiliations with international organisations like International Association of Schools of Social Work and regional organisations like Asian Regional Association of Social Work. In addition to these national level organisations, there are associations of trained social workers functioning at the level of School of Social Work. For example, Lucknow University Social Work Alumni Association has been looking after the interests of its alumni and publishing *Lucknow University Journal of Social Work.*

It is thus self-evident that we have been gradually heading onwards professionalisation in Social Work. However, a word of caution need be pronounced here because social workers in this country are lacking in sincere devotion and dedication to the cause of suffering humanity, forgetting their professional ethics, becoming too much after money and keeping self-interest even above the service which is the basis of their existence. In such a situation a danger has developed that the profession may degenerate into an occupation and wide-spread distrust regarding its utility may develop in the minds of the people. It is, therefore, the need of the hour that professional social workers must become cautious and disciplined, and render their services to the people from the core of heart—not merely for the sake of financial returns but for their commitment to serve—by applying the scientific knowledge and technical skills which they learn in course of their professional education, and thus must demonstrate that their work is undoubtedly superior to that of lay workers so that the confidence of the public in their utility may be further strengthened, and the profession may grow and develop in an atmosphere conducive to its functioning.

II

SOCIAL WORK: CHANGING FASHIONS

Notably in the West, particulary in U.K., concern for human welfare, and the giving of service, has a long history, and is an integral part of Christian and humanistic philosophies. Welfare work has developed through the church, voluntary social services and the Poor Law. But social work as a skilled and paid occupation, for which there is training, is a twentieth-century phenomenon. To write about changing fashions is therefore to look at the growth of social work over the last few decades, and particularly at the period since 1945. In the first part the development of social work is traced, noting, prior to 1971, its organisational fragmentation, and the extent to which social workers were employed in non-social work agencies. The second part considers a few of the dilemmas of social work practice, and draws attention to the potential for conflict between the values of the social worker and the priorities of the administrator.

Social Work Organisation

Here we donot intend to write a brief history of social work, but to look at a number of salient points which have led to the establishment of social work in social services departments. The process has not been a direct one. In a rather indistinct way it is possible to see something of a pendulum swing, from large general-purpose agencies to small specialised ones and back again. Another path traces social work from its tentative beginnings as an appendage to wider services through to fragmented independence and then unification.

In the first phase, that is the move to small specialised groups with developing independence, it may be worth picking out four themes.

1. Decline and Fall of The Poor Law

In so far as the state had any involvement in welfare work towards the end of the last century, it was to be found in a growing policy of protecting children and the general provisions of the Poor Law. The gradual demolition of the Poor Law spanned several decades until its final demise in paragraph 1 of the 1948 National Assistance Act, and although there was little social work to be siphoned off from it, the decline and discrediting of the only broadly-based public welfare organisation during the 1920s and 1930s deprived the growing social work profession of a natural home. The views and pressures expressed in the Minority Report of the 1905-9 Poor Law Commission played a part in this process, and Donnison draws attention to an interesting organisational aspect of the changes. 'In their plan for the break-up of the Poor Law, the Webbs-those inveterate technocrats — proposed a wholesale eviction of laymen ... and their replacement by paid professional and administrative staff...'

Social work may have been threatened with homelessness, but the basis is set for a new group of employees. Donnison quotes a contemporary critical commentator suggesting that we shall all become 'sheep shepherded by an enormous and apparently irresponsible bureaucracy. . . .'

2. *Fragmented Growth*

As Poor Law provisions diminished so new services emerged, narrower in individual scope, though cumulatively broader, and culminating in the intensive developments of the period immediately after 1945. In the earlier period, before and during the Second World War, there was growth in state activity in housing, health and education. In each of these services it was realised that some of the users were in situations needing more than the regular arrangements of the agency. Some tenants of council housing had difficulty keeping up with rent because of a whole range of upsets outside the direct concern of housing. Health and education services found the same difficulty that some of the problems presented to them reflected more than just health or educational issues, and indeed that the health and educational aspects could not be tackled properly without taking wider concerns into account. This, of course, is a highly simplified version of what happened, but it serves to illustrate why the major social services looked around for help with the personal welfare needs of their customers, and finding nothing, began to employ their own staff for the purpose. The result was that much of the early growth of social work took place under the sponsorship and control of other kinds of service organisation, with the continuing absence of a unified base.

3. *Social Work Specialisations*

The picture offered to the Labour Government in 1945 was of personal welfare services either in process of development or well established, under a variety of controlling organisations. Housing and education welfare are examples of the former; hospital social work an example of the latter. Indeed, psychiatric social work was already showing as the elite service of the profession. There is no indication that the government gave any consideration to a unified social work service at that time, or had moved from the preference of the Webbs for specialised services to meet special needs. In any event, housing, health and education kept their welfare workers, the new National Assistance Board employed some of its own, the link between health and social work was extended into community provisions for the mentally ill (under the control of a medical officer of health), and the needs of children, the handicapped and the elderly were met by the introduction of two new local authority departments: Children's and Welfare.

This set the pattern for post-war growth of social work organisation, fragmented, partly under social work control, partly an appendage to the major social services. The 1960s saw expertise and efficiency on narrow fronts, but also poor co-ordination and large sectors of unmet needs. Crucially from the organisational point of view, social workers were in small clusters, whether running their own system or responsible to a larger agency. Not only was there no opportunity to gain experience of management in agencies of the size of social services departments, but also social work practice reached high standards of effectiveness in small compact organisations.[4]

4. Children's Services

While all these developments were in progress there was widespread sensitivity to the particular needs of children, and looking back it is clear that many welfare initiatives were either in the direct interests of children or an extension of attitudes and provisions which had first been justified in relation to children. Perhaps the most obvious example of this is the emergence of the probation service out of concern for children who were being subjected to the full severity of the penal services.

The second phase, or, if one is using the pendulum idea, the return swing, starts with the situation in the 1960s. Looking back, this decade is seen as a period of growing self-confidence inside social work ranks, a golden age for some workers, a time when we approached a high quality of performance in narrow sectors of provision. At the time people seemed less aware of the strengths of the services, more bothered by the weaknesses. The important weaknesses were only organisational in part, a recognition of the unevenness of provisions stemming from the administrative fragmentation, the islands of privileged services in an ocean of unattended needs. Centrally, however, the forward-looking focus of the period was on the need for some guiding theme for social work, a relevant sense of direction to draw together the diversity of social work functions into an effective problem-solving profession. The theme was found in the family; the family as the basic unit of society, as the natural network of personal aspirations and dependencies, as the necessary framework for self-sufficiency, as the desired setting of all right-thinking people, and therefore as the appropriate focus for social work services.

Social work skills and practices could be equated with the reality of personal needs, the stigmatised nature of client status could be overcome, and social work could come of age, given this acknowledgement of the central place of the family. By the time the Seebohm Committee was set up it was clear that a unified focus for social work was closely linked to the issue of whether or not there should be administrative unification. Indeed, these years saw the gradual decline and increasing criticism of the concept of the family as a sufficiently accurate reflection of social circumstances, in proportion to the growing identification of the family as justification for large-scale service organisations.

It is illuminating to look back to the work of the Seebohm Committee and to parliamentary debates leading up to the passage of the Social Services Act, 1970, to see what were the main issues of the time, what objectives the reorganisation was intended to attain, and what sort of development was envisaged for social work by the architects of social services departments.

The plan to replace a fragmented system by a unified one was the corner stone of the proposals. Unifying the organisational structure was seen as consistent with and in natural sequence to the way social needs were understood at that time. Fragmentation 'clearly militates against the prospect of helping a family or individual with multiple needs through a single social worker or through a close-knit professional team with comprehensive responsibilities'. Neither the Seebohm Committee nor the members of Parliament debating the Local Authority Social Services Bill queried the validity of the family as an adequate unifying factor of personal needs. Indeed, there is little evidence of any detailed analysis of the assumptions made about family-based needs, whether their scope or nature. 'Its [the Committee's] references to needs, though forceful, are secondary to a discussion of administration....' It was asserted that a larger organisation would offer an improved equation between needs and services, but beyond some specific concern about whether or not certain small agencies should be included (child guidance is an example), the matter was not taken up. There was little investigation of the interlocking span of human needs, the possible relationships between personal needs of a kind traditionally helped by social work, and education, housing, social security or health, although the potential difficulties were taken up in parliamentary debates.

The crucial arguments for unification were internalised and organisational. Fragmentation was seen as leading to buck-passing, sometimes with a view to getting rid of burdensome clients, and sometimes through disagreement or lack of clarity about the extent of departmental responsibilities. The theme of accountability is a recurring one. 'Placing responsibility for social care on one committee and department would provide a clear and evident system of accountability.' Good co-ordination becomes the anticipated virtue of the new unified agency. Under the old system 'co-ordination between the various agencies is considered deficient, with the result that families and individuals have received less than adequate service and scarce resources have been inefficiently deployed'. 'But an integrated social services department will ease problems of collaboration as the number of separate units involved is reduced, and above all as issues of responsibility are clarified.'

It also had simple faith in the greater efficiency of the larger organisation — 'For instance, an organisation with a total budget of £100, 000 should be able to do more with it than the sum of the achievements of two separate organisations, each with £50, 000' — as did parliamentary speakers—'One of the great advantages of the Seebohm system is that it provides for the maximum efficiency and humanity in the use of our resources.' One of the ways in which this greater efficiency would show itself would be in the quantity of work to be undertaken, but improved quality and more adaptability were other factors. Quality was seen particularly as related to staffing: 'a reformed organisation should, in part, be Justified by its greater ability to increase the recruitment and training of appropriate staff, and to deploy them better'. Adaptability was anticipated from the increased freedom with which the personal social services could move resources around: 'An integrated social services department will impose fewer boundaries and require less arbitrary classification of problems.'

The arguments of the Seebohm Committee were overwhelming. There were important flaws in the fragmented system, and social services departments would give a better service to more people — easier access, a broad span of services to be obtained with greater convenience and efficiency than before, and a more coherent relationship between people's needs and the organisation of the services.

Social Work Practice

The development of social work in the last few decades has, in part, been a quantitative one. Despite restrictions on public spending, the general pattern has been one of an increasing employment (and training) of social workers. Any changes in the practice of social work therefore have to be set in the context of almost continuous pressure to recruit more staff and catch up with basic training. There are several important components of this context. Social workers have not been recruited solely for social work practice; many of the better qualified and more experienced ones have moved into the newly created administrative establishments of social services departments. Teams of frontline staff are frequently made up of new people, a mixture of trained and untrained, although the proportion of qualified staff in social services area teams is increasing, there is a dearth of experience. In short, front-line teams have not had that combination of theoretical preparation and experience which would enable them to play as dominant a part in the late 1970s as their predecessors played in the 1960s, in the development of social work practice.

The pressure on recruitment derives from the need to fill a host of new posts (mostly administrative and advisory) and meet a growing level and range of demand for services. Concern with these pressures, with getting social services departments through their birth pangs and handling new service legislation, has inevitably detracted from closer consideration of the way practice is moving. There has been little room for experiment (at least that which has no primary concern with improving efficiency), and much of the discussion of new ideas has been frustratingly confined to the classroom rather than getting a detailed airing in the agencies.

Within this rather limiting setting it is possible to identify a number of developmental themes.

1. Specialist or Generalist

Earlier in this chapter we noted how the organisation of social work had first taken solid root in a variety of separate agencies, sometimes as autonomous groups, more often within a larger structure. Out of its growing strength and through recognition of the range of its potential had come pressure for organisational merger and unification. Social services departments brought together, with a view to integration, the diversity of practices and specialisations that had hitherto characterised social work services. This movement finds a close parallel within social work theory, beginning with a strongly based cluster of specialisations and then growing (or is it reacting?) out of narrow boundaries into the idea of general purpose work.

The theoretical justification of each approach is clear and compelling. Much of the criticism of the old Poor Law (in the Minority Report) concerned its lack of sensitivity towards the nature of people's problems, and it came to be felt (e.g. by the Webbs) that a proper response to personal and family need was to analyse it down to its component parts and then provide an expert service to meet each of the parts. By having specialised agencies and staff it would be possible to offer an expertise relevant to each aspect of the need. For the social worker, specialisation offered scope for developing a depth of knowledge and experience in a chosen field, which in turn could be translated into a particularly skilled service to the customer.

Further, a specialised social worker was in a better position to join a team of allied specialists, and it is in the health care team setting that this view reached its greatest fulfilment. Certainly in the period after the end of the Second World War it was noted that specialisations needed to be knitted together to form a coherent whole, but this could be achieved by such devices as the case conference, without any basic restructuring. Some inefficiencies (multi-visiting by social workers of a single client is the commonly stated example) were tolerated, and some clients were passed around from office to office, but this was accepted as an unavoidable snag to what was otherwise a highly competent service. Specialisation guaranteed quality.

The case for general purpose social work follows similar lines to that for a general purpose organisation. The basis of social work should be its appropriateness to the needs of the client, seeing the client as a whole, not in disconnected segments. Of course there were outer frontiers for social work which would recognise the areas of concern of other services-health, housing, education and income maintenance — but within those frontiers there should be no demarcations.

The client would get the best treatment if a single social worker was involved and had a comprehensive picture of what was needed. Further, the concept of the general purpose social worker allowed a desirable move away from a problem-based categorisation of society, towards a patch system, the linking of a single worker with a geographically and socially defined community. It has been an important tenet at government level for many years that categorising people by their problems invited stigmatisation, whereas a community approach could minimise it: this belief has been widely accepted amongst social workers. Recognition was given to the difficulties of being an expert, all-round social worker, or having knowledge and experience across wide stretches of activity, but it was argued that most circumstances did not require specialist services, and where these were necessary, a specialist adviser could be consulted.

With the benefit of hindsight it seems that neither of these polar positions is satisfactory, and there has been some move back to specialisation. However, it will be argued later that an issue which began with social workers debating ways of giving service, has now been taken over as an administrative concern with more efficient ways of deploying resources and with keeping control over professional staff.

2. Social Work or Social Service?

One of the reasons put forward by senior staff of social services departments as to why social worker cannot take responsibility for such things as their method of practice, is that the task of the departments is only partially a social work one. It involves many other things — residential and day care provisions, home helps, domiciliary services which do not need the efforts of a social worker, and so forth — and the responsibility of management is to take a balanced overview.

This is a reasonable argument in the sense that it is important to ensure that national objectives are being met, but it begs some questions. Is it inevitably the task of the administration to take the overview, rather than that of the range of service personnel in the agency? Is administration just another segment of a social services department, with its own sectional interests? Does a concern to meet national objectives necessarily involve interference in professional matters about methods of treatment? What has happened to the vision of a single organisation representing, first and foremost, the interest of a unified social work service? Is there any better prospect for effective social work in the context of general social services than in liaison, with, say, health services? Chapter 6 looks further at the relationship of social work to social service.

A point being implied here is that whatever the original intentions, social services departments no longer represent unified social work, but exercise control over and denial of many forms of social work. This is illustrated by noting the context of the remaining themes to be discussed in this section. The theoretical platform, or philosophical base, for social work practice, and the way social workers identify the focus for their intervention, have both been and remain of great importance to new social workers contemplating their future. Yet they are issues of limited relevance to agencies who see their staff as employees first and social workers second. Staff of social services departments can hold whatever views they wish, as long as they practise within boundaries set out by the agency. This has tended to undermine philosophies and to limit flexibility of intervention.

3. *Focus of Social Work Intervention*

This has had its impact on the focus of social work intervention. Is the client to be seen uniquely and alone, in a small group, or as part of a community programme? In part the identification in social work method of case, group and community work has been to suggest different approaches to meeting a client's needs. For some workers they have been mutually exclusive alternatives, for others a range of interventions which can operate together in the client's interest. However, there is a further dimension to be considered once intervention extends beyond the individual client. Up to that point the limit of treatment objectives is to help the client to adjust to the surrounding community, its laws, conventions and expectations. Beyond it, the focus of intervention can move to the community itself, to trying to provide an environment suited to the individual. Flexibility can be demanded of social institutions as well as of individuals. But whatever the strength of this development within social worker ranks, it has little place as yet in practice. It creates too much complexity, and too many dangers. Can social services departments be flexible enough to allow their social work staff a range of approaches to clients, or will they continue to use control mechanisms such as case allocation procedures to ensure uniformity? Can social services departments accept the possibility that the focus of action and pressure to change may not rest solely on the clients, but could extend to many of the organisations of society, including the social service agencies themselves?

Here tried to indicate the extent of changes in recent years in ideas about the organisation and practice of social work. These are, in themselves, sufficient to create real difficulties for social workers. Yet additionally these changes reflect uncertainties at a very basic level about the way services should be structured, and how their staff should operate. Given such changes and uncertainties, any group with a clear idea of how to proceed must be well placed to gain a strong position.

Coming to the case of India, here it is pertinent to note that Social Work is much sought-after profession, which have gathered momentum with emergence of a full crop of NGOs and voluntary organisations. With abundant fund-flows from various sources-state or otherwise--community development is being much emphasised.

Here in this book we will take Gandhian perspective of social work as main theme. All vital issues of the theme are portrayed in subsequent chapters.

REFERENCES

1. D. Donnison *et al. Social Policy and Administration Revisited*, revised edn. (Alen and Unwin, London, 1975), p. 21.
2. Department of Social Welfare, Ministry of Education and Social Welfare, Government of India, *Handbook on Social Welfare Statistics*. 1976, New Delhi, pp. 332-33.

3. HMSO, *Parliamentary Debates, Standing Committees* (Vol. 11, session 1969-70), Committee B, sitting 1, column 5.
4. Home Office, *Report of the Committee on Children and Young Persons* (HMSO, London, 1960), Cmnd. 1191.
5. J.K. Whittaker, *Social Treatment* (Aldine, Chicago, 1974).
6. Marshall, *Social Policy*, Chapter 5, especially pp. 74-6.
7. P. Seed, *The Expansion of Social Work in Britain* (Routledge and Kegan Paul, London, 1973).
8. P. Boss, *Social Policy and the Young Delinquent* (Routledge and Kegan Paul, London, 1967), p. 30.
9. P. Corrigan and P. Leonard, *Social Work Practice Under Capitalism* (Macmillan, London, 1978), and P. Halmos, *The Personal and the Political* (Hutchison, London, 1978).
10. P. Townsend, *Sociology and Social Policy* (Penguin Books, Harmondsworth, 1976), p. 202.
11. R. Fletcher, *The Family and Marriage* (Penguin Books, Harmondsworth, 1962).
12. Shastri, Raja Ram, *Social Work Tradition in India*. Welfare Forum and Research Organisation, Varanasi, 1966, pp. 2-3.
13. *The Family and the Young Offender* (HMSO, London, 1965). Cmnd. 2742.
14. T. Hancock Nunn, *The Minority Report* (National Poor Law Reform Association, undated), p. 10.
15. Wadia, A. R., "Ethical and Spiritual Values in the Practice of Social Work", in A. R. Wadia (ed.), *History and Philosophy of Social Work in India*, Allied Publishers Private Limited, Bombay, 1961, p. 15.

2

Social Work Perspective of Gandhian Philosophy

Today there is being observed fresh-interest in Mahatma Gandhi and Gandhian philosophy. A multifaceted wide spectrum person, Gandhi is judged by different people and different scholars according to their own point of view. As such often a question is being raised—What was Mahatma Gandhi? Was he a social worker, sociologist, political leader or just a spiritualist?

It is very difficult to assess and answer. Gandhi did not present his views in a systematic manner to make them theories. His views also changed from time to time as he had dynamic personality. He did not want to theorise only, he also experimented with all his views practically. He tried to present Indian point of view of various problems. He has himself written "People say that my views have changed and today what I say is quite different from what I had said years ago. Reality is this that the circumstances have changed. I am the some but my words and actions are according to circumstances. The atmosphere in which I live gets developed and due to my self being a `Satyagrahi' I react to that." (M.K. Gandhi, *Young India*)

Mahatma Gandhi had said again and again that there is nothing like Gandhism. Nevertheless we see some continuous currents of thoughts in his various philosophical considerations. Today 'the Collected Works of Mahatma Gandhi are available in 100 volumes. Much has also been written about him. We see the undercurrent of some basic values in all his works in spite of his claim of not propounding any ism (Gandhism). Some common stands can be traced in his thoughts such as:

1. The concept of spiritualisation of every worldly affair whether it is politics, property or power.
2. Use of Indian and Vedic philosophy to validate his thoughts.
3. The ideal of interdependence of mankind in spite of his views of self-reliance.
4. Disapproval of any formal or legal authority like police, court, government or even state whether it is Indian or foreign rule.
5. The concept of totality in every sphere specially for independence struggle. He felt that at independence struggle was not to be launched without social welfare, education and self-reliance programmes.

Coming to some most 'basic concepts' of Mahatma Gandhi, a student of Social Work should always remember that Gandhian thoughts are more relevant to social development than to social welfare. He has given us a new school of thought leading to social development which has detailed description of both means and ends.

On Religion and God

Religion for Gandhi was very broad and liberal. He has said "To me religion means truth and ahinsa or rather truth alone because truth includes ahinsa.... the students should be trained to cultivate the habit of understanding and appreciating the doctrines of various great religion of the world..... in this respect religion stands on the same footing as culture. Just preservation of one's own culture does not mean contempt for the others but requires assimilation of the best that there may be in all the other cultures, even so should be the case with religion."

His religious ideas were not revolutionary. He was quite traditional on certain matters. Answering Radhakrishnan's questions, he says plainly "My religion in Hinduism which for me is the religion of humanity and includes the best of all the religions known to me.... I often describe my religion as religion of Truth. Of late, instead of saying "God is Truth," I have been saying "truth is God" .... to be true to such religion one has to lose oneself in continuous and continuing service of all life. Realisation of truth is impossible without a complete merging of oneself in and identification with this limitless ocean of life. Hence, for me there is no escape from social service. In this scheme there is nothing low, nothing high. For all is one, though we seem to be many." (Gandhi quoted by R.N. Mukharjee)

It is quite obvious that his ideas are at times, too philosophical. His views are basically emotion based. He said "If I stop believing in God I would die at once." "God is love and truth for me. God is character and morality, God is fearlessness, God is light and a source of life. But He is not only this He is above all and beyond all. God is conscience. To the extent that He is atheism among atheist." (Gandhi quoted by Radhakrishnan, 1938)

Remarkably, due to his views about God and religion that he declined material world and material achievements. He was against cosumerism mainly because he wanted to promote the ideals of self denial, control of palate and control of animal passions. His philosophy about religion and God can be taken as the foundation of other philosophical considerations in his chain of thoughts.

On Ideal Society

Mahatma Gandhi had a clear and vivid dream about an ideal society (not utopian) as a social organisation. His ideal society was based on the following concepts.

(a) Ram Rajya

Basically Gandhiji has taken Ram Rajya as a rule of justice and social justice both. It will not be a rule of one emperor or one king. It would be a democratic state where extreme simplicity would prevail in education, medical treatment, agriculture, international relations and trade. Too much consumption and large scale production is against the spirit of Ram Rajya. He took 'Ram Rajya' as an idiom and not in the literal sense of it.

Mahatma Gandhi gave his own definition of Ram Rajya. He explained it as a moral based social system. It is apt to quote RN Mukherjee who explained Ramrajya would have minimum control of state. Everybody would be more concerned to his duties and less interest in the show of rights. This way every one in Ram Rajya would care for duties in place of rights, service in place of selfishness, sacrifice in place of rights, service in place of selfishness, sacrifice in place of possession, whether he is a part of masses of administration."

(b) Stateless Democracy

Gandhi took state as an organised and centralised form of violance. Mahatma Gandhiji took the idea of stateless democracy from Tolstoy. He felt that self reliance is the gist of independence though he thought that a loose type of state structure would be required at least for the time being because some criminal elements might be three and state is required to fight against them. What type of state like organisation they will have in this Utopian society? Answering to this Mahatma Gandhi has written at one place "I believe there is no use to ask such a question. If we will be working hard for such a society, slowly it would develop to some extent. Euclid had said that a line is without breadth but nobody could make such a line. Nobody will every make it but still progress is only possible when we keep the imaginary line in mind.... There is no stateless democracy in the whole world, if it is possibly built it may start from India."

Mahatma Gandhi said very clearly that the real meaning of *Swaraj* is to remain free from government control whether it is local or foreign. It is quite clear that Mahatma Gandhi was knowing that stateless democracy is rather impracticable. He was in favour of state having as small role as possible. To him state was a necessary evil. He was not in favour of state, therefore he was against police organisation, crime, punishment and even army.

In 1922 when he was himself in prison he prepared a scheme for jail reform. He had written in *Harijan* in 1940 "Every criminal is a diseased person and we should treat him in the same way." He further wrote "This (crime) is a symptom of diseased mind.... Haveli's (Jails) would not be required. A poor country like India cannot bear the expense of this type of prison."

(c) Swadeshi or Self-Reliance

Another pillar of Gandhian thought is his concept of self reliance or 'Swadeshi.' Swadeshi is usually identified with the use of khadi but it is not so. As Gandhiji has expressed "It does not mean merely the use of what is produced in one's own country. That meaning is certainly there in Swadeshi. But there is another meaning implied in it which is far greater and much more important. Swadeshi means reliance on one's own strength .... own strength means the strength of own body, own mind and own soul." He took vow that he would not use cloth made by foreign companies. He also associated self-reliance with Swaraj (independence). He had discussed "India cannot be free so long as Indian voluntarily encourages or tolerates the economic drain which has been going on for the past century and a half. If India could make a successful effort to stop that, she con gain Swaraj by that one act." In his views Swadeshi is a system of self-reliance which has social, economic and political aspects.

While discussing Swadeshi, Mahatma Gandhi went to another extent. He thought that trade within the country should also note be encouraged. People should use the things which are available nearby. Therefore he was in favour of cottage industries and not heavy industries. He also thought of maximum decentralisation of political power, economic resources and judicial system.

(d) Village Republic

Gandhiji believed that all the power should be decentralised. He was afraid that after independence even Indian rulers might become dictators therefore he was greatly concerned with the massive decentralisation of all the powers. More than India, he wanted to see village as a republic. He was against heavy industries and highly sophisticated means of production and communication because he wanted every village to be independent of the outside (other's) influence. He writes "My idea of village Swaraj is that it is a complete republic, independent of its neighbours of its own vital wants and yet interdependent for many others in which dependence is a necessity."

This is quite clear that he thought of village as a basic unit to democratic decentralisation of power. He was more concerned about the judicial system. He condemned the modern system courts, lawyers and police. He suggested a traditional manner of panchayat in place of British judicial system, "The government of the village will be conducted by a Panchayat of five persons annually elected by the adult villagers—male and female, possessing minimum prescribed qualifications. These will have all the authority and jurisdiction required..... this Panchayat will be the legislature, judiciary and executive combined to operate. Any village, can become such a republic today without much interference even from the present government." All these statements indicate that Mahatma Gandhi was not thinking of political freedom without participation of grassroots level citizens. He was very much interested in the revival of *Panchayat Raj System* which existed in India during ancient and medieval period, but was destroyed by British rule.

(e) Trusteeship Principle

Gandhiji was somewhat impressed by socialism but he tried to develop a union of capitalism and socialism. He was against the wide gap between rich and the poor. Socialism teaches that wealth should be snatched from the rich people can should be distributed equally but Mahatma Gandhi showed another path, as he has written "There is no other choice than between voluntary surrender and consequent acquisition of the real happiness of all on the one hand and on the other the impending chaos into which, if the capitalist does not wake up in times, awakened but ignorant famishing millions will plunge the country and which, not even the armed forces, that a powerful government can bring into play, can avert." (Gandhi quoted by J.D. Sethi, 1979)

Undoubtedly, trusteeship is most original among all the Gandhian thoughts. We do not see tradition of trusteeship in the history anywhere in the whole world. However, like Euclid's definition of a point he knew that absolute trusteeship is also unattainable. Not only this, Sethi has rightly pointed out "Trusteeship like other Gandhian concepts is not absolute but relative in space and time and to the need of the society. Nevertheless it remains an absolute ideal the full concept of which becomes clear as we reach near it." (J.D. Sethi, 1979)

In fact, concept of trusteeship has emerged due to three points i.e. non-violence, Swaraj and equality. They are interwoven. Like Marx Gandhiji was also against capitalism. He was in favour of abolishing it yet for him it was not the end which was important but means were equally or even more important. He says "If the state suppressed capitalism by violence it will be caught in coil of violance itself." (*Harijan, March* 31, 1946)

Practically, Gandhi wanted to use all societal resources or the masses but in this process rich would have to face anger and violence of the masses which will be against the spirit of this venture. Therefore, rich people should be persuaded to surrender their wealth voluntarily in the interest of the public. He was also interested in the related issues such as:

1. What will be the method of abolition?
2. Upto what extent would capitalism be eliminated?
3. What it is to be replaced by?

Certainly, the proper answer is, with the help of persuasion, capitalism would be replaced by the system of trusteeship which means owners of the means of production would still own them but will not use for their own profit. They will act as trustees and the profit will be used for public because everybody's (even capitalist's). Gandhi felt "Accumulation by private persons was impossible except through violent means. If doctrine of trusteeship is followed the poor masses will get rid of the selfish capitalist owner and equally selfish bureaucrat who runs nationalised industries. It is thrust or movement towards social self-management of industry whether privately or publicly owned." (Sethi, *op. cit.*, p. 147)

In fact, Gandhiji had given six principles for understanding the concept of Trusteeship:

1. It is based on the faith of human nature that human being are not selfish.
2. There should not be any private property.
3. Even then legislative regulation of ownership and use of wealth should be organised.
4. If would be state regulated ownership where wealth will not be used for any selfish motive.
5. Minimum and maximum wages should be fixed.
6. Production would be based on the need not on greed. (Gandhi quoted by Sethi)

The entire description makes us think that Mahatma Gandhi was keen to establish the system but he himself knew it was rather a bold step and it would lead to topsy-turvy change. Moreover it is based on persuasion and not compulsion, therefore, it will take very long to get implemented. It is not true if we say that trusteeship has not been experimented.

Vinobha Bhave and Jai Prakash Narayan in the form of *Bhoodan and Gram dan,* started it but it turned out to be a flop system. It is because Gandhi had assumed that rich people are so good that they will be persuaded easily and not resist to this great sacrifice. He also thought that trusteeship organisation will work on cooperative basis. They will work for fulfilling the needs, not for greed, and everybody would share the fruit of production and development.

In other theories of Gandhiji also we see that, Gandhiji was believing that every human being is a saint of Mahatma. Similar over confidence about the virtues of human being is visible in his other theories too. V. Jagannadham had said "His concept of trusteeship was a product of the inherited culture in India. It reflects his concern for fraternity rather than equality." (Jagannadham, *op. cit.*, p. 162)

As J.D. Sethi has raised some question on the doctrine of trusteeship, a brief description on his curiosity is given as follows:

1. Other economic systems aim at profit maximisation, revenue maximisation and net income maximisation. It is also having any single producible maximum?
2. Three is a confusion about the nature of market which could be competitive, monopolistic and oligarchic etc. Trusteeship is perhaps not following anyone of those models then what model would they follow.
3. The theory has no answer as to how will a trusteeship firm adjust to environment changes, change in demand, raw material and technology etc.
4. What will be the nature and degree of competition. What economic law will govern it.
5. It claims to end the conflict between worker and management thought it is very difficult but even if it comes true it is quite possible that both these parties exploit the consumers jointly. (Sethi, *op. cit.*, pp. 155-57)

Though we do not have answers for these questions but we imagine that Mahatma Gandhi thought of simple economy and not this type of highly sohphisticated economic system.

Basic Education Scheme (Nai Taleem)

Though himself product of British system of education Gandhi developed his own system of basic education and implemented it too, and he was very confident about the results.

He claims "I have given many things to India but this system of education together with its techniques is, I feel the best of them. I do not think I will have anything better to offer to the country."

In 1937 a council of all the famous educationist was organised. In this meeting held at Wardha he kept his proposal which was published in Harijan on 2.10.1937. It discussed some characteristics of "*Nai Taleem*" such as:

1. Seven years free and compulsory primary education.
2. Mother tongue as the medium of instruction.
3. Handicraft as the basis of education (which means learning through activity).
4. The ideal of self sufficiency in education.
5. The ideal of citizenship.
6. More emphasis upon freedom.
7. Based on non-violence.

Right from the very beginning people started criticising his scheme. The main criticism being:

1. It will make schools only a production centre.
2. Raw material will be wasted by the children.
3. Marketing the products would be another problem.
4. It will have too much emphasis on handicraft. It will narrow down student's vision only to a particular cottage industry.
5. Expectation from teachers is too much but they are not given due importance.

But Gandhiji was devoted to his idea of Basic Education. Only one month before his death in December 1947 he said that basic education "is based on truth and non-violence in individual and collective life. Education is that which gives true freedom, untruth and violence lead to bondage and can have no place in education."

In the real sense we can observe that basic education is also a part of his undercurrent philosophy of truth, non violence, less consumption, swadeshi (or self reliance), physical labour and cottage industries promotion.

The most significant point is the importance of primary education, which is still not recognised fully by the planners and policy makers.

Welfare and Development of Untouchables

One of the pioneers of social justice in our country, Gandhi's idea of equality and fraternity was not a lip service, he took a very bold step both theoretically and practically in the field of Harijan welfare.

It is significant to note here that Mahatma Gandhi and Dr. Ambedkar had a great disagreement in Round Table Conference in 1931 where Dr. Ambedkar pleaded that government should not take untouchable as a part and parcel of Hindu population. But Gandhiji opposed this idea and he thought that it would be a disgrace to Hindu community if untouchables formed their separate group. Mahatma Gandhi had a tendency to empathise with untouchable because he was "himself treated as untouchable on racial ground in South Africa. Gandhiji felt the gravity of caste segregation of Harijans in Hindu society and rebelled against this form of injustice vigorously."

Commenting on caste system he said" ... as it is practiced in Hinduism today is in my opinion a sin against God and man and is therefore, like a poison slowly getting into the very vitals of Hinduism... The sooner, therefore, it is ended, the better for Hinduism, the better for India, and perhaps better for mankind in general."

He renamed them as Harijan (children of God). Mahatma Gandhi was of the opinion that untouchability is not part of original Hinduism. Those who did not stop eating cow were perhaps called untouchables. But now scavengers should be considered not untouchables but protectors of humanity as he describes at one place. "Mother cleans the dirt of child, therefore, she is considered pure, a sister serving a patient picks up very smelly waste of the patient, we respect her. Then why those who are always cleaning excreta and keep us healthy should not be worshipped. Therefore, he wanted everyone to clean is own toilet so that he should not feel that this profession is inferior. Besides this, Mahatma Gandhi was always practicising equality with untouchables. He started institutions where Harijan cooks were appointed and Harijan students stayed with the caste Hindus though come of the donors opposed it very vehemently, but he continued his struggle fill he could guarantee equality for Harijans in the guideline of Indian constitution.

On Sarvodaya

While working as a lawyer in South Africa in 1904 his friend Mr. Polak gave Gandhiji a book written by Ruskin *'Unto this Last.'* Some teachings of the book were as follows:

1. That the good of individual is contained in the good of all.
2. That a lawyer's work has the same value as the barber's. All have the same right of earning their livelihood from their work.
3. That a life of labourer, that is the life of the filler of the soil and the handicraftsman, is the life worth living.

In 1904 itself Mahatma Gandhi practised Sarvodaya principles. His paper *Indian Opinion* started giving monthly allowance of £3.00 per head to all the workers irrespective of colour, nationality, qualification or status.

His belief on equality and on the principle of Sarvodya (good for all) persisted throughout his life. He was not in favour of majority rule rather he believed in total consensus. He used to say "Wipe every tear from every eye."

In the opinion of V.K.R.V. Rao "Sarvodaya the welfare of

all, is a classless society based on the destruction of the individuals who constitute the classes, a system of production that does not fall to make use of science and technology for creating an economy of abundance but does not in the process either kill individual initiative or freedom of development nor create a psychology of ceaseless striving for more and more of material goods, a system of distribution which will ensure a reasonable minimum income for all and, while not aiming at a universal equality of an arithmetical kind, will nevertheless ensure that all private property and talents beyond the minimum will be used as a trust for the public good and not for individual aggrandizement."

A careful analysis of this description reveals that Sarvodya includes the doctrine of trusteeship in it. Gandhism (if there is anything like that) is manifested in the fullest form in the theory of Sarvodaya. Let us see what are the components of Sarvodaya.

(a) Mahatma Gandhi believed that the country should be divided into small units of villages and towns. They will have their own Sarvodya programme because national level Sarvodya programmes is not possible.

(b) If people will reduce their needs then communities and villages will be more self sufficient. More consumption will lead to more production and all this may take us to colonialism and later on to war. Sarvodya wants production for need not for greed.

(c) Science and technology should not work for mass production it should work for small units. Small industries should be promoted in place of heavy industries.

(d) This social system of Sarvodya should be based on basic education theory of Mahatma Gandhi which revolves around physical labour and skill learning.

(e) In this system end would not justify the means. Means are equally or even more important. It is because ultimate achievement is not important in Gandhian approach but small achievement during the process are small targets for him. He has sometimes admitted that the desired goal might be imaginary like Euclid's point but struggling to achieve that is our aim in doing so we will achieve many other things and nearness to this imaginary point also.

We see that Mahatma Gandhi, who is known as a great political leader and freedom fighter, fought against Britishers because he found foreign rule unethical and unjust. He found it against 'good for all' According to him his *Sarvodya* United with *Satyagrah* can face and defeat exploitation and injustice. He rightly thought that exploitation cannot be the basis of god relationship. He was not against foreign rule only. He was against exploitation and corruption due to political power. Explaining this he wrote at one place. "There can be no living harmony between races and nations unless the main cause is removed namely exploitation of the weak by the strong. We must revise the interpretation of the so-called doctrine of the survival of the fittest.'

On Social Development

Gandhi had a strong feeling against modern civilisation based on industrial growth and development. Nehru's idea of public ownership could also not convince him. In 1940 he wrote "My own view is that the evil are inherent in industrialism and no amount of socialisation can eradicate them." In other words his idea of social development was much different from industrial and economic growth and development. His idea was constituted on:

1. Rural oriented development based on cottage industries.
2. Physical labour which was considered superior than mechanical labour.
3. Decentralisation of power which is inherent in that system.

4. Social justice and equitable distribution which is to be achieved but without violence.

Gandhi's disciple Ramachandran asked him. Are you against machinery Bapuji? Gandhi replied with a smile "How can I be when I know that even this body is a most delicate piece of machinery. The spinning wheel itself is a machine; a little tooth pick is a machine. What I object to is the craze for machinery, not machinery as such. The craze is for what they call labour saving machinery. Men go on saving labour till thousand are without work and thrown on the open street to die of starvation, I want to save time and labour, not for a fraction of mankind but for all... Today machinery merely helps a few to ride on the back of millions." (*Young India,* Nov. 13, 1924)

All his theories can be understood in totality not in isolation India has not adopted his approach barring giving some privilegs to cottage industries. It is because consumerism, mass production and profit making have their own advantages. Moreover, India has to compete with the rest of the world. She cannot remain isolated, he also felt that pauperism leads to moral degradation.

Therefore he wanted to have economic activities for fulfilling the needs. He had his own vision of economic development. Here it will not be irrelevant if we discuss the concepts of economic development according to Mahatma Gandhi. K.J. Charles had presented if in a nutshell. According to him the major tenets of Gandhian economics can be considered under the following heads.

1. Theory of happiness.
2. Limits of industrialisation.
3. The role of machinery.
4. Decentralisation.
5. Bread-labour.
6. Theory of Trusteeship. (1983, p. 94)

Gandhiji opines that happiness is the "deliberate and voluntary reduction of wants." This alone promotes real happiness. He was also in favour that "the means of production of elementary necessities of life remain in control of masses." (*Young India*, Nov. 15, 1928)

So far as limits of industrialisation are concerned Gandhi felt that industrialisation amounts to exploitation of underdeveloped countries industrialised countries. Moreover large scale methods of production would lead to mass unemployment specially in thickly populated countries like India. Not only this, the high cost investment will be beyond the reach of poor nations. Finally non renewable resources of the earth may even get exhausted because he felt that resources are enough for human needs but not for human greed. (Young India, Aug. 6, 1925)

Earlier Mahatma Gandhi was so much against machinery that he says "It represents a great sin. I cannot recall a single good point in connection with machinery but later he was moderate in this regard. He wrote "Mechanisation is good when the hands are too few for the work." Much later on October 5, 1945, he wrote to Nehru that his ideal village would have "railways, post and telegraph and the like." (Nehru, *op. cit.*, pp. 506-07)

Mahatma Gandhi has always propagated the importance of physical labour like Russian writer T.M. Bondaref and Tolstoy. He envisaged about simple village life based on village republic where people will be busy in agriculture and small scale industries. He has written in a letter to Nehru "My ideal village will contain intelligent human beings. They will not live in dirt and darkness as animals." He always felt that political and economic power will not be in the hands of few but it will be decentralised to the maximum extent.

Comming to trusteeship coming to though it may take as part of economic reforms but basically it is a pature of social development ideal. A famous disciple of Mahatma Gandhi has discussed trusteeship like this. "Trusteeship provides a means of transforming the present capitalist order of society into an equalitarian one. It gives no quarter to capitalism buyt gives the present owning class a chance of reforming itself. It is based on the faith that human nature is never beyond redemption." (Pyarelal in *Harijan*)

While examining Gandhian thoughts on economic reform and development we feel that Mahatma Gandhi is not as rigid as people think of him. Moreover, his economic thoughts were basically social thoughts. Consequently we cannot divide his thoughts in various components.

Remarkably, one fact that surprises the readers of Gandhian philosophy that is the validity of some thoughts. We may take them almost as a forecast in some cases specially in the case of exploitation caused by developed industrialised countries to poor and underdeveloped nations. His forecast is also valid in the case of non-renewable sources which may be exhausted due to capitalist greed. Today we know that chemical fertilisers are harmful to ozon layer but Gandhi and Vinoba always preached about natural manures, they gave the idea that we should not over cultivate.

The relevance of Gandhi today is a big question. In 1969 the noted historian Nihar Rajan Ray had remarked "The Gandhian way of life has been obliged to confine itself in a handful of workers in half a dozen voluntary organisations." But this idea is an underestimation of Gandhian philosophy. People like Vinoba Bhave started Bhoodan Gram dan and Jai Prakash Narayan started total revolution in Bihar. A.B. Singh has written ". . . .renewal of Gandhian social movements is most visible in the environment movement led by Baba Amte, Chandi Prasad Bhatt and Sunder Lal Bahuguna. In relying heavily on Gandhian method of hunger strike (*Bhookh Hartal*) the walking tour (*Padyatra*) and non violent protest *(Satyagraha)* these leaders have acknowledged their allegiance and debt to Gandhian thought and ideology."

There is no doubt that industrialisation, urbanisation and

westernisation are grabbing India today and Gandhian ideals are lagging behind. Gandhian dreams are unattended but by the side of the deep and wide ocean of modern industrialisation a narrow stream of Gandhian thoughts is also flowing. It is not correct to ay that Gandhism is non existent. Actually, not knowingly, many western thinkers had discussed Gandhian philosophies e.g. Nobel Laureate, Paul Samuelson has developed a concept of New which means New Economic Welfare (something more than just economic growth). He discussed "More growth can be a cancer, a malignancy. What we want is welfare."

It is felt that people do get convinced with Gandhian approach but it is very difficult to be followed. Denial of consumerism and extreme of simple life is perhaps not the dream of masses. Right now Indian masses are trapped by consumerism. But still many of us do realise the element of truth in Gandhian thoughts.

Modern Social Work and Gandhian Social Work

No doubt, it will be exaggeration if we claim that Gandhian philosophy has coloured professional social work a great deal. By and large they have remained as the banks of the same river which go together but do not meet. Nevertheless social work profession has got some peripheral influence from it. But current revival of Dandhiam has compelled society and social work to reconsider Gandhian Social Welfare Scheme.

Here we are describing main similarities and differences for a comparative study.

(a) Similarities

(1) First as far as the ultimate aim is concerned both Gandhian constructive worker and professional social worker, work to help people. They do not want to promote parasites in the society. They believe in self help and mutual help and not in charity.

(2) Both of them believe in training for social workers but professional social worker believes in formal

and structured training whereas Gandhian worker believes in less theoretical and more flexible training.

(3) Both of these categories of workers believe in social justice and distribution of societal resources on the basis of that. Both of them believe in social change and planning but professional social worker wants it in a scientific manner and Gandhian worker believe in the voluntary surrender of wealth from haves.

(4) They have an agreement on the issue that social welfare should be started in small groups. It may be a village or a community. They do not want to work on nation wide programmes. Though sometimes it is inevitable specially when they are working as planners and policy makers. This does not mean that global issues like disarmament, political exploitation, exite of refuges, violation of human rights and environmental preservation are not the concern of professional social workers or Gandhian constructive workers. Both of these tribes of social workers are interested in all these but when it comes to actual working they select small areas (may not be small issues).

(5) The approach of both of them is secular and without any discrimination of caste, colour, religion, religion and sex. They want to emphasise equality among all human beings.

(6) Both of them believe in the purity of means and they want to have every achievement with proper process.

(7) Both of them take individual as a focal point. In this way they are against socialism, they want to take individual as a unique unit of the society. Discussing the society of his dreams Gandhiji wrote "Life will not be a pyramid with the apex sustained by the bottom. But it will be an oceanic circle whose centre will be the individual always ready to perish for the

village the latter ready to perish for the circle of the villages till the last, the whole, becomes one life composed of individual .... sharing the majesty of the oceanic circle of which they are integral units." The views of professional social workers are also not so different. Professional social work also respects individualism a lot.

(8) Both of these types of workers believe in persuasion and not in compulsion. They believe that people should not be compelled to change. There should not be any drastic change.

(9) Both professional social worker and Gandhian constructive worker believe that social work can and should be a full time occupation. If needs total involvement of the worker. It should not be treated as a hobby.

(10) Practically three objectives of social work are restoration, provision of resources and prevention of social problem. Gandhian workers work on the same parameters through their priorities are some time different.

(11) Both of them use social action as a popular method. They believe in the democratic way of disagreement and agitation it can be a procession, dharna, strike, non-cooperation, *satyagraha,* even to the extent of sacrificing one's life. In the changing socio-political milieu social activism is more and more used. That is basically social action which is used by both the schools of thought.

(12) Both the approaches believe in team work. Help seekers may or may not be a team but helpers are usually working with a team. It may be a team of various type of helpers or various organisations and service agencies. Liaison with them is very important. Social workers and Gandhian constructive workers

take extra care that they should have a team behind them.

Major Differences

Now the main difference between a Gandhian social worker and professional social worker.

(1) Whereas professional social workers take social welfare work as a career, as a source of livelihood. They clearly distinguish between professional and personal life of the worker. Gandhian worker do not have this professional attitude. They believe in sacrifice and self-denial. They do not believe in distinct personal life of the worker.

(2) In professional social work client and worker relationship is professional and to the point, whereas Gandhian worker is just like a family member of the clients. He has tender and personal relationship with them.

(3) Gandhian social workers find a spiritual satisfaction in helping others. They do social service as a moral duty but professional social workers take it as an obligation for better and just social system.

(4) Activities introduced by Gandhian workers are not so innovative they work for popularising cottage industries, environment preservation activities and prohibition but professional social workers organise all sorts of programmes.

(5) Professional social workers are more scientific and systematic. They would like to collect complete information about any problem before they start working for it, but Gandhian workers have already fixed priorities in social service area. Though currently sometimes they use some facts and figures for convincing public and government but generally they do not have any survey or research before starting activities.

(6) Professional social workers are not working for classless society. They do not imagine that everybody should get the same pay and have absolute equality. Rather professional social workers feel that monetary incentive is an important device to improve efficiency. But Gandhian social workers believe that the pay of a barber and an advocate should be the same.

(7) Professional social workers are not against consumerism and better standard of living but Gandhian social worker work for a simple life with basic needs fulfilled.

(8) Professional social workers are not against private ownership of the property and sources of production. But Gandhian view are in favour of cooperative ownership and trusteeship of all the means of production.

(9) Gandhian social workers are more often interested in poor, downtredden and ignorant rural masses or under privileged Harijans but professionals social work accepts everyone as a client. He may be rich or poor. His problem may be bedwetting or extreme poverty, every person with a need may become a clients for professional social work.

(10) Professional social work is not against industrialisation, urbanisation and westernisation, rather it is a product of complex urbanised and industrialised society. But Gandhism takes urbanisation and industrialisation as a disease. Gandhians believe that industrialisation widens the gap between rich and poor. It actually makes poor much more miserable and poor.

Summing Up

In the end we can say that it was possible for professional social work to get influenced by Gandhian thoughts but due a number of reasons both these remained distinct and aloof.

Gandhism could not provide an indigenous touch to imported social work.

However, indirectly some effect of Gandhian thoughts has been imbibed by Indian society and government. We can see this impact in our constitution, particularly on Directive of Principles of State Policy and Fundamental Rights. Social worker's concern for socially deprived people, ideal of intimate family ties, concept of nutrition and health care for everyone, fight for social justice, decentralisation of power, efforts to minimise the gap between rich and poor and the concept of communal harmony look like echo of Gandhian thoughts. It is quite surprising that the issues which were noticed by Mahatma Gandhi in their infancy now have become monsters, like over exploitation of the land, problems of chemical fertilisers and insecticides, unplanned growth of the cities, rivers pollution and negative role of police, government and the state. It is quite true that Gandhian concepts have become more meaningful in changing set up. Mahatma Gandhi was always against the massive planning based on industrialisation.

Much later in 1981 it was realised by Victor S. D'Souza, who says "(Planning) has dismally failed in solving some of basic problems of our country such as poverty and unemployment, malnutrition and illiteracy. Some of the most embarrassing consequences of development planning have been that the gap between the rich and the poor has been widening and the proportion of the people below the poverty line has been increasing." D'Souza and many others are of the view that this type of massive planning cannot provide social justice, it will only help those who are already little developed.

Discussing the same situation (late) Prof. Sugata Dasgupta has written about white revolution in India "(It) has not failed to deprive the children of their dues. Its great contradiction lies inpersuading the parents to buy nylon clothes, fancy umbrellas and transistors at the cost of their own offspring. The history of development of the past three decades has proved, if proof was needed, that the village doctor has looted the village more that the village bully has ever done. Neither have the extension experts been able to solve the problem of hunger, nor has the well meaning banker failed to reduce the peasantry into utter destitution." He further writes "Our poverty and scarcity are, therefore, our only insurance against misery and starvation... so that we do not produce more than enough only to lose the bare minimum."

There is a small section of social workers who believe in the benefit of poverty and scarcity. With the help of these thinkers professional social worker may come closer to Gandhism. We do not imagine that the whole tribe of social workers is going to be coloured by Gandhian thoughts in the coming days but certainly more importance will be given to Gandhian social work in future.

Though, will not be correct if we say that there is a particular type of revival of Gandhian thoughts but today's social worker and social scientist think about Gandhian approach more seriously. While discussing developmental planning Chakravorty has rightly mentioned "Gandhian approach has received a certain measure of support in recent writing of ecologist and ecologically minded economists (Before) Gandhi and his disciples looked more like moralising old men than like people who could be expected to change the direction of society." (Chakravorty, *op. cit.*, p. 8)

But currently we see a drastic change in the situation and in all works of life resurgence of Gandhism is being noticed. Modern professional social work is not untouched of it. Gandhian social welfare plan is being pondered over seriously.

REFERENCES

1. A.B. Singh, (1991) "Towards Gandhian Philosophy of Social Development in India" *Journal of Social Work* Vol. VIII (Lucknow: Dept. of Social Work Lucknow University), p. 69.
2. Gandhi, 23 January 1935 quoted by S. Radhakrishnan, *Contemporary India* (London: Allen and Unwin, 1938), p. 21.
3. Gandhi, *'Harijan'* 1.9.1940.
4. Gandhi, 'New Year' in *Indian Opinion* 2.1.1909.

5. Gandhi, 'The Secret of Swaraj', '*Young India*' 19.1.1921.
6. Gandhi 'Question Box', *Harijan* 26 July 1912.
7. Gandhi, *Harijan* 6 Feb. 1931 quoted by J.D. Sethi, *Gandhi Today* (New Delhi : Vikas Publishing House Pvt. Ltd., 1979), p. 138.
8. Gandhi, *Hind Swaraj,* 1908.
9. Gandhi, Yervada Mandir Chapter VI 1930 quoted by Charles, *Total Development.* 1983, p. 95.
10. Gandhi, *Young India,* 13 Nov. 1924, pp. 85-86.
11. Gandhi quoted by S.K. George and G. Ramachandran, *Economic Peace* (Wardha : 1952), p. 148.
12. Gandhi, quoted by R.N. Mukherjee, *Social Thought,* p. 416.
13. Greek Dorothy (1974), "An Interview with Paul Samverson *Spain,* June.
14. Jaggannadham, *Administration and Social Change* (New Delhi: Uppal Publishing House, 1978), p. 161.
15. J.B. Kriplani, *Gandhi—His Life and Thoughts* (New Delhi : Sangram Books, 1979), p. 368.
16. J.D. Sethi, *Gandhi Today,* p. 139.
17. K..J. Charles, *Total Development* (New Delhi: Vikas Publishing House Pvt. Ltd., 1983), p. 94.
18. Mahatma Gandhi, *Young India* quoted by Ravindra Nath Mukherjee, *Social Thought* (Mousoorie Saraswati Sadan 1965), p. 369.
19. Mahatma Gandhi, *Young India,* 6 December 1928.
20. Mahatma Gandhi, *Harijan Sewak,* 15.9.1946.
21. M.K. Gandhi, *Trusteeship* (Ahmedabad: 1960), pp. 3-49.
22. M.K. Gandhi, *The Problem of Education* (Ahmedabad, 1949).
23. Mahatma Gandhi quoted by K. Arunachalam, "Sarvodaya Approach to *Social Development Aspect of Social Education* ASSWI pp. 25-26.
24. Mirza Ahmed (1991), "Social Development and Human Rights" *Journal of Social Work* (Lucknow), p. 3.
25. Nehru, *A Bunch of Old Letters,* 1958, pp. 506-7.
26. Pyare Lal, *Harijan* 25 Nov. 1952.
27. Ramchandra Guha, "Guardians of the Gandhian Way," *Indian Express* Magazine Section October, 7, 1990), p. 4.

28. Sugata Dasgupta, "Local Community and New Economic Order", *Perspectives on Voluntary Action*, pp. 25-26.

29. Sukhamoy Chakravarty (1987), *Development Planning* (Delhi: Oxford University Press), p. 8.

30. Victor S. D'Souza (1991), Harnessing Lok Shakti for Development" *Perspectives on Voluntary Action* (New Delhi: NIPCCD Publication), p. 3.

31. V. Jagannadham, *Administration and Social Change* (New Delhi: Uppal Publishing House, 1978), p. 162.

32. V.K.R.V. Rao, *The Gandhian Alternative to Western Socialism* (New Delhi: Bhartiya Vidya Bhawan Publication, 1958), pp. 47.

3

Gandhi on Dalits

On Elimination of Untouchability

In the wake of current Dalit dilemma, many so-called thinkers or Dalit think-tank or leaders blame Gandhiji for his thoughts on Harijans (Dalits). It is said Gandhi betrayed them. But this has been a biased and opportunistic criticism. Undoubtedly, Gandhiji was a great champion who was deeply concerned with the cause of Harijans and their upliftment.

The disease of untouchability is fairly old in our society. It generated social hatred and discriminatory feeling of high and low, and as a result the later category suffered for centuries in the hands of the former. Time and again, ceaseless efforts were made by social reformers to alleviate the status of down-trodden and bring them to a level by which they could breathe and subsist with some confidence in the society.

Untouchability in India, as the race and colour problems in the West, rested upon the idea of the superiority of one section of people over another on account of their birth. A Brahman might be as poor as the untouchable, but he was not ill-treated by our society on that account. Gandhi called these so-called religious sanctions as a serious stigma on the fair name of a society which have deep-rooted culture and historical traditions to support its identity.

This was, however, a most complex problem, the complete or satisfactory solution of which could not be evolved in spite of efforts by prominent personalities including social reformers, educationists and political leaders of our society. For example, Buddha, Mahavira, Kabir, Nanak, Dayanand and others played their social and religious role at one time or the other. Besides numerous socio-religious reform movements had deep linkage with the cause of the untouchables who were labelled as a serious stigma on the fair name of Hinduism.

To begin with, the very idea of social discrimination dawned on Gandhi in South Africa where he engaged himself against the discriminatory attitude of the South African Government against Indians. The problem was akin to that of untouchability as the migrants were treated as inferior to the local population which enjoyed numerous basic rights legally denied to Indians. As a youngman Gandhi began to realise how much hellish was their life which had weakened their social and moral fabric essential for the growth of physical and economic faculties of human beings. In India, too, he was confronted with this problem when he came back to his motherland in 1915, during the second year of the World War I. For him the reconstruction of the life of the nation was of utmost significance. This could be achieved by alleviating the social status of the untouchables. He always called untouchability as a cruel and inhuman institution. It violated human dignity. He did not believe that the imperial ambitions of Britain were alone responsible for our slavery, but it was the neglect of our national duty which was primarily responsible for it. A reformed India, he stated, would be a free India.

Untouchability in its extreme form always caused him so much pain, because he considered himself to be a Hindu of Hindus saturated with the spirit of Hinduism. As he always regarded it at an excrescence in Hinduism, he had even no hesitation in renouncing Hinduism itself. To remove untouchability was a penance that caste Hindus owed to Hinduism and to themselves. Thus the purification required was not of untouchables, but of the so-called superior castes. The apathy of the high-caste Hindus worried him much. He, however, dealt with them as best as he could.

During his discussion with Harijans, at Ahmedabad, he opined, "this is a movement for the purification of Hinduism. Think what contribution you can make to it. If you bestir yourselves, if you shed your unclean habits, if you reform your way of living, irrespective of what the high-caste Hindus do, I assure you their superiority of birth will automatically disappear, Superiority consists in clean and pure living and I assure you that in spite of your unclean occupations you can live cleaner and purer lives than the rest of us. Yours is a service without which the community cannot do. I want you to be conscious of the dignity of your profession, to learn to practise it in a dean manner and I am sure you will be able to dictate your terms. Depend on yourself, stand on your own legs and work your own salvation". (*Harijan,* July 29, 1933)

Time and again, Gandhi asked the Harijans to magnify their own faults so that they appeared to be as big as mountains and then make constant efforts to overcome them. In it lay the key to obtaining the rights which they wanted. 'Never believe that since others have the same faults we need not mind our own. No matter what others do, it is your dharma to overcome the feelings which you find in yourselves .... You will not be able, at the behest of others, to overcome what you yourselves do not look upon as failings. Hence, it should suffice to say that you should shake off whatever faults you can find in yourselves.'

In the process of regeneration of the nation, Gandhi waged an incessant and systematic war. 'If we are children of the same God how can there be any rank among us.' For him, there was only one *varna* in India—the *Sudras.* Indeed the *Sudras* are those who serve. He wished that all the Hindus voluntarily call themselves *Sudras.* He was critical of any person who would claim superiority over fellow-men. In his opinion there was no such thing as inherited or acquired superiority.

He was happy and felt satisfied to call himself a scavenger, a spinner, a weaver and favourer. He wrote in the *Harijan,* 'I have intentionally described myself as a *Bhangi.'* In man-made social ladder I want to be at the bottom."

He indeed was much pained to see the appalling plight of untouchables in various regions of the country. Its eradication greatly agitated his mind and he devised ways and means, from time to time, through his speeches and writings. He wrote in *Navajivan*, 'By passing resolutions and talking about their problem we have raised hopes in them. It was absolutely necessary to do this. It was necessary also that hopes should be raised in them and to tell those antyaja friend that what has happened should be sufficient answer to them. Another answer can be that they lay the entire burden on me. I can understand the sting in their words. They accuse me of being satisfied with the more or less that I do myself and of being gullible enough to be taken in by others who only befool me. However, if I do something, there are others who may be doing less but still they do it'.

Mahatma Gandhi Christened Dalits as Harijans as men of God and believed that all the religions of the world describe God pre-eminently as the Friend of the friendless. Help of the helpless and Protector of the weak. He stated that the rest of the world apart, in India who could be more friendless, helpless or weaker than the forty millions or more Hindus of India who were classified as 'untouchables'. If, therefore, any body of people could be fitly described as men of God, they were surely these helpless, friendless and despised people. He opined, 'when Caste Hindus have of their own inner conviction and, therefore, voluntarily, got rid of the present day untouchability, we shall all be called Harijans; for according to my humble opinion, Caste Hindus will then have found favour with God and may, therefore, be fitly described as His men'. (*Harijan*, Feb. 11, 1933)

II

Remarkably, Gandhi had the apprehension that "If we came into power with the stain of untouchability unaffected, I am positive that the 'untouchables' would be far worse under that Swaraj than they are now, for the simple reason that our weakness and our failings would then be buttressed up by the accession of power." Through his speeches in public and writings in *Young India* and *Harijan,* he emphasised the problem of untouchability and its removal from its roots. He hated untouchability with his entire soul.

The Mahatma had the feeling that in Hinduism there was no sanction for treating a single human being as untouchable. The *Bhagavadgita* has never taught that a *Chandala* was in any inferior to a Brahmana. 'A Brahmana ceases to be a Brahmana, immediately be becomes insolvent and considers himself a superior being.' Gandhi regarded himself a Sanatani Hindu, because he obeyed the eternal precepts of the faith as embodied in the Shastras as he understood them. He had no doubt that there are many interpolations in the Smritis and the other scriptural books. He rejected as interpolations everything in the Smritis or other writings that was inconsistent with Truth and Non-violence or other fundamental and universal principles of ethics.

He opined, 'The idea of superiority and inferiority is repugnant to the most elementary principles of morality. A Brahmana who considers himself superior to any single creature of God ceases to be a Brahmana. If we are children of the same God, how can there be any rank among us ?.... What will happen to the body, if these members begin to quarrel about rank ? . . . . The verses in the Smritis about Sudras deserve to be summarily rejected as being contrary to the spirit of humanity.' (*Harijan,* Sept. 28, 1934)

Gandhi was quite sure in his mind that untouchability would not be removed by the force even of law. It could only be removed, he opined, when the majority of Hindus realized that it was a crime against God and man and were ashamed of it. In other words, it was a process of conversion, i.e.. purification, of the Hindu heart. The aid of law had to be invoked when it hindered or interfered with the progress of the reform as when, in spite of the willingness of the trustees and the temple-going public, the law prohibited the opening of a particular temple.

"There are innumerable castes in India. They are a social institution .... This institution has superadded to it restrictions which, in my opinion, are undesirable and are bound to go in course of time .... The difference, therefore, between the caste system and untouchability is not one of degree, but of kind. An 'untouchable, is outside the pale of respectable society. He is hardly treated as a human being. He is an outcasts hurled into an abyss by his fellow-beings occupying the same platform. The difference, therefore, is somewhat analogous to the difference between heaven and hell". (*Harijan*, Feb. 11, 1933)

Gandhi assessed the social position of untouchables as follows: "Socially they are lepers. Economically they are worse than slaves. Religiously they are denied entrance to places we miscall 'houses of God'. They are denied the use, on the same terms as the Caste Hindus, of public roads, public schools, public hospitals, public wells, public taps, public parks and the like .... The wonder is that they are at all able to eke out an existence or that they still remain within the Hindu fold. They are too downtrodden to rise in revolt against their suppressors. ... It is only ceaseless effort that can raise these downtrodden fellow beings from degradation, purify Hinduism and raise the whole Hindu society and with it the whole of India". (*Harijan*, March 18, 1933)

In matters of inter-dining and inter-marriage, the Mahatma opined that marrying and dining were matters of individual concern and no one had a right to ask to choose a girl for wife or to dine with anybody against his will. He, however, elaborated his point thus: "But my answer is at the same time 'yes' because if a person refused to take food touched by another person on the ground of untouchability or inferiority, he is observing untouchability. In other words, untouchability cannot constitute any ground for restraint on interdining or marriage."

An important organisation, known as the Harijan Sevak Sangh which was not a part of the Congress, was the outcome of the fast, the Mahatma undertook in 1932 when he was in jail.

GD Birla was its President and Thakkar Bapa its Secretary. ...'it is the duty of Harijan workers and Caste Hindus to do sweepers' work themselves. . . . These reforms do not cost much. They require intelligence, hard work and love of an ideal. We may not relegate sweepers' work to one particular class. Therefore all should learn it in the same way as cooking. Each person should be his own sweeper. If this ideal were to be put into practice in society, the miserable condition of sweepers would at once be rectified'.

The system of forced labour exacted by petty landowners from Harijans and other backward classes is almost prevalent in India. The petty landlords are mostly Hindus. 'It is the privilege of Harijan Sevaks, no matter to what organisation they belong to befriend Harijans, to study their condition in detail, to approach Savarna Hindus and show them as gently as possible what their duty is towards those whom they have treated as outcastes of society and deprived even of legal rights.'

It is significant to note that Gandhiji always preached to the Harijans cleanliness, abstention from carrion-eating and intoxicating drinks and drugs, necessity of taking education themselves and giving it co their children, also abstention from eating the leavings from Caste Hindus' plates. He stated, 'On the contrary, I suggest to Caste Hindus that the shortcomings are not inherent to Harijans but that they are due to our criminal neglect of—even deliberate suppression of— these brethren of ours .... We must approach Harijans as penitents or debtors, not as their patrons or creditors extending generosity to the undeserving'.

On Dalit Education

Notably, Gandhi recommended that common schools and wells should be opened where the existing ones were not available for Harijans either owing to the violent and successful opposition of the neighbours or some other unavoidable cause: Harijans, he opined, could not be left uncared for in matters of necessary services till public opinion had ripened. 'National schools, to be worth the name in terms of Swaraj for the attainment of which they have been brought into existence, must be conducted with a view to advancing the national programme in so far as it is applicable to educational institutions. Thus, for instance, national schools must be the most potent means of educating the 'untouchables' and abolishing the curse of untouchability from the schools. Whilst in theory the (present national) schools are open to the 'untouchables' very few, as a matter of fact, have untouchable children in them .... I have no hesitation in advising that teachers should run the risk of closing down their schools if the condition of running them requires the exclusion of untouchables.

As such Gandhiji emphasised the fact that preliminary training should consist in teaching Harijan children manners, good speech and good conduct. 'A Harijan child sits anyhow; dresses anyhow; his eyes, ears, teeth, hair, nails, nose are often full of dirt; many never know what it is to have a wash.... Their lesson should begin for the first three months with teaching them cleanliness. They should be taught also how to eat properly .... If this preliminary training is to be given in all Harijan schools, pamphlets giving detailed instructions for teachers in their languages should be prepared and distributed, and inspectors of schools be required during their inspection to examine teachers and pupils on this head and to send full reports of the progress made in this direction'.

Also Gandhi warned the Hindu brethren against the tendency which he saw of exploiting the suppressed classes for a political end. He stated that to remove untouchability was a penance that Caste Hindus owed to Hinduism and to themselves. The purification required was not of "untouchability" but of the so-called superior castes. There was no vice that was special to the "untouchables", not even dirt and insanitation. 'It is our arrogance which blinds us, superior Hindus, to our own blemishes and which magnifies those of our downtrodden brethren whom we have suppressed and whom we keep under suppression .... That religion and that nation will be blotted out of the face of the earth which pins its faith to injustice, untruth or violence.

God is Light, not darkness. Gad is Love, not hate, God is truth, not untruth. God alone is great. We His creatures are but dust. Let us be humble and recognise the place of the lowliest of His creatures. Krishna honoured Sudama in his rags as he honoured no one else. Love is the root of religion.'

For the opening of the roads was not the final but the first step in the ladder of reform. Temples in general, public wells, public schools must be open to the untouchables equally with the Caste Hindus. 'I want my Harijan brother, if he wishes, to share this temple worship with the millions of his co-religionists the so-called Caste men. It is the latter's duty to throw open their temples to their Harijan brethren. Temple worship supplies the felt spiritual want of the human race. It admits of reform. But it will live as long as man lives.'

The Mahatma regarded untouchability as the greatest blot on Hinduism. He developed this feeling when he was a child. He described how he did not like numerous Hindu customs which promoted the feelings of high and low in Indian society. He regretted that Hinduism had sinned in giving sanction to untouchability, and Indian society had suppressed 'our brethren'.

"I regret untouchability as the greatest blot on Hinduism. This idea was not brought home to me by my bitter experience during the South African struggle. is not due to the fact that I was once an agnostic. It is equally wrong to think—as some people do-that I have taken my views from my study of Christian religious literature. These views date as far back as the time when I was neither enamoured of, nor was acquainted with the Bible or the followers of the *Bible*.

"While at school I would often happen to touch the 'untouchables', and as I never would conceal the fact from my parents, my mother would tell me that the shortest cut to purification after the unholy touch was to cancel the touch by touching any Mussalman passing by. And simply out of reverence and regard for my mother I often did so, but never did so believing it to be a religious obligation. After some time we shifted to Porbandar, where I made my first acquaintance with Sanskrit. I was not yet put into an English school, and my brother and I were placed in charge of a Brahmin, who taught us *Ramaraksha* and *Vishnu Puja*. The text *"Jale Vishnuh Sthale Vishnuh"* (there is the Lord present in water, there is the Lord present in earth) has never gone out of my memory. A motherly old dame used to live close by. Now it happened that I was very timid then, and would conjure up ghosts and goblins whenever the lights went out and it was dark. The old order, to disabuse me of fears, suggested that I should mutter the *Ramaraksha* texts whenever I was afraid, and all evil spirits would fly away. This I did and, as I thought, with good effect. I could never believe then that there was any text in the *Ramaraksha* pointing to the contact of the untouchables as a sin. I did not understand its meaning then, or understood it very imperfectly. But I was confident that *Ramaraksha,* which could destroy all fear of ghosts, could not be countenancing any such thing as fear of contact with the untouchables.

"The *Ramayana* used to be regularly read in our family. As Brahmin called Ladha Maharaj used to read it. He was stricken with leprosy, and was confident that a regular reading of the *Ramayana* would cure him of leprosy, and in-deed, he was cured of it. 'How can the *Ramayana'*, I thought to myself, 'in which one who is regarded now-a-days as an untouchable took Rama across the Ganges in his boat, countenance the idea of any human beings being untouchable on the ground that they were polluted souls ?" The fact that we address God as the 'purifier of the polluted' and by similar appellations, shows that it is a sin to regard anyone born in Hinduism as polluted or untouchable—that it is Satanic to do so. I have hence been never tired of repeating that is a great sin. I do not pretend that this thing had crystallised as a conviction in me at the age of twelve, but I do say that I did then regard untouchability as a sin. I narrate this story for the information of the Vaishnavas and orthodox Hindus.

"I have always claimed to be a Sanatani Hindu. It is not

that I am quite innocent of the scriptures. I am not a profound scholar of Sanskrit. I have read the *Vedas* and the *Upanishads* only in translation. Naturally therefore, mine is not a scholarly study of them. My knowledge of them is in no way profound, but I have studied them as I should do as a Hindu and I claim to have grasped their true spirit. By the time I had reached the age of 21, I had studied other religions also.

"There was a time when I was wavering between Hinduism and Christianity. When I recovered my balance of mind, I felt that to me salvation was possible only through the Hindu religion and my faith in Hinduism grew deeper and more enlightened.

"But even then I believed that untouchability was no part of Hinduism; and that if it was, such Hinduism was not for me.

"True Hinduism does not regard untouchability as a sin. I do not want to enter into any controversy regarding the interpretation of the *Shastras*. It might be difficult for me to establish my point by quoting authorities from the *Bhagavat* or *Manusmriti*. But I claim to have understood the spirit of Hinduism. Hinduism has sinned in giving sanction to untouchability. It has degraded us, made us the pariahs of the Empire. Even the Mussalmans caught the sinful contagion from us, and in South Africa, in East Africa and in Canada, the Mussalmans no less than Hindus came to be regarded as pariahs. All this evil has resulted from the sin of untouchability.

"I may here recall my proposition, which is this: So long as the Hindus wilfully regard untouchability as part of their religion, as long as the mass of Hindus consider it a sin to touch a section of their brethren, Swaraj is impossible of attainment. Yudhishtira would not enter heaven without his dog. How can, then, the descendants of that Yudhishtira expect to obtain Swaraj without the untouchables ? What crimes for which we condemn the Government as Satanaic have not we been guilty of towards our untouchable brethren?

"We are guilty of having suppressed our brethren; we make

them crawl on their bellies; we have made them rub their noses on the ground; with eyes red with rage, we push them out of railway compartments—what more than this has British rule done ? What charge that we bring against Dyer and O'Dwyer may not others, and even our own people, lay at our door ? We ought to purge ourselves of this pollution. It is idle to talk of Swaraj so long as we do not protect the weak and the helpless, or so long as it is possible for a single Swarajist to injure the feelings of any individual. Swaraj means that not a single Hindu or Muslim shall for a moment arrogantly think that he can crush with impunity meek Hindus or Muslims. Unless this condition is fulfilled we will gain Swaraj only to lose it the next moment. We are no better than the brutes until we have purged ourselves of the sins we have committed against our weaker brethren.

"But I have faith in me still. In the course of my peregrinations in India I have realised that the spirit of kindness of which the poet Tulsidas sings so eloquently, which forms the cornerstone of the Jain and Vaishnava religions, which is the quintessence of the *Bhagavat,* and which every verse of the *Gita* is saturated with— this kindness, this love, this charity, is slowly but steadily gaining ground in the hearts of the masses of this country.

"Many a fracas between Hindus and Mussalmans is still heard of. There are still many of those who do not scruple to wrong one another. But as to the net result, I feel that kindness and charity have increased. The Hindus and Mahommedans have become godfearing. We have shaken ourselves free from the hypnotism of law courts and Government schools and no longer labour under any other hallucination. I have also realised that those whom we regard as illiterate and ignorant are the very people who deserve to be called educated. They are more cultured than we, their lives are more righteous than ours. A little study of the present day mentality of the people will show that according to the popular conception, Swaraj is synonymous with Ramarajya— the establishment of the Kingdom of Righteousness on earth. If it can bring any comfort to you, my untouchable brethren, I would say that your question does not cause so much stir, as it used to do formerly. That does not mean that I expect you to cease to have misgivings about the Hindus. How can they deserve to be not mistrusted having wronged you so much ? Swami Vivekanand used to say that the untouchables were not depressed, they were suppressed by the Hindus who in turn had suppressed themselves by suppressing them.

"I suppose I was at Nellore on the 6th of April. I met the untouchables there and I prayed that day as I have done today. I do want to attain *moksha.* I do not want to be reborn. But if I have to be reborn, I should be born an untouchable, so that I may share their sorrows, suffering and the affronts levelled at them, in order that I may endeavour to free myself and them from that miserable condition. I, therefore, prayed that if I should be born again, I should do so not as a Brahmin, Kshatriya, Vaishya or Sudra, but as an Atisudra.

"Today is much more solemn than the sixth. It is hallowed by the memory of the massacre of thousands of innocents. And I prayed, therefore, also today that if I should die with any of my desires unfructified, with my service of the untouchables unfinished, with my Hinduism unfulfilled, I may be born again amongst the untouchables to bring my Hinduism to its fulfilment.

"I love scavenging. In my Ashram, an eighteen-year-old Brahmin lad is doing the scavenger's work in order to teach the Ashram scavenger cleanliness. The lad is no reformer. He was born and bred in orthodoxy. He is a regular reader of the *Gita* and faithfully performs *sandhyavandana.* His pronunciation of Sanskrit verses is more faultless than mine. When he conducts the prayer, his soft, sweet melodies melt one into love. But he felt that his accomplishments were incomplete until he had become also a perfect sweeper, and that if he wanted the Ashram sweeper to do his work well, he must do it himself and set an example.

"You should realise that you are cleaning Hindu society. You have therefore to purify your lives. You should cultivate the habit of cleanliness, so that no one may point his finger at you. Use alkali ash or earth if you cannot afford to use soap to keep yourselves clean. Some of you are given to drinking and gambling which you must get rid of. You will point your finger at the Brahmins and say that even they are given to these vices. But they are not looked upon as polluted as you are. You must not ask the Hindus to emancipate you as a matter of favour. Hindus mast do so, if they want, in their own interests. You should, therefore, make them feel ashamed by your own purity and cleanliness. I believe that we shall have purified ourselves within the next five months. If my expectations are not fulfilled, I will think that although my proposition was fundamentally correct, yet I was wrong in my calculation; and I will again say that I had erred in my calculation.

"You claim to be Hindus; you read the *Bhagavat.* If, therefore, the Hindus oppress you then you should understand that the fault does not lie in the Hindu religion but in those who profess it. In order to emancipate yourselves you shall have to purify yourselves. You shall have to get rid of evil habits like drinking.

"If you want to ameliorate your conditions, if you want to obtain Swaraj, you should be self-reliant. I was told in Bombay that some of you are opposed to N.C.O. and believe that salvation is only possible through the British Government. Let me tell you that you will never be able to obtain redress by discarding Hindu religion and courting the favour of a third party. Your emancipation lies in your own hands.

"I have come in contact with the untouchables all over the country; and I have observed that immense possibilities lie latent in them of which neither they nor the rest of the Hindus seem to be aware. Their intellect is of original purity. I ask you to learn spinning and weaving, and if you take them up as a profession, you will keep poverty from your doors. As regards your attitude towards the *Bhangis* I will repeat what I said at Godhra. I cannot understand why you should yourselves countenance the distinction between Dheds and Bhangis. There is no difference between them. Even in normal times their occupation is as honourable as that of lawyers or Government servants.

"You should now cease to accept leavings from plates, however clean they may be represented to be. Receive grain only—good, sound grain, not rotten grain—and that too only if it is courteously offered. If you are able to do all I have asked you to do, you will secure your emancipation, not in four or five months, but in so many days.

"The Hindus are not sinful by nature—they are sunk in ignorance. Untouchability must be extinct in this very year. Two of the strongest desires that keep me in flesh and bone are the emancipation of the untouchables and the protection of the cow. When these two desires are fulfilled, there is Swaraj, and therein lies my own *moksha*. May God give you strength to work out your salvation." (*Young India,* May 4, 1921)

Again it is pertinent to note here that in a huge assembly of students at Nagpur on 9 November, 1933, the Mahatma stated that he was not confined to Hinduism, and if untouchability was removed from the Hindu heart, he expected far-reaching consequences and a great change in Indian society. The barrier of untouchability, he said, was a great hindrance towards achievement of any kind of unity. He was, however, not sure if his dream about the removal of untouchability would be achieved during his life.

"I know this tussle between English and Hindi is almost an eternal tussle. Whenever I have addressed student audiences, I have been surprised by the demand for English. You know, or ought to know, that I am a lover of the English language. But I do believe that the students of India, who are expected to throw in their lot with the teeming millions and to serve them, will be better qualified if they pay more attention to Hindi than to English. I do not say that you should not learn English; learn it by all means. But, so far as I can sec, it cannot be the language of the millions of Indian homes. It will be confined to thousands or tens of thousands, but it will not reach the millions. Therefore,

I am delighted when the students ask me to speak in Hindi.

"You, both the speakers, have spoken of me in terms, which if I believed to be true of myself, I do not know where I would be. But I know my place. I am a humble servant of India, and is trying to serve India, I serve humanity at large. I discovered in my early days that the service of India is not inconsistent with the service of humanity. As I grew older in years, and I hope also in wisdom, I saw that the discovery was well made, and after nearly 50 years of public life, I am able to say today that my faith in the doctrine, that the service of one's nation is not inconsistent with the service of the world, has grown. It is a good doctrine. Its acceptance alone will ease the situation in the world and stop the mutual jealousies between nations inhabiting this globe of ours. You have said truly that, in taking up this war against untouchability, I have not confined myself to Hinduism. I have said more than once that if untouchability is removed in its fulness from the Hindu heart, it will have far-reaching consequences, inasmuch as it touches millions of human beings. As I said last night to the great meeting in Nagpur, if untouchability is really removed from the Hindu heart, that is, if the high caste Hindus purge themselves of this terrible taint, we shall soon discover that we are all one and not different peoples. Hindus, Muslims. Christians, Parsis, whatever we may call ourselves. We shall feel the unity, once the barrier of untouchability is removed. As I have often said, untouchability is a hydra-headed monster, appearing in many shapes. Some of them are very subtle. If I have jealousy for any human being, that also is a species of untouchability. I do not know if my dream about the removal of untouchability will be fully realised while I am living. And those who are religiously inclined, those who believe not in formal religion but in the essence of religion, cannot but believe in the removal of a subtle type of untouchability that affects the lives of a vast mass of humanity. If Hindu hearts can be purged of this evil, our eyes of understanding will be more and more opened. It is not possible to estimate the gain to humanity when untouchability is really removed. You can now have no difficulty in understanding why I have staked my life for this one thing.

"If you, the students who have assembled here, have followed me so far and understood the implications of this mission of mine, you will soon extend the help I want from you. Many students have written to me asking what part they can take in helping this movement. It is a surprise to me that students are obliged to ask this question. The field is so vast and near you that you need not ask the question as to what you may do and what you may not. It is not a political question. It may become one, but for you and me, for the time being, it is not connected with politics. My life is governed by religion. I never lost sight of the principle that governs my life when I began dabbling in politics. As this is a humanitarian campaign, students must devote a part of their spare time, if not the whole, to the service of thousands of Harijans. By giving me this magnificent purse you have certainly equalled the brightest records of students' meetings which I have addressed in my many peregrinations throughout the length and breadth of India. But I want much more from you. I have found that, if I get many helpers who can give their spare time, much work can be done. This work cannot be done by hired labour. With hired labour we cannot go to Harijan quarters and sweep their roads, enter their houses and wash their children. I have described in the columns of the *Harijan* what students can do. A Harijan teacher has shown what a Herculean task it is for him to tackle. Even wild children are better than Harijan children. Wild children are not sunk in utter degradation, as the Harijan children are, nor do they live in such filthy surroundings. This problem cannot be tackled by hired labour. No amount of money can enable me to do this. It must be your prerogative. It is an acid test of the education received by you in schools and colleges. Your world will not be measured by your ability to make faultless English speeches. Your worth will be measured by the service you render to the poor and not by Government posts worth Rs. 60 or Rs. 600 that you may have got. I wish you would do this work in the spirit I suggest. I have not met a single student who has said that he cannot spare one hour per day. If you write your diary from day to day, you will find that you waste many a precious hour in the 365 days of the year. If you want to turn your education to good account, you will turn your attention to this work while this hurricane campaign lasts. Erstwhile students are serving Harijans within a radius of 5 miles round about Wardha. They are doing good silent work; therefore, you do not know them. I invite you to see their work. It is hard but pleasurable. It will give you joy, greater than your cricket or tennis. I have repeatedly said that money will come if I have real, intelligent, honest workers. As a boy of 18 I began my education in begging. I have seen that money can be found easily if we have the right kind of workers. Money alone will never satisfy me. I would ask you to pledge yourselves to devote a definite number of spare hours to Harijan service. As you, Mr. President, have said, I am a dreamer, I am indeed a practical dreamer. My dreams are not airy nothings. I want to convert my dreams into realities as far as possible. Therefore, I must hasten to auction the gifts I have received from you." (*Harijan,* Nov. 17 1933)

There was much difficulty in running schools for Harijan boys. In spite of allurements of fee-concessions and scholarships to them, their attendance in the schools was not up to the mark. The Mahatma suggested ways and means for the improvement of their lot by devising novel schemes by the teachers attached to these schools. "One who is responsible for the management of over twenty-five Harijan schools writes a long letter stating the difficulties experienced in the management of the schools and ask how I would conduct them if I had the direct management thereof. I need not recount his difficulties which he has described carefully. What I am about to say is an attempt to answer them.

"While we are bound to give scholarships and other help to those Harijan boys and girls who attend the established schools, there is no reason whatever slavishly to reproduce the mode and methods of those schools in the ones under our own management.

"We have to recognise that we get Harijan children with great difficulty to attend any school at all. We cannot expect any degree of regularity in them and, thanks to our past criminal neglect, they are so unkept that we have, in the beginning stages, to handle them in a manner wholly different from the ordinary.

"On first admission their bodies have to be minutely examined and thoroughly cleaned. Their clothes might have to be cleaned and patched. The first daily lesson, therefore, will for some time consist of applied hygiene and sanitation and simple needlework. I should use no books probably for the whole of the first year. I should talk to them about things with which they are familiar and, doing so, correct their pronunciation and grammar· and teach them new words. I should note all the new words they may learn from day to day so as to enable me to use them frequently till they have them fixed in their minds regularly. The teacher will not give discourses but adopt the conversational method. Through conversations he will give his pupils progressive instruction in history, geography and arithmetic. History will begin with that of our own times, and then, too, of events and of persons nearest us, and geography will begin with that of the neighbourhood of the school. Arithmetic will begin with the sums applicable to the pupil's houses. Having tried the method myself, I know that infinitely more knowledge can be given to the pupils through it, and without strain on them, than can be given through the orthodox methods, within a given time. Knowledge of the alphabet should be treated as a separate subject altogether. The letters should be treated as pictures which the children will first be taught to recognise and name. Writing will follow as part of the drawing lesson. Instead of making daubs of their letters, pupils should be able to make perfect copies of the models placed before them. They would not, therefore, be called upon to draw the letters till they had acquired control over their fingers and the pen. It is criminal to stunt the mental growth of a child by letting him know as much only as he can get through a book he can incoherently read in a year. We do not realise that, if a Child was cut off from the home life and was merely doomed to the school, he would be a perfect dumee for several years. He picks up information and language unconsciously through his home, not in the schoolroom. Hence do we experience the immense difference between pupils belonging to cultured homes and those belonging to uncouth homes, which are no homes in reality.

"In the scheme I have adumbrated, the schoolmaster is expected to treat his occupation seriously and feel one with his pupils. I know that, in putting the scheme into operation, the want of schoolmasters of the right type is the greatest difficulty. But we shall not get the right type till we have made the right beginning...." (*Harijan,* Nov. 10, 1933)

REFERENCES

1. *Harijan, 29* July 1933.
2. *The Collected Works of Mahatma Gandhi,* Vol. LV, p. 364.
3. *Harijan,* 11 February 1933.
4. *Harijan,* 28 September 1934.
5. *Harijan,* 23 September 1939.
6. *Harijan,* 11 February 1933.
7. *Harijan,* 18 March 1933.
8. *Young India,* 4 May 1921.
9. *Harijan,* 17 November 1933.
10. *Harijan,* 10 November 1933.

4

Social Work Through Harijan Sevak Sangh

Gandhi's constructive programme was devoted to social reform and development of the backward communities. His aim was to regenerate a new spirit, a new thinking and self-reliance amongst the Harijans. This kind of feeling, he believed, would greatly enhance their prestige and self-respect. They could raise their heads by becoming economically stronger by hard work and incessant labour.

He was deeply concerned with the stigma of untouchability. It was made clear at numerous meetings and through his writings that untouchability was a cruel and inhuman institution. It always violated human dignity by compelling untouchables to do work which was unclean and degrading. It was opined that untouchability was against the spirit of democracy which made no distinction among citizens of a free country. It also raises economic problems. The untouchables were the poorest section of Indian society. Their avenues of employment were strictly limited. They lived apart, in unhygienic surroundings, on the outskirts of villages and cities. Though they were Hindus and believed in and worshipped Hindu gods and godesses, they were not allowed to enter Hindu temples. Public institutions like schools, hostels, etc., were closed to them. (J.B. Kripalani, *op. cit.*,)

To boost up the work for the upliftment of Harijans, Gandhi laid the foundation of the Harijan Sevak Sangh. Its main function was the removal of all such disabilities which hampered the progress and development of Harijans. As it consisted of dedicated workers it did remarkable work. So far so, Gandhi brought a Harijan family in the Ashram and he adopted their daughter as his own. He also offered his blessings on the eve of marriages which were celebrated between Harijans and Caste Hindus. A few such marriages were celebrated in his own Ashram.

It is pertinent to note that in an article on 'Task before Harijan Sevaks', Gandhi stated that the growing number of reformers should be active in the execution of various programmes and should not sit still. Rather they should demonstrate that change by their visible conduct. He was sure that the change to full self-reliance would never come unless all the workers realised that this was essentially a religious movement.

"Though I have concurred in the policy of centralisation I have always desired, as I have no doubt the Board too has desired, decentralisation at the first opportunity. But that could only be done when the Provincial Boards were ready and able to raise their own funds, I would love nothing so much as that every village had its Harijan Board and was able to find its own funds. When that day comes, it will also be one of complete abolition of untouchability in every shape and form. For the present it has to be unfortunately admitted that the cause is still led by a handful of earnest reformers scattered all over the country. Not all of them are able to raise funds locally nor are they all sure of the policy to be followed. I use the word policy deliberately. For while everyone knows the goal, even-one does not know the grave limitations under which the reformer labours. The slightest error of judgment, a hasty action or a hasty word may put back the hands of the clock of progress. Policies have, therefore, to be cautiously evolved in the light of experiences daily gained by the few who have no other thought but that of serving Harijans and riding Hinduism of its greatest blot." (*Harijan*, 17 Aug. 1935)

"Ever since the inauguration of the Harijan Sevak Sangh, the central organisation has been feeling, every properly, the provincial branches. But the time has certainly arrived for the branches to stand on their own and be self-sustained even though it may be at the sacrifice of a part of their programme. The work in each province, and for that matter in each district or taluka, should be an unequivocal demonstration of active Savarna support. For the chief mission of the Sangh is to touch the Savarna heart and change it.

Supposing the central organisation had collected from two or three reformers a crore of rupees, and with it established branches all over India to cover it with schools and hostels for Harijan boys and girls, it would not have hastened the day of the doom of untouchability. For the Savarna heart would remain as stony as ever. Supposing conversely that without cost of a single pice, by some stroke, of good fortune, the Savarna heart was changed and untouchability became a thing of the past, the whole object the Sangh would be fulfilled. For in that case every public school, place of worship and other institutions would be open to Harijans precisely on the same terms as to Caste Hindus. That day may be far off or much nearer than many people expect. Anyway that is the goal of the Harijan Sevak Sangh, and never the opening of separate schools, wells, temples and the like for Harijans and consequent perpetuation of untouchability. At present these things are undoubtedly done, but they are done only as a means to the end. They have become necessary because the Savarna heart is slow to change.

"The growing number of reformers must not sit still and make protestations of removal of untouchability from themselves. They must demonstrate that change by their visible conduct. The spending of their purse for the Harijan cause is a tangible proof of the change and, therefore, an essential part of the programme. But immediately it becomes a corner confined to a few individuals who salve their conscience by liberal donations, it ceases to be a token in the manner indicated by me. Hence it becomes a matter of duty for the Central Board to invite the attention of the branches to this fundamental part of the programme and for the branches to appreciate it and prepare the way to becoming wholly self-reliant. Indeed the burden has been progressively thrown on provincial boards of financing their own institutions. But the time has come for definite and decisive action in the direction.

"This change to full self-reliance will never come unless all the workers realise that this is essentially a religious movement. We are a nation spending lavishly for causes which the masses believe to be religious. One has only to go the places of pilgrimage to have an ocular demonstration of the fact. A study of the history of religious endowments will reveal the tragic story of fortunes being entrusted to them by credulous millions without ever caring to know-how they were spent. It is enough for people to believe that they pay their mite to a cause which in their opinion is religious. Harijan workers have a cause that is wholly religious in the best sense of the term. If they have a living faith in it, if they do not move mountains, they will at least get from their surroundings enough for the institutions in their charge." (*Harijan*, Oct. 10, 1936)

Q. *The Harijan Sevak Sangh is looked upon as a part of the Congress. But very few Congressmen are Harijan workers. Why?*

A. The Sangh is not a part of the Congress. It was the outcome of the fast I undertook in 1932 when I was in jail. The meeting of Hindus drawn from every class, which was held under the Presidentship of Pandit Malaviyaji and which gave birth to the Sangh, deliberately decided to keep the organisation separate from the Congress and non-political. It was this quality of the Sangh that enabled Seth G.D. Birla to become its President and Shri Thakkar Bapa its Secretary. Nevertheless there are ought to be many Congressmen in the Sangh, because practically all reformers are drawn into the Congress fold. But it is true that there are plenty of non-Congress persons in the Sangh. It is also true that those Congressmen who are only interested in politics do not come into it. It is, therefore, sometimes wrongly thought that Congressmen do not take an interest in the Sangh. It is the duty of every Congressman to remove untouchability, root and branch, from his life.

Q. *Harijan service has really developed into mere Harijan uplift. Practically no work is done among Caste Hindus for the removal of untouchability. What is the remedy for this?*

A. Experience shows that propaganda among Caste Hindus can only be successfully carried out by influential persons whose words carries weight with the general public. Such persons are hard to find. But it is within the capacity of every Harijan worker to carry on mute propaganda. Our Caste Hindu workers are often satisfied with mere uplift work among the Harijans, which is not sufficient. Many workers, while they do not observe untouchability themselves, are unable even to convert their own families. How then can they influence the outside world? Moreover it is my confirmed opinion that every Harijan worker has to make a point to beg for even one pice for Harijans from those Caste Hindus with whom he comes in contact. If all devoted themselves, heart and soul, to this task, very good results would ensue.

Q. *Should not the Sangh take upon itself the service of those Harijans who have been converted to Christianity or Islam and are yet treated as untouchables? Are we not out to remove untouchability root and branch and, therefore, help all who come under its sway?*

A. This question has already been answered in the columns of *Harijan* but must bear repetition so long as it is raised. The moment untouchability is utterly banished from Hindu society it will, *ipso facto,* disappear from elsewhere too. Whatever the merits or demerits of the case, it is clear that our interference with converts will be the cause of strife with Muslims and Christians. Such converts have either broken off all contacts with, or they have been in their turn boycotted by Hindus. They have thrown in their lot with other sects whose leaders will not allow them to maintain their old contacts. Hence the Harijan Sevak Sangh quite rightly decided from its inception to confine its area of work to Harijans who had not left the Hindu fold. A convert, having left his original fold, is no longer guided or controlled by it.

Q. *What should be the attitude of the Sangh, if Harijan boys wish to enlist in the army?*

A. They should be allowed to do so. They may not be controlled by the Congress policy or Ahimsa. They must be given absolute freedom of choice.

Q. *Harijans are of opinion that Caste Hindus who are sympathetic to their cause should not use those temples where they are not allowed entry.*

A. They are right. It is the bounden duty of Harijan workers not to go where Harijans are not allowed and likewise to dissuade Caste Hindus.

Q. *Harijans are legally entitled to send their children to many educational institutions as also to draw water from public wells. But public sentiment still militates against this being put into practice. Should Harijans resort to the law courts for justice in these matters or wait patiently until the Caste Hindus are converted?*

A. Where there is no danger of violence being done to them, the Harijans should exercise their legal right and where necessary, resort to law courts. Harijan workers must continue agitation among Caste Hindus and not rest content with mere legal rights.

Q. *Is it not essential to reform the insanitary methods employed by sweepers for cleaning latrines and scavenging?*

A. It is not necessary. What is more, until this is done the condition of sweepers will remain pitiable. To this end it is the duty of Harijan workers and Caste Hindus to do sweepers' work themselves. No Caste Hindu will employ the methods used by sweepers. He will do the work scientifically. For example, he will never remove excreta in a basket or carry it on his head; he will cover excreta with dry earth and remove it in a metal vessel. He will avoid touching dirt with his hands as far as possible; he will clean the vessel with water and a rod; he will bathe immediately after doing the work; he will wear special clothes when scavenging. These reforms do not cost much. They require intelligence, hard work, and love of an ideal. We may not relegate sweepers' work to one particular class. Therefore, all should learn it the same way as cooking. Each person should be his own sweeper. If this ideal were to be put into practice in society, the miserable condition of sweepers would at once be rectified. (*Harijan*, 10 May, 1946)

Here it is remarkably that the Harijan Sevak Sangh was mainly concerned with the welfare work. The members were also advised to organise unions or even induce hartals, not from political motives or for such purposes, but for bettering the social or economic position of Harijans. 'The Harijan Sevak Sangh, however, being a non-political organisation should never put expediency before its primary duty towards the Harijans.'

Q. *The Communist Party as successfully organised sweepers' unions and helped them to secure their rights through hartals, etc. But the Harijan Sevak Sangh's activities are confined mostly two welfare work. It cannot, therefore, successfully compete with the Communists for popularity among the Harijans. Don't you think that in view of this, the Harijan Sevak Sangh ought to alter its policy and method of work?*

A. We must be guided in our policy by our sense of right, not by the lure of winning cheap popularity. If the Harijan Sevak Sangh is convinced that it is working on the right line, it will keep on to it, regardless of what others might or might not do. 'Thus we may organise unions or even induce *hartals*, not from political motives or for such purposes, but for bettering the social or economic position of Harijans.

Q. *The feeling is gaining ground among the Harijans that the Congress is showing more solicitude for Muslim demands than for the just rights of the Harijans. What have you to say to it?*

A. The Congress being a political organisation is likely to be more susceptible to political pressure, which the Muslims are in a far stronger position to exert than the Harijans. If it succumbs to that pressure, it will pay the price for it. The Harijan Sevak Sangh, however, being a non-political organisation should never put expediency before its primary duty towards the Harijans.

Q. *Would you advise the so-called Savarna Hindus to start, even under the present circumstances an agitation in selected places for securing elementary civic and social rights for the Harijans? Would you for this purpose advise the Harijan Sevak Sangh to organise Satyagraha against the Savarna Hindus if necessary?*

A. I would not advise the Sangh as an organisation to offer Satyagraha against the Savarna Hindus, but I would certainly not only advise but expect members of the Sangh in their individual capacity to organise such Satyagraha in their respective places. I shall certainly support any such move on their part if it is undertaken in the proper spirit. It is their duty.

Q. *Would you, in the absence of popular Governments in the provinces, advise the Sangh to carry on a vigorous and energetic programme of temple entry for Harijans?*

A. I could. I understand it is being done even at present but at a rather slow pace. I would certainly like its tempo to be stepped up.

Q. *Should not the Harijan Sevak Sangh try to secure for the Harijans political power by demanding due representation for them on Grama Panchayats, municipalities and Legislatures?*

A. Certainly it ought to. No effort can be too great for it.

Q. *Should not the Sangh give instructions in the essentials of Hindu religion in the Harijan hostels and in Harijan gatherings of adults?*

A. It ought to be the primary duty of the Sangh to give to Harijan children and adults a grounding in the essentials of

Hindu religion. If they were brought up in ignorance of these, they would not continue to remain in the Hindu fold, and the responsibility for it would rest on those who had failed to give them the necessary instructions.

Shri Sitaram Shastri of Vinaya Ashram, Guntur, asked whether the Sangh ought not to specially train a body of missionaries to carry on propaganda work among the Savarna Hindus. He was prepared to start a training centre for that purpose in his Ashram if he were given adequate help.

Gandhiji, however, had grave doubts as to the practicability of the suggestion. In fact the question had actually been raised by Shri Ghanashyamdas Birla several years ago and dropped after full discussion. He would be quite satisfied if at least the members of the Sangh would fully come up to the ideal.

Gandhiji was next asked: "Ought not we to set up a precedent for having Harijan representatives in the Sangh or at least one member in the Executive Committee of the Sangh?" In reply he referred to the history of the birth of the Harijan Sevak Sangh at the conclusion of the Poona Pact, which resulted in the modification of the decision of the MacDonald Government, on the question of the representation of the minorities. 'It was felt that if the rot was to be effectively stopped Hinduism ought to be completely rid of the curse of untouchability. This called for a real change of heart and repentance for its past sins on the part of Hindu society. It was to that end that the Harijan Sevak Sangh was formed.

"I am, therefore, opposed to both the propositions," proceeded Gandhiji. "I know that under the present arrangement some Harijans are included in the Board of the Sangh. But this was a concession to Thakkar Bapa's weakness. I have described the Harijan Sevak Sangh as an organisation of penitent sinners. Its object is to call upon the so-called Savarna Hindus to do expiation for having harboured untouchability. The inclusion of a Harijan in the Sangh would be mere *eye-wash* and make-believe, as his would be a mere voice in the wilderness. Before long, he would himself heartily wish to be out of it. I say this from my personal experience of the way in which committees function. I know the Sangh cannot always keep up to the mark. It is, of course, open to the Sangh to alter its scope and give Harijans a majority in its Executive Committee or appoint a competent body of representative Harijans to act as a Board of Advisors and Supervisors and keep the Sangh on the alert and on the right track."

Gandhiji was next asked to give his opinion on the recent work in the Gwalior State to enlist the services of the Sadhu community in the cause of Harijan uplift. Gandhiji replying said he had grave doubts to the correctness or advisability of the step. It seemed to him to smack of politics. He would welcome the assistance of true Sadhus, if it was available. But he confessed, he looked in vain in the country for Sadhus of his conception. Such Sadhus as he saw disappointed him. There might be here and there honourable exceptions and their help would be welcome. But he was frankly sceptical of the possibility of utilising Sadhus as a body for their work. Even if they tried the experiment, he was afraid they would come to the parting of the ways before long.

Another friend asked whether a portion of the Kasturba Memorial Trust Fund ought not to be earmarked for Harijan sisters. Gandhiji's reply was that they could have the whole of it if they could show the capacity to utilise it. No special earmarking of a part was, therefore, necessary.

The questions and answers finished, Gandhiji addressed a few general remarks to those assembled to give his diagnosis of the relative sluggishness of the Harijan Sevak Sangh's activities and his remedy for the same. "I am responsible for the policy of conducting Harijan uplift work through the agency of the Savarna Hindus. They had to do expiation. All of them, I argued to myself, could help with money even if they could not, owing to lack of necessary qualifications, render direct service. For instance, they might not be able themselves to do teaching work, but they could engage a competent teacher to give education to Harijan children. That would be one way of doing expiation. They would be able to penetrate Harijan society and help in its progress." He knew there were sceptical critics, who questioned whether this kind of work could lead to the eradication of untouchability. He himself was at one time among the doubters. But he had since realised his mistake. He owed a debt of gratitude in this respect to the late Shri Devdhar, at whose activity he had at one time looked askance and which he had even criticised. A year's experience, however, had cured him of his conceit and taught him humility. He realised that if he confined himself exclusively to doing propaganda among the Savarna Hindus with a view to their conversion, he might have to wait till the Greek Kalends and in the meantime the actual uplift work among the Harijans would remain hopelessly bogged. His own experience has since convinced him that if they could only have sufficient workers with the requisite purity and devotion and spirit of sacrifice to work among Harijans, untouchability would become a thing of the past, even if the Savarna Hindus were left severely alone. But that would mean that they must become Harijans at heart and live and labour among the Harijans as Harijans. "But can the members of the Harijan Sevak Sangh truthfully claim to have eradicated the last trace of untouchability from their own hearts? Are their professions altogether on a par with their practice?" he asked.

A member asked as to what his criterion was in that respect. "Are you married?" questioned Gandhiji in return. "I happen to be", replied the puzzled interlocutor. "Then have you an unmarried daughter?" resumed Gandhiji. "If you have, get for her a Harijan bridegroom not to satisfy her lust but in a purely religious spirit and I shall send you a wire of congratulations at my expense."

"You will now realise," continued Gandhiji, " why the Harijan Sevaks are unable to move the hearts of the Savarna Hindus. The reason is that they have not that fire of faith in their hearts, impatient hunger for service which is the first essential for an effective appeal. Let but a handful of Savarna Hindus go forth in that true missionary spirit and they will leaven the entire

Hindu mass. But not even a whole army of missionaries so-called will produce any effect upon them." It needed a Malaviyaji to make such a missionary. He (Gandhiji) could not convert his own sister. And if he could not, argued he, how could he blame others? That would show how hard and thorny was that path. It was, however, open to them if they felt that they had the necessary qualification, to try the experiment for themselves in their locality.

The reason for this partial failure, Gandhiji proceeded to explain, was also that the approach of most of the members of the Harijan Sevak Sangh to their mission was not unmixed with political motives. If they really wanted to penetrate the hearts of Savarna Hindus, they ought to be filled with a purely religious spirit. Mere dialectics was a poor weapon for this kind of work. As it was, they were too much weighed down by inertia, heedlessness and woodenness of mind.

"The other method is more fierce and not altogether free from danger," continued Gandhiji. "It is the method of fasting." He himself had before condemned fasting when it seemed to him to be wrong or morally unjustified. But to shirk a fast when there was a clear moral indication was a dereliction from duty. Such a fast had to be based on unadulterated Truth and Ahimsa." (*Harijan*, 28 July, 1946)

Further, what should be the qualifications of members of Harijan Boards and what should be the number constituting them are the questions often asked. Only those will be included who are eager to serve the cause and whose presence will promote the usefulness of the Board to which they belong and whose capacity for service will be increased by their being members of a Board.

No one should allow himself or herself to be a member of a Board unless he or she:

(1) believes in the uttermost removal of untouchability;

(2) pays something to the Board according to his or her capacity;

(3) does some definite Harijan service, e.g., having a Harijan in his or her home as a member of the family, or at least as a domestic servant, or his teaching a Harijan or Harijans, or paying a regular visit to Harijan quarters and cleaning them, or, if he or she is a doctor, treating Harijan patients free of charge, etc.;

(4) sends to the Board a diary containing a record of his or her service from month to month.

If some such conditions are observed, there need be no restriction on the number of members. The more, the merrier. Such Boards will meet to take notes, exchange experiences and solve mutual difficulties. They will never waste time in fruitless discussions.

There may be Advisory Committees attached to the Boards. These will lay down for themselves some minimum qualifications. Naturally the qualifications of Advisors will be less stringent than those of members of regular Boards.

"What if members with the qualifications I have described cannot be found is the natural question arising from the bare mention of them. I must repeat the answer I have given often enough before now. The persons invited by the Central Board to form Sanghs in their own provinces will, in the absence of members having the necessary qualifications, perform the service through agents. "Act True" must be the motto of every Harijan Board, and there should never be any departure from the wholesome maxim." (*Harijan,* Nov. 9, 1934)

Mahatmaji had suggested the formation of Advisory Committees of Harijans to assist Harijan Sevak Sangh Boards consisting of Caste Hindus. On being asked for guidance in this matter by a Harijan correspondent, Gandhiji replied:

> "I should suggest the formation of compact, small representative Committees who would truly represent the opinion of local Harijans. They would frame rules for the

conduct of their proceedings and formulate their expectations of Savarna Hindus and generally watch the proceedings of Harijan Boards. These Advisory Committees, wherever they are formed, would advise Harijan Boards of their existence and show their preparedness to help the latter. If the Boards are sincere in their desire to discharge their debt, that is, to serve Harijans, they will establish the friendliest contact with the Advisory Committees, and perfect co-operation and harmony will prevail. There may be friction in the beginning because of mutual suspicion. Harijan Boards, being naturally better organised and better off in every respect, will have to exercise tact in handling what may appear to be extravagant demands. Advisory Committees would endeavour to be considerate. The more considerate they are, the better able they will be to help themselves. From their ability to conduct themselves in a dignified manner, they will learn the art of asserting themselves if the occasion ever arises. For they should know that Savarna Hindus will never be able to discharge their debt except with the co-operation of Harijans. But the question of asserting themselves does not arise just yet, because the vast mass of Harijans have been rendered so completely helpless that they have no power of resisting injustice, even if they wanted to. Let me explain what I mean. Harijan Boards have three functions, to raise the economic, social and religious status of Harijans, or to put it in another way, to remove the difficulties that Savarna Hindus have for centuries put in the way of Harijans raising their heads in any department of life. Thus the Harijan Boards have to provide wells, scholarships, boarding houses, schools and social amenities, wherever the need arises. In all these, the general body of Harijans simply take the help wherever it is offered. Advisory Committees can, therefore, help the cause and themselves by making useful suggestions to the Boards and also rendering such help as they themselves can to those whom they represent. Thus only will they acquire the power of asserting themselves. In short, Advisory Committees will best help the cause by taking up internal reform and causing an awakening among the Harijan masses, so that they may begin to realise that they are men and women entitled to the same rights as are enjoyed by the other members of the society to which they belong." (*Harijan*, April 20, 1934)

Further, at Rajahmundry a deputation of Harijans met Gandhiji and had a long talk with him. They agreed, among other things, that, as they had sufficient men among them who were enlightened and efficient, they should be entrusted with the reins of the Harijan Sevak Sangh. Caste Hindus, they said, might help in the work, but the office bearers should be all Harijans. Gandhiji gave them the following reply:

"One important question that you have raised is that the Harijan Sevak Sangh should be principally manned and managed by you. That shows that you have not followed the pages of the *Harijan*. That shows also that you have not understood the origin of the Board. The Board has been formed to enable Savarna Hindus to do repentance and reparation to you. It is thus a Board of Debtors, and yon are the creditors. You owe nothing to the debtors, and therefore, so far as this Board is concerned, the initiative has to come from the debtors. You have to certify whether the debtors discharge their obligation or not. What you have to do is to enable and help them to discharge their obligation; that is to say, you can tell them how they can discharge their obligation you can tell them what, in your opinion, will satisfy the great body of Harijans. They may or may not accept your advice. If they do not, naturally they run the risk of incurring your displeasure. A debtor may go to a creditor and say to him, 'I have brought so much money, will you take it?" The creditor may say, 'Off you go; I want full payment or none.' Or the creditor may say, 'What you have brought is not part payment, but worse.' All these things you, creditors, can do. And so, when this Board was established and some Harijan friends wrote to me, I told them that Harijans should form themselves into Advisory Boards or Boards of Inspection. I want you to understand this distinction thoroughly. You will please see that there is no desire not to accept your advice or co-operation or help. I am only putting before you the true and logical position. This is a period of grace that God has given to Caste Hindus, and it is during this period of grace that they have to prove their sincerity. And I am moving heaven and earth and am going about from place to place, simply in order that this obligation on the part of Savarna Hindus may be fully discharged."

A member of the deputation then suggested that the Board should appoint Advisory Committees of Harijans of its own selection. Gandhiji, 'as a fellow Harijan by choice', showed them the danger underlying this suggestion and said, "Do not ask the Board to select a Committee of Harijans; but select your own Committee and say to the Board, you have selected these members and it should carry on correspondence with them. There is another danger in the suggestion. There may be factions and divisions among you. Different committees may be appointed by different factions. The Board may recognise all of them. But that will be unfortunate. Let there be no quarrels among you. Present a united front to the debtors. The debtors may put you against one another, though the Board, if it is worth its name, will not do that, The Congress has been able to present a united front. Today, the Congress is full of simple men like you and me. You should have a body of business-like men who will put down with a strong hand all quarrels among you. Then you will dominate the Board without being on it. Do not be easily satisfied. Tell the debtors you are not going to be satisfied with 5 shillings in the pound but that you must have 20 shillings in the pound. This is not a matter for bargaining". (*Harijan,* Jan. 5, 1934)

Again, Gandhiji, recommended a 'Harijan Day' to be fixed under the auspices of the Harijan Sevak Sangh. It should be a day of sanitation and cleanliness. The poorest could do this by denying themselves a meal or a portion thereof. House to house collection was to be made by the members. The literature should be sold or given away as the exigency of the time might require.

In a sacred cause like the Harijan cause, a special day should be one of greater dedication, prayer and intensive work. I should divide the day somewhat after this style:

1. I should begin the day from 5 A.M. with prayer and

set apart for the cause some money or cloth or grain according to my means. The poorest can do this by denying themselves a meal or meals or a portion thereof without feeling the slightest deprivation. Preferably donations in kind should be converted into cash. Where this is not possible, they should be given to the most deserving and needy Harijans.

2. The work of the family Bhangi, if there is any, should be wholly done by the family or at least shared with him. This will enable one to understand the nature of the service that the Bhangi performs and may also lead to an improved method of performing such services. Not many persons have any consideration for the 'knight of the broom' at the time of using the sanitary conveniences. If we had no untouchability in us and if we even occasionally shared the work with the Bhangis, we would have a different method of working the home sanitary system.

3. Having done these two things, we are ready for corporate effort for the day, which should open with house to house collection of donations in cash or kind. This work should be finished by a given hour. The donations should be handed to the local committee, which will in its turn, hand the collection to the superior committee till it reaches the headquarters of the province. Collectors should take with them a judicious section of literature including leaflets, pamphlets books and even copies of *Harijan*, English or vernacular edition as may be required. The literature should be sold or given away as the exigency of the moment may require. But each committee should bear the cost of the literature ordered by it. If extra copies of the *Harijan* required, previous advice should be given to the publishers so as to enable them to print extra copies.

4. Harijan quarters should be visited in each place and they should be cleaned wherever necessary. Meetings

of Harijan should be held and their wants noted. They should be advised as to the part they have to play in the removal of untouchability. Dr. Deshmukh's authoritative opinion should be used in support of the plea for the giving up of carrioneating. Children can arrange meetings and excursions for Harijan children. Possibilities of inauguration of improved methods of sanitation should be explored. It is neither difficult nor expensive if the people will shoulder the burden willingly. In the end it means a visible addition to the health and wealth of the community.

5. The day should be wound-up by a general meeting of both Savarnas and Harijans to pass resolutions, pledging the meeting to the removal of untouchability and emphasising the desirability of permissive legislation regarding temple entry.
6. Where public opinion is favourable, public wells and private temples should be opened to Harijans.

An accurate report of the work done should be sent to the Central Committee. (*Harijan,* April, 15, 1933)

Hardly has the great central organisation of the Servants of Untouchables Society (Harijan Sevak Sangh) made the commencement, when complaints against it and the provincial organisations have cropped up. They come chiefly and naturally from Harijans. One of these correspondents sent to me some time ago an able letter, undertaking to give details if I desired. I took him at his word and asked him to give me details; and the letter he has sent me in reply is abler than the first. It will compete with any well written report of an inspector. It contains a summary of reports of every organisation claiming to work in the writer's province for the uplift of Harijans, and after giving me sufficient details, his one conclusion about all the organisations practically without exception is:

> "They are run principally by Caste men who have their own axes to grind or who are in need of some occupation that

> would maintain them decently. The utmost that some of these have done is to fling a few scholarships at Harijan boys. Some others have been great at delivering lectures. All have come to us as patrons. Hardly has anyone come as a friend and equal, let alone as a servant. Your provincial organisation is no exception. It is difficult for a Harijan to approach its chief man without fear and trembling. He is always in danger of being met with a frown."

My correspondent is also not without suggestions, which may be summarised thus:

> "If you are to take advantage of the great awakening that has taken place, you must concentrate upon primary education on a mass scale. You will not drive out the ignorance of ages without spreading that education. We shall certainly help, but seeing that Caste Hindus want to remove untouchability and make us one with them, there is no better way of employing their money and their labour than in imparting this education."

It is necessary to know the Harijan mind in any programme of work that may be taken up. Caste Hindus, for whom removal of untouchability is a matter of penance and purification, have undoubtedly to do much more than open schools everywhere. I have discussed elsewhere where such schools may be opened. The conduct of Caste Hindus would be generally tested by its reaction upon the mass mind of the Harijans. If we have really changed towards them, they will feel the change in a thousand ways. Our activity, I mean that of Caste Hindus, will affect every department of their lives. Even in the remotest village we are interdependent, so much so that this interdependence cannot be dissolved all at once, even if we desired it, without resulting in the greatest harm to the nation in general; and this interdependence, which is today that of slave and master, will never be corrected unless there is absolute religious equality. It is a tremendous task, but as we progress towards the goal, the truth must dawn upon every Caste Hindu that there is no halfway house between abject slavery and perfect religious equality. Hence my bumble insistence upon temple entry without losing sight of the other things we must do.

My correspondent is bitter in discussing what he considers to be the extravagant management of the different organisations that have come under his lash. As an expert organiser that I may claim to be, I have been generally guided by the rule that the cost of administration, that is, overhead charges, should never exceed 10 per cent of the receipts—5 per cent being the ideal—the balance going to the cause which brought the organisation into being. I suggest this test to the Central Board and the Provincial Boards and all other independent Harijan organisations run by Caste Hindus. Let it not be said of us that we spend more on running the organisations than upon Harijans themselves. Let us see to it that, out of every Rs. 100 received as donation for the Harijan cause, Rs. 90 go straight into the pockets of Harijans. Therefore, our officials should be largely volunteers, never highly paid wherever paid service is required. Wherever it is possible, we should get Harijans. We should select candidates and train them. The correspondent says that peons in the organisations inspected by him are not drawn from the Harijan ranks.

Let every organisation for the service of Harijans introspect itself in the light of the criticism I have condensed and the suggestions I have made. (*Harijan,* March 13, 1933)

'I have repeatedly said that this work can be done only by those who sincerely believe untouchability to be a stain on Hinduism. This is a movement requiring the change of heart of millions. It cannot be led to success by any political manoeuvres. It can be done only through self-purification. This is a great sacrificial fire in which we have to burn our load of sins and come out purified. Those who do not take to this work with faith and spirit will fail to move the hearts of millions. We shall be nowhere if we deceive ourselves or the Harijans. The success or failure of this movement depends on our getting the right type of workers. We are on our trial today. If we miss today the opportunity that God has given us, we may never hope to get the opportunity again in this generation. What we refuse to do voluntarily today we shall have to do in future perforce, and we shall repent for having lost this opportunity. I pray to God that we may come out successful from this trial and save Hinduism and ourselves from destruction. (*Harijan,* Dec. 1, 1933)

"Injustice is being done all the word over, but we have given to it the sanction of religion. These distinctions have not been created by God. The Harijans are on the lowest rung of the ladder not because of any inherent defects but only because they have been kept down by the so-called higher castes. God had bestowed on them the same talents that He had given us, but we deny them the opportunities for using them. They should surely have the same rights and privileges and the same opportunities of growth that we enjoy.

"We are now awake to the wrong we have done to them, and the least we can do by way of penance now is to contribute money for their uplift and to share with them all the amenities of life that we have created for ourselves. We are all creatures of the same God and, therefore, equal in His eyes.

"From the money that you give for this cause, you will reap a hundred-fold, for it is like grain sown in good, manured soil. The money spent after luxury and lust is, on the other hand, wasted like grain sown in barren soil.

"I am told you have suffered heavily. But you should know that no nation has ever come to its own without having passed through the severest fire of suffering. Voluntary suffering only adds of our strength. I, therefore, congratulate you for having suffered. But I should also like to remind you that one of the causes that add to our sufferings is this curse of untouchability. We have oppressed the weak. We reap as we have sown. It is for us now to undo the wrong we have done to the Harijans and remove the yoke of serfdom from their shoulders.

"Caste Hindus must first ask you to forgive the wrongs they

have done to you. But I should also tell you, as a Harijan by choice, that you should give up your evil habits, especially carrion and beef-eating. The whole world looks upon carrion with abhorrence. And beef-eating should be given up because that is a *sine qua non* for a Hindu. The cow is the giver of plenty, and by killing her we kill ourselves. Then, I would urge you not to accept leavings. And above all, you should abolish the distinctions of high and low that have crept in among yourselves. And these things you should do, not in a bargaining spirit but because they are good in themselves. I would, therefore, ask you also to give up drink, irrespective of the fact that many other Hindus drink." (*Harijan*, Dec. 1, 1993)

> "A friend writes:
>
> 'I observe that there are some people in the Harijan service organisations not working in the spirit in which you want them to, that is, merely for the sake of serving Harijans. They are seeking its shelter in order to satisfy other ambitions .... I know that you do not desire civil resistance to be mixed up with Harijan service organisations. If you propose to make any public use of the letter you may emphasise this last point and make it clearer ....'

"I am thankful to the friend for giving me the benefit of his experience. It is a most difficult task to keep a big organisation like the Servants of Untouchables Society with branches all over India free of all self-seekers and time-servers. I have discussed the subject fully with Seth Ghanshyamdas and Thakkar Bapa. I know that they are both anxious to keep the organisation as pure as possible. Personally I can do no more. It was because of my utter helplessness that I undertook the fast of 21 days. On discovering impurities amongst Harijan servants, I saw that it was no use merely writing about impurities. I was searching for a way out of the difficulty. The reader should believe me when I tell him that the fast was the last thing in the world that I was thinking of, but as I have described in these pages, it came to me all of a sudden and gave me great relief. I know that it did much good. But, how far could the fast of a single mortal go? Hence it was that I developed the idea of a chain of such purificatory fasts. The idea has by no means been dropped. It comes to me again and again, But it does not admit of a mechanical organisation. Several co-workers are ready to inaugurate or take part in the chain after it is inaugurated, but I have not yet found the way to begin it. The proper way will have to come to me or to the co-workers before the chain can be begun. Meanwhile I can only reiterate my conviction that untouchability will not be removed root and branch except through the service of men and women who take it up for its own sake and in a religious spirit. Unless we have a fair number of such servants throughout the length and breadth of India, we will never succeed in changing the hearts of millions of human beings. The *Savarna* Hindus are at one end, Harijans at the other, and the evil custom of ages, which has assumed the dignity of religious tenet, will not be uprooted without penance and purification. Whilst it gladdens my heart that thousands of people flock to the meetings that are being held in towns and villages and that they willingly give their pices as a token of their approval of the movement, I am painfully conscious of the fact that, if the thousands were suddenly called upon to enforce in their own lives what they seem to approve by their attendance at these meetings, they would fail to respond. not from want of will, but from sheer inability. I have discovered this again and again amongst my closest associates who have frankly confessed their inability to enforce immediately in their conduct what they knew was the right thing and what they knew had to be done immediately. They had to put up a brave fight against their traditional repugnance. The mere intellectual grasp that untouchability is an evil, corroding Hinduism, and that belief in it is tantamount to disbelief in God, His goodness and His Fatherhood, is not enough to destroy the monster. The vicarious penance of the comparatively pure is needed to bring about a change in the hearts of both *Savarnas* and Harijans.

"A movement, so grand and so pure, so religious and so humanitarian, must not be exploited by anybody for his own end. Certainly, not for its political consequences. It will be discovered, as the movement progresses, that the political approach can only end in accentuating the strife. It can only add to the confusion already existing and add one more, if not many more warring parties, to the existing ones. May God save us and save the movement from such a calamity!

"So far as the connection of civil resistance with the movement is concerned, I am as emphatic as ever that Congressmen who desire to offer active civil resistance should not accept office in the various organisations, and much less can they be used for serving the purpose of civil resistance. Civil resistance is a unique weapon, it does not admit of alloy. It is a weapon of the fearless and, therefore, needs no shelter; but it has to be wielded in the open daylight. 'Therefore, whilst Congressmen who are also civil registers on active service may do, as they are bound to do, such service to the cause as they can, they may not belong to the Servants of Untouchables Society or any of its branches. By holding office in the organisations they will harm both civil resistance and the Harijan cause. It would be like a man going to a temple to pray and using the act of worship for advancing civil resistance. Neither God nor man will be cheated in that manner and, as I have said often enough in these columns, the great reformation of Hinduism will not be brought about, if it is to depend purely upon Congressmen. For, much as I would like to think that every Indian is a Congressman, I know that such is not the case. Nor is every Hindu a Congressman, if only because every Harijan is not a Congressman. Therefore, a Harijan organisation must in the very nature of things be strictly non-political and non-party and should contain in it both Congressmen and non-Congressmen, office-holding being restricted to those who are not active civil resistors and who will not exploit the office secretly or openly to advance the cause of civil resistance." (*Harijan,* Nov. 24, 1933)

"A correspondent sends me the following questions for answering:

1. In the propaganda against untouchability, should a worker make use of the Hindu Shastras and religious

texts to show that Hinduism does not sanction untouchability as we practise it today?

2. Should a Harijan sevak, even in his private capacity, take part in inter-dining functions?
3. Should a Harijan who is employed as a domestic servant sit at meals alongside all the members of the family?

"These three questions, the correspondent says, have been seriously discussed in the columns of a newspaper and the readers have been advised that Harijan workers should serve with all seriousness, I, therefore, beseech you, to purify your hearts of the sin of untouchability, to treat Harijan boys and girls as if they are your own children, brothers and sisters. We have for long ages suppressed Harijans and today if we sacrifice our all for their sake we shall be only making some slight and tardy reparation for all the wrongs inflicted upon them in the name of religion. Therefore, whatever you give, whether it is a trinket or heavy piece of jewellery or silver, I want you to give as merely a token of your determination to rid yourselves of this taint of untouchability, the idea that you are high and somebody else is low. May God give you wisdom to see this very simple truth and enforce it in your life. Now you can give the things, whether jewellery, or silver or paper, whatever you want to give." (*The Hindu,* Jan. 15, 1934)

Remarkably, in an address presented to him at a public meeting held at Calicut on 13 January, 1934, Gandhi replied:

"I am much obliged to you for these addresses that have been presented to me this evening and I thank you for the self-restraint you have imposed upon yourselves by not desiring to read those addresses to me. Only you have thereby appreciated the fact that I have been going from one place to another from day to day, now for over two months, and at the end of the day I am, therefore, fatigued. You, wise men that you are, have appreciated this fact and absolved me from the duty of having to listen to these addresses. You having exercised this self-restraint, naturally it was up to me to read those addresses and be prepared. But I must say to you that I had no notion whatsoever that I was to have all these addresses nor have I been given copies of these addresses. Had I been given copies I would certainly have read them. However I have no doubt whatsoever that these addresses contain nothing more than what I have noticed in the numerous addresses that I have been receiving throughout these two months or more. Almost without exception they have expressed to me great joy, not only their sympathy with the cause that I am espousing for the time being but they have in these addresses signified their intention, nay their determination, of doing everything that these various bodies of gentlemen or ladies could possibly do in their own sphere to advance the Harijans' cause.

"It has given me a great deal of satisfaction and joy to discover that there is consensus of opinion on the part of the intelligentsia. I would have been painfully surprised if it had been otherwise. Not only has it been so with reference to the intelligentsia but as far as mere assent goes, I have found to my great delight the masses also are equally with this movement. I am not easily self-deluded. I have no doubt that I have, must have, my due share of self-delusion or else life perhaps would be a positive burden to most of us if not to all of us. But due allowance having been made for self-delusion I can say that all these scenes that I witness every day cannot possibly be a matter of masses or classes coming to me to signify their praise or their satisfaction for services that I might have performed in a previous life or in days gone by. This life has rushed and with me it has rushed with such rapidity that it is impossible for me to have a photography of the events that have happened and, that being the case, I should be intensely surprised and also disappointed that these classes and masses had signified not only their satisfaction and their sympathy by their presence at these meetings but also give me donations more or less and had done certain acts also as a consideration for those services. I would let that pass by. I am assuming that all your addresses contain a serious and solemn pledge that you are determined to do everything that is humanly possible for you to do to render the reparation that is overdue to the Harijans. Malabar, if one were to draw the untouchability map of the whole of India, I suppose will easily wear the black crown and Malabar would be the blackest spot so far as untouchability is concerned. It is a matter of regret but it is no use ignoring the fact. I would turn this blackness to good account and I would invite you to gird up your loins and make such Herculean effort that at the end of the struggle it may be possible to say of Malabar that Malabar had been in the vanguard of progress in this battle against the monster of untouchability. Let it be said of Malabar that Malabar counted no sacrifices too great for removing this evil of untouchability. And what could be a better and more sacred reminder for this meeting than the portrait of Mr. K. Madhavan Nair?

"I had the pleasure of knowing him long ago. When I first visited Calicut I had the honour of being introduced to him but I must confess that I did not know him so intimately as I came to know him when he paid me a visit at Yervada. I came into very intimate touch with him, and when Mr. C. Rajagopalacharia was here and the Guruvayur referendum was going on, naturally I was corresponding with him as with other friends almost from day to day. Then Smt. Urmila Devi and my wife came, into close contact with Mr. K. Madhavan Nair. My wife is a simple woman. She knows nothing, she does not know the English language, certainly she does not know Malayalam, but she was able to tell me in her very simple language that she was very much struck by the simplicity of his character. She merely strengthened the impression that Mr. Madhavan had left on my mind and that impression is still indelible. I have the most vivid recollection of my contact with him and what struck me most was his transparent humility. This is his faithful picture and I congratulate the artist on presenting the citizens of Calicut with this picture. I think there you can easily see humility written in his features. I don't think that the artist has enhanced the transparence of his humility. I think the artist is incapable of doing that. To look at Mr. Madhavan Nair and look at the living eye would give you a better illustration of that humility. The whole of his behaviour is on the picture. Mr. Madhavan Nair is in front of me today as I saw him in Yeravda. He stands vividly before me and this is the one peculiar impression that he left on me.

"I discovered also that he was a man of very few words. You do not find many people who are economical in the use of language or their words. In his contact with me Mr. Madhavan Nair showed this quality in a supreme degree. His letters were compact, nice, neat and the briefest possible. Whatever he had to say he expressed in a few words and he had finished. That was the man. If you were to recall the men who had died in body but are even now still living, you will discover that they are living not because of their intellectual gifts but because of virtues which you and I and every one of us can cultivate if we have the will and if we will make the necessary effort in order to cultivate them. Therefore, I would say you will be doing wrong to the memory of the man whom I have described as I have known him, if you think that you have performed your duty by calling upon me to unveil his portrait and for having witnessed this ceremony and having heard a few words in praise of his memory; nay, you will be doing wrong. But you will be doing the right thing if you will treasure this as a perpetual reminder to you that you also would like to be if not wholly at least somewhat like Mr. Madhavan Nair. At the end, to put a finishing touch, Mr. Madhavan Nair died in harness so far as the Harijan cause is concerned. He was a true co-worker in the Harijan cause which is a matter of self-purification, repentance and reparation. I give you my evidence that Mr. Madhavan Nair, when he took up this cause, had the spirit in him, for every act that he did in connection with the Harijan cause was an act of sacrifice, repentance and reparation. There was no meanness about anything that he did. May his memory ever remain in ray heart and in your own hearts.

"I thank you once more for having presented me with addresses. Since I think that this is not the proper time for auctioning these addresses, I hope that tomorrow you will help me to realise some money from these addresses because I know that Calicut will not send me away with disappointment." (*The Hindu*, 15 Jan. 1934)

REFERENCES

1. *Harijan*, various issues.
2. J.B. Kripalani, *Gandhi: His Life and Thought*, Delhi, 1970, p. 383.
3. *The Hindu*, 15 January 1934.

5

Gandhi and the Tribals

As we have seen, Gandhi was deeply concerned with the pathetic situation of Dalits whom he christened as Harijans. But he was aware of the problems of *Adivasis* (i.e. tribals) also.

In this chapter we give an elaborate account of the political perception of the tribal question revealed by Mahatma Gandhi's attempt to understand it and by the interaction of various viewpoints within the parameters of the nationalist movement and its programme of social reform. The Mahatma's pre-occupation was with the development of a technique of social action based on non-violence (satyagraha). He took up only a few major issues, such as national freedom, untouchability, communal unity and rural reconstruction and sought to develop through the implementation of the programmes revolving around them the people's collective will, *lok shakti,* as the supreme solvent of social ills.

The tribal (adivasi) problem, as such, did not claim his attention until the early 1940s, but he exercised the imagination of the tribal people, as of other segments of the rural community, and his life and mission became known through the adivasi welfare programmes implemented by a number of organisations. A number of social movements among the tribes were influenced by him. Two key figures, Amritlal Thakkar, popularly known as Thakkar Bapa, and Verrier Elwin, who shaped free India's 'tribal policy, came in close contact with him. Thakkar Bapa was a life-long collaborator, and he in a way influenced the Mahatma's interest in the tribal problem.

In consonance with this line of thinking, he reminded Thakkar Bapa, who was preoccupied with the tribal problems, of the Hindus' duty towards the harijans rather than the tribals, and persuaded him to accept the secretaryship of the Harijan Sevak Sangh:

> There is no limit to your greed. By all means satisfy it to the top of your bent. Your secretaryship surely is no hindrance.... You can give as much of your time as you like to the Adivasis while discharging your duty as Secretary of the Sangh. You do not want to tell me that you want to resign even after that latitude.... But the eradication of the sin of untouchability calls for the moral force of the pure in heart. Do not forget that the irreligion of untouchability is today being sanctioned as religion. *That is not so in the case of Adivasis* [italics mine]. I do not mind therefore your dedicating yourself to the service of the Adivasis, but it must not be at the cost of the Harijans. (Pyarelal, *op. cit.*)

Bapa yielded to the Mahatma's advice. He would, however, often yearn to go back to his first love, the tribals. Gandhiji, who did not "depreciate the service of the Adivasis" but thought that the service of the Harijans must have the first claim on the Hindus", reminded him:

> Our ancestors have sinned grievously by putting Harijans virtually out of the pale of Hindu society. It is our sacred duty to give them once again an honoured place amongst outselves. The work is nothing less than that of reforming the current Hindu religion. No, Thakkar, while you and I live, that must be our primary duty.
>
> Everything else must come after, however important it may be in itself. All you can do is to leave a large part of the actual work to your colleagues and confining yourself to general supervision, give as much time to the Adivasis as you can spare, but the responsibility for the Harijan Sevak Sangh will lie on you. Neither of us can divorce ourselves from that work. (SG Vaze, *op. cit.*)

Gandhiji was sensitive to the social and moral aspects of conversion among the illiterate rural masses including the tribals. He believed that there was no such thing as conversion from one faith to another. Religion was a personal matter between an individual and his God:

> It is a conviction daily growing upon me that the great and rich Christian Missionaries will render true service to India if confine their activities to humanitarian service without the ulterior motive of converting India, or at least her unsophisticated villagers, to Christianity, and destroying their social superstructure, which notwithstanding many defects has stood now from time immemorial the onslaught upon it from within and from without.... Every living faith must have within itself the power of rejuvenation, it if is to live. (Gandhi, Christian Missions: *Their Place in India,* p. 78)

Gandhi was not so much against conversion, as against the methods of it. "The methods of conversion must be like Caesar's wife, above suspicion. No nationalist government will antagonise Christians but only oppose insidious ways of undermining it".There was no point in the missionaries weaning away the tribals from their animistic faith and superstitions; they should be allowed to develop according to their laws and compulsions.

C.F. Andrews, on the other hand, justified proselytisation as a means of conferring on tribes freedom from primitive terrors and savageries. He wrote to Elwin, a supporter of Gandhiji's views on conversion:

> And I cannot at all agree with Bapu that most forms of "religion" which are really evil in their essence, are not to be condemned, and those who practise them are not to be converted. I believe in South India the devil worship is absolutely hideous in some of its forms and utterly unworthy of man made in the image of God.

And he warned Elwin:

> Have you not gone too far in following Bapu about "conversion"? I fully accept that these hill tribes must be free from the suspicion and fear that you must have some ulterior motive. But the joy which we have in our own hearts owing to the love of Christ must find its expression,

> because it is the one motive power in our own lives. Bapu would seem to suggest that even to wish in one's own heart to give to another that joy, which has been the strength and stay of one's own life, is itself wrong. (Quoted in *Tribal World of Verreer Elwin*)

Remarkably, Andrews was perhaps as logical as Gandhi, but to the latter the right of the individual to shape his destiny according to his own will and judgement was an article of faith. Gandhiji, however, admired the missionary spirit. Speaking in the vastly different context of what one could do with the tribal people of the north-west, he said in 1946:

> I would accept a challenge of conquering tribal areas, but as a non-violent man I would not bribe them nor kill them: I would serve them. Have not the missionaries allowed themselves to be eaten by cannibals? (Tendulkar, p. 28)

Notably, in the early forties, Gandhiji showed an awareness of the tribal problem, and he was the first and foremost of the national leaders to have done so. The tomes of the Congress resolutions did not contain a word about the tribal issue;• probably there was no attempt to identify the issues in the times of the all-consuming struggle for independence, when the tribal issue was considered a minor part of the wider social and economic challenge.

As a significant phenomenon, in December 1941, Gandhiji drew up the 13-point reconstruction programme. In January 1942, it was enlarged to include tribal welfare as the fourteenth item, reportedly at the instance of Thakkar Bapa. But Gandhi was no less with it; for in the meanwhile, he had come to realise that tribals were materially no better than the harijans, that the former constituted a sizeable segment of the population, and that the danger of their neglect and de-nationalisation was real. This was a departure from his old point of view:

> The Adivasis are the original inhabitants whose material position is perhaps no better than that of the Harijans and who have been long victims of neglect on the part of the so-called high classes. The Adivasis should have found a special

> place in the constructive programme. Non-mention was an oversight.... The Christian missionaries have been more or less in the sole occupation of the field. Great as his labour has been it has not prospered as it might have because of his ultimate aim being the Adivasis' conversion to his fold and thus becoming de-Indianised. Anyway, no one who hopes to construct *Swaraj* on the foundation of non-violence, can afford to neglect even the least of India's sons. Adivasis are too numerous to be counted among the least. (*Harijan*, Jan. 18, 1942, p. 5)

Notably, soon there followed the most disarming admission to have come from the foremost national leader, and in a vein so characteristic of him. He laid stress on the interdependence of various elements in the composite life of the nation and on the unity of all sections and all communities of this vast land of ours. As he said:

> Adivasis have become the fourteenth item in the constructive programme. But they are not the least in point of importance. Our country is so vast and the races are so varied that the best of us, in spite of every effort, cannot know all there is to know of men and their condition. As one comes upon layer after layer of things, one ought to know as a national servant, one nation whose every unit has a living consciousness of being one with one another. (*Harijan*, Feb. 15, 1942)

Remarkably, nothing hurt the nationalist in Gandhi more than the segregation of various communities, particularly the tribals, under the dangerous spell of the policy of the 'isolation and status quo. The Act of 1935, he recalled, separated tribals from the rest of the inhabitants. The excluded areas were placed under the government's direct administration; the adivasis were put into water-tight compartments and classified as tribal people by the government. "It was a shame", he told social workers, "that they had allowed them to be treated like that. It was up to them to make the Adivasis feel one with them".

In strategically situated Assam, in 1946, he reminded the people that "it was their shame, that the Adivasis should be isolated from the rest of the nation of which they were an inalienable part". Assam was a vast field for the constructive programme, which could serve as an effective instrument for bringing the tribals into the national fold. If a social worker was "prevented from rendering silent service to the Adivasis, he should prefer to go to prison because prison going would ever in itself advance their cause". (Tendulkar, *op. cit.*, p. 12)

Mahatma's Impact on Tribal Movements

Definitely the Mahatma's interest in the tribal problem crystallised at a late stage in his life, his influence on tribal movements was wide. In the course of his itineraries through the length and breadth of the country, he came in contact with the tribes and spoke to them in a language that was familiar to them. In September 1925, he passed through the tribal regions of Bihar, and made the first acquaintance of the Hos at Chaibasa and of the Mundas at Khunti (Ranchi); he was impressed with the colony of the *bhaktas* (Tana and Birsait bhagats) who believed in khaddar and nearly four hundred of them plied their *charkhas* most assiduously and sang their *bhajans* in a chorus. The spinning wheel had preceded the Mahatma. This was repeated seventeen years later at the Ramgarh Congress (1941). The visit made a profound impression on social movements among they Chotanagpur tribes.

Now to recall in brief the development of the tribal *bhagat* movements (bhagatism). A few of these movements arose in the medieval period under the impact of the Hindu *bhakti* movements spearheaded by Chaitanya who had passed through Jharkhand and by Kabir. In the wake of the growing contacts with Vaishnavism and socio-reform movements among the tribes, many bhagat cults came into existence, particularly among the Oraons, Santals, Mundas and Bhils. The bhagats attacked spirits and witchcraft, preached devotion to a personal God (often a Hindu deity), enjoined the observance of cleanliness and laid down a new code of moral conduct.

It is apt here to note that to the Hindu peasantry steeped in the medieval *bhakti* tradition, the Mahatma appeared like a *bhakti* preacher, and to the tribals like a bhagat. He spoke in predominantly *bhakti* idioms of *Ram rajya,* of the efficacy of *Ram nama,* of the service of the *Daridranarayan* (God in the shape of the poor) at his evening prayer meetings. Did he not also speak, a tribal bhagat would nod approvingly, of temperance, purity and of a personal God, as one of their own bhagat leaders (cf. Birsa Munda to the Mundas)? But the Mahatma also spoke of something more, of independence and freedom (swaraj), of a new order, of a new moral idiom. So new dimensions were added to tribal movements.

Now to some prominent movement, the Tanabhagat movement among the Oraons, the Haribaba movement among the Hos and allied tribes, and the Rajmohini movement among the Gonds, which reflected the impact of Gandhi.

The Tanabhagat movement among the Oraons started as a reformative movement after the First World War, but it assumed a political overtone when it came in contact with the Congress movement in Chotanagpur. To traditional bhagat idioms of purity, temperance and teetotalism were added new ones such as swaraj, Gandhi raj, non-payment of taxes, *ahimsa,* etc. The tribals seized upon these idioms to express their agrarian "hunger". The Tanabhagats refused to pay land tax, because Gandhi raj had arrived and the land belonged to them. They lost in consequence their land, but they remained, above twenty thousand of them or so—a small fraction of the Oraon community—a solid phalanx of the followers of the Congress and Gandhi, in the most unfavourable circumstances, pitted against the missionaries and the establishment.

Large numbers of them courted imprisonment, trekked long distances to attend the sessions of the Congress held in different parts of the country, propagated the message of the spinning-wheel and the National Flag, all the while hoping that when swaraj would come, they would not pay rent, and would get back all the land they had lost to the aliens, a familiar cry of the Sardar movement among the tribes in the 19th century. The Mundas' reaction to Gandhiji's Chotanagpur tour in 1925 who saw a similarity between their own Birsa and the Mahatma was understandable. A Santal leader in 1928-29 in Hazaribagh proclaimed himself as a disciple of Gandhi, exhorted his people to eschew meat and drink and wear the sacred thread like the Hindus. He declared that Gandhi raj would replace British raj and that Gandhi raj would bring ease and comfort and that the bullets of the Government soldiers would become harmless like water. The Santals refused to pay the *chowkidari* tax, and displayed the Congress flag.

The Mahatma crept into the bhagat's rituals. Some practised a secret ceremony: the father in the family would collect some rice and a few pice, make them into three packets for Gandhi, Durga and Kali, leave the packet for a short while by the side of a tank, throw Gandhi's packet into water and pick up the remaining two. No explanation of this queer practice, which was officially reported, was available.

Among the Hos, one Duka Ho, called Haribaba in 1930, proclaimed himself as one of the "most intimate disciples of Gandhi". The reign of Gandhi had arrived, his message ran, and this was to be celebrated with dance and feasts and by shouting "The British are no more: victory to Gandhi Mahto" The movement grew into a gigantic operation against village spirits and witchcraft before it subsided with the arrest of Haribaba and his colleagues. (Suresh Singh)

Notably, a bhagat movement developed among the Gonds of Surguja after the Mahatma's death. In 1951 Rajmohini, a Gond woman, driven to the extremity of hunger in a famine, went out to collect roots and tubers for her starving family. Exhausted, she lay unconscious. According to one of the versions put out by the workers of the Bapu Dharam Sabha Adivasi Seva Mandal, she had a vision of Mahatma Gandhi. Returning home she went on a fast for twenty-one days. Her prayer was granted, rain fell, peace and prosperity returned to her people. She turned a preacher. She called upon her people, in true bhagat tradition, to give up eating meat and telling lies and to follow the path of truth.

Adivasi Welfare Programmes

As we have seen, from the early 1920s a number of organisations for the welfare of the tribal people came into existence. Though they did not owe their origin to Gandhi, they were modelled on the rural reconstruction programme that Gandhi had drawn up. The Bhil Seva Mandal (1922) was organised by Thakkar Bapa in the wake of the famine in the Panch Mahal to promote the welfare of the Bhils through education imparted from a network of residential schools (ashrams), and to provide debt relief, eradication of drinking habits and inculcate cleanliness and purity in life. In the process, the Bhils came closer to Hindu Vaishnavism.

In the thirties, Shakti Ashram in Assam (1931) and Barama Ashram (1936) were founded. In the forties, a number of organisations were formed on the model of the Bhil Seva Mandal: Andhra Sramik Dharma Rajya Sabha (1942); Vanavasi Seva Mandal, Mandla (1944); Adivasi Seva Mandal, Tohana; Adimjati Seva Mandal (1944), Santals and Paharia Seva Mandal (1942), etc.

The apex organisation, Bharatiya Adimjati Seva Sangh was established by Thakkar Bapa in 1948 firstly to promote social, economic and educational advancement of the tribal communities, including nomadic and de-notified tribes to enable them to take their legitimate place in the national life of the country as equal citizens; and secondly to co-ordinate the activities of the bodies engaged in similar activities. This body is non-political, and it does not engage itself in any proselytising activities.

Remarkably, organisations—have a multi-pronged programme for the welfare of the tribes: (i) education through ashram schools assisted by the grant of stipends; (ii) medical relief through ayurvedic dispensaries; (iii) village and cottage industries; (iv) promotion of khadi and spinning; (v) debt-relief; and (vi) forest co-operative societies. Items (iii) and (iv) were taken out of Gandhiji's reconstruction programme, as was the philosophy and the context.

These centres projected powerfully the image of Gandhi as *disum aba* (father of the nation) and brought a sizeable section of the tribals, apart from the bhagats, into the mainstream of the national movement. These organisations became the channels for communication of the ideas of nationalism and freedom to the tribal people. A nationalist perspective on tribal problems thus emerged in contra distinction to the isolationist standpoint of the missionaries and the officials. In the course of time, the approach of these organisations came to be identified too closely with the stance of a political party, and this together with other constraints handicapped their secular development.

Gandhi and Bapa

While Thakkar Bapa's heart lay with the Mahatma, his head was with the Servants of India Society, from whose ranks he rose. Though a conscience-keeper of Gandhi, he disagreed with the latter's assessment of the relative merit of the harijan and tribal positions, and continued to highlight with characteristic humility and clarity the hardships of the latter, which he thought were worse than those of the former. This could be explained by the background of his life, his life long service of the tribals and his first hand experience of their problems. Amritlal Thakkar joined the Servants of India Society in 1914. A terrible famine that broke out in the Panch Mahal region populated by the Bhils saw him organise his first relief work. He fell in love with the people—it was love at first sight—and since then the Bhils held "primacy of place in his heart", and aroused his "tenderest concern and foremost love".Another famine afflicted the object of his love in 1922, and he founded the Bhil Seva Mandal in 1923, the forerunner of the Adivasi welfare organisations to be launched from a nationalist platform. He conducted many inquiries into the social and economic condition of the tribal people. In 1925 he spent about six months investigating the problems of tribals of Central Provinces, Assam and Chotanagpur. He stayed mainly in the Bhil area till 1932, when Gandhiji asked him to shoulder higher responsibility regarding harijan welfare.

With the assumption of office by the Congress Party in

some states, he was called upon to draw up a programme for the welfare of the tribals. In 1939, he toured the tribal tracts of Bihar, Orissa, Central Provinces and Assam extensively, drew up schemes for uplift of adivasi/harijan communities and conducted enquiries into their condition. He also' organised welfare work among the Bhils in Khandesh. In October 1940, he became a member of the Aboriginal Welfare Board which was set up in Bihar. When the Interim Government took over, he prepared a five-year adivasi welfare plan for Bihar and Central Province. He was appointed a member of the Advisory Sub-committee of the Constituent Assembly formed to enquire into and report on the political, economic and social set-up to be accorded to the hill-people of Assam.

He summed up his analysis of tribal problems in the Kale Memorial Lecture (1941), which he first categorised into (i) poverty, (ii) illiteracy, (iii) ill-health, (iv) inaccessibility of the areas inhabited by the tribals, (v) defects in administration, and (vi) lack of leadership. The adivasis were the poorest section of the Indian population, not excepting the harijans.The harijans, for all the disabilities and discrimination they suffered, always "lived with us" and became "part and parcel of our town and village life". In contrast, we "hardly felt' the existence of our aborigines. The "kaliparaj" the dark people, were held in contempt; they were neglected for ages; they laboured under very hard primitive conditions of life, waging an unequal fight against disease and exploitation by the advanced sections of our people.

Secondly, nobody except the missionaries, least of all Hindus, took care of them; it was the love and affection of Christians that attracted him:

> True, we Hindus rarely show that love and sympathy to the distressed and semi-wild people of our country, which we human beings should show to one another. On the Other hand we shun them and even hate them as if they were not creatures of God with the same feelings and passions as ourselves. Whose fault is it if such people find consideration, love and happiness amongst people of another religion, and so embrace it? (Thakkar Bapa, *op. cit.*)

Thirdly, tribals enjoyed far less protection and were much less organised than the harijans. While the latter enjoyed representation in proportion to their population under the Act of 1935, the tribals had only a 'bare modicum of representation" (only 24; Assam 9; Bihar 7; Orissa 5; and Bombay, Madras, C.P. one in each of the three). in C.P. where the aboriginal population was very nearly equal to the harijan population, and one-fifth of the total population, only one seat was reserved for the aborigines against twenty for harijans. In local boards hardly any representation had been given, except by the Bombay 'Government. In Orissa, out of the five seats reserved, four were filled up by nomination; nomination to provincial legislatures bad been discarded in all other provinces.

Bapa joined issue with the isolationist school of policy-makers which comprised "anthropologists and British members of the I.C.S. and other Government officers". The isolationists, according to him, believed in "keeping the aborigines in their areas, untouched by the civilisation of the plains" because they feared that contact with the Hindus of the plains would (i) break the solidarity of the tribal society; (ii) spread the contagion of social evils such as untouchability, early marriage and purdah into tribal areas; (iii) expose the tribals to the temptation of imitating only the lower strata of the Hindu community of the plains, and (iv) bring about demoralisation and pose danger of being eventually contained as another depressed community. As Dr. Hutton, the chief-exponent of this school, wrote:

> The opening up of the communications involving contact at many points and often practical settlement of tribal country, alters the aspect of any agricultural changes that may have been taking place. Generally speaking it substitutes conflict for contact—not necessarily a conflict of arms, but of cultures and of material interests. Attempts to develop minerals, forests or land for intensive cultivation can only be made at the expense of the tribe whose isolation is thus invaded. Again, the exploitation of minerals not only involves the tribal land but generally the introduction of an alien population, usually of an extremely mixed character and not infrequently exceptionally dissolute.

Thakkar Bapa protested against such efforts to isolate the tribals from the Hindus. "To keep these people confined to and isolated in their inaccessible hills and jungles was like keeping them in glass cases of a museum for the curiosity of purely academic persons". He, however, reiterated that "safeguards must be instituted to protect the aborigines from exploitation by the more advanced people of the plains, as had been done with regard to non-alienation of land". He argued:

> But how can the aborigines realise their present backwardness and work for their own economic, social and political progress if there is no contact with people more advanced than ourselves? When contact is advocated, I do not for a moment suggest that large populations of the plains should be transplanted to aboriginal regions and made to live amidst and dominate the Adivasis. Also, I do not discountenance the need for protection of aboriginal interests against any possible exploitation by some sections of the advanced people of the plains. What I mean to say is that a healthy comradeship should develop between the aborigines and the non-aborigines and each should profit culturally from the other and in course of time work hand in hand for the welfare of India as a whole,. I am one of those who strongly advocate reservation of seats, but in a general electorate, for the Adivasis in the legislatures and Local Boards for some time to come. All the same, I feel that there is no cause for getting alarmed over imaginary evils resulting out of the contact with non-aborigines and their civilisation.

Sharply reacting to the proposal regarding the creation of self-governing tribal areas, he pleaded for unity and "assimilation":

> In fact, it is unjust and wrong to call the indigenous social workers "interventionists". It would be proper to call them advocates of the policy of assimilation. The aborigines should form part of the civilised communities of our country, not for the purpose of swelling the figures of the followers of this region or that, but to share with the advanced communities the privileges and duties on equal terms in the general, social and political life of the country. Separation and isolation seem to be dangerous theories and they strike at the root of national solidarity. We have already enough communal

> troubles and should we add to them instead of extinguishing the existing ones and seeing that we are all one and indivisible? Safety lies in union and not in isolation. Nationalists cannot but view with concern and regret statements like the...one from Dr. Hutton. (Kale Lectures, p.)

Energetically repudiating the charge that indigenous social workers and nationalist politicians were the "interventionists', who approached the aborigines with the feelings of a morally and socially superior person and brought with them social evils and taboo with regard to food (such as beef-eating), he reminded that these evils were dying in the plains and there was no likelihood of their being carried to the aboriginal society. Care should be taken that contagion of social evils like untouchability did not spread into aboriginal areas.

He reminded the isolationists of their perfect silence over and non-objection to "Christian missionaries' close and uncontrolled contact with tribals, introduction of the Roman script for tribal dialects, spread of Christian propaganda, migration of thousands of tribals to tea-gardens from their natural surroundings on low wages".

Bapa appreciated the Salvationists' and other missionaries' good work, and modelled his own organisation and programme on theirs, but he sharply differed with them in other matters. He pleaded for greater protection and for making available safeguards under the Indian Constitution for non-Christian aborigines, because there was none to look after them in the Constituent Assembly. The representatives of Christian tribals charged him with seeking to bring about a division among the tribes between Christians and non-Christians. He also felt that the aboriginal children should be taught through the medium of provincial languages and through the medium of tribal dialects in lower classes, introduction of the Roman script for Khasi language should be discouraged because it presented innumerable complexities and estranged the feelings of the major communities, besides having many technical disadvantages.

Bapa disagreed with Verrier Elwin, that incorrigible romanticist, who favoured continuance of the *jhum* with some alterations and restrictions because it was almost a religious necessity for some of the tribals. "The argument" that some tribals did not "plough the land because they considered it a sin to lacerate the womb of *dhartimata*", could not justify the practice any longer. In *1945*, he protested against the plan of B.R. Ambedkar under which all communities except aborigines were to get proportionate representation; this amounted to political disenfranchisement of the tribals, on the ground that they did not possess the political capacity to exercise political power for their own good. Bapa reminded people that there were 112 adivasi graduates. Thakkar Bapa thus built up the nationalist perspective on the tribal question. In doing so, he was sharply critical of the official and missionary efforts to isolate the tribals from the mainstream of national life. But the choice of the phrase "assimilation" was unhappy, because Bapa did not advocate complete absorption of the tribals at the cost of their individuality.

Gandhi and Elwin

Before Verrier Elwin took up his work among the tribals, he was involved for a brief spell from 1928 to *1932* with the national movement and came close to Gandhiji who wrote to him:

> Son you have become of your own choice. I have accepted the responsible position. And son you shall remain to the end of time.

This was not to be. Elwin who was earlier enamoured of working among the untouchables in Gujarat was advised by Sardar Vallabhabhai Patel and Jamnalal Bajaj to leave the harijans alone and establish himself among the adivasis.

Elwin saw no contradiction in the Christians associating themselves with the freedom movement under the stewardship of Gandhi without losing distinctiveness of their own religion. After "long discussion and much, good advice from Gandhi", he resigned from the Christian Seva Sangh, and took a "plunge in the dark". In the company of Thakkar Bapa, he toured the Bhil area, and decided to settle down among the Gonds at Karanjia. To this phase belonged some of his writings in which he sought to establish that it was the right and duty of the Christians to overthrow a foreign or despotic government; in a similar vein he praised khadi to the skies.

Elwin's honeymoon with the national movement came to an unhappy end in 1932, when he offered, in return for the passage to India, to confine himself entirely to his work among the Gonds and to take no part in the civil disobedience and any other political movement. Gandhiji called him "*naram*", and added that "these adjectives could be applied to you in certain circumstances". He, however, consoled him: "It is enough for me to know, as I do know, that you regard no sacrifice, too great for the pursuit of truth".

Notably, from 1932 onwards, and particularly in the forties, when Gandhi reached the pinnacle of his career, Elwin's links with him weakened, "though his affection for him never wavered". From an enthusiast of the khadi programme, he turned into its critic.

In July 1937, he wrote to Gandhiji that the utility of spinning for Gonds or other tribes was questionable; in areas where cotton did not grow spinning seemed artificial and uneconomic. Secondly, the Mahatma's view on prohibition was damaging to the tribals. Thirdly, his philosophy of sex-relations and his excessive emphasis on diet, jarred on tribal susceptibilities. These were only minor points, and yet these led Elwin to "deprive himself of the warmth of his affection and strength, when he reached his highest stature during his later years, but it was a feeling about Truth that kept me from going to see him". (Elwin, *Religious and Cultural Aspects, of Khadi,* p. 85)

Yet there were two points on which Elwin's stand coincided with Gandhiji's. The first was his view that Christianity and British imperialism were not convertible terms; this was against the view of the establishment that Christianity should have nothing to do with the policies of the Congress and Gandhiji, and that deviation from this would amount to treachery to Christ and the emperor. Elwin was for the grant of independence to India.

The second was the attitude to conversion which has been mentioned earlier. It could also be partly explained by the influence of mystical literature on Elwin, which made him look at religion not "as a matter of saving of your and other's soul"—in times of famine many missionaries at one time undoubtedly took advantage of people's hunger to change their religion—but as a quest for spiritual reality. This attitude was also strengthened by his experience in Gandhiji's ashram "which made it impossible to believe in an exclusive form of Christianity", and once exclusiveness was taken out of Christianity or for that matter any religion, a great deal goes out of it.

In the forties, his views on conversion became stridently polemical. In a paper called "The foreign missionary danger" (1944), he highlighted "the rapid pace of conversion of tribes and the danger of the conversion within a few years of the entire aboriginal population in to a querulous, anti-national, aggressive" minority community, with none of the old virtues and few of the new, which will be a thorn in the side of the future Government of India"; and he advocated the prohibition of proselytisation as in many other free countries:

> Change of religion is actually harmful to the aborigines. It destroys tribal unity, strips the people of age-long moral sanctions, separates them from the mass of their fellow countrymen and in many cases leads to decadence that is as pathetic as it is deplorable, the methods employed are questionable. There is economic exploitation, exploitation of ignorance and social exploitation. Therefore missionaries should be withdrawn from tribal areas. (Elwin, *Truth about India Can We Get,* p. 56)

About the place of the tribes in Indian society, Elwin as mentioned earlier, indignantly denied having been an isolationist; he affirmed that he had only condemned the policy of isolation. But the confusion arose out of the inept pharase, "the National Park", that he coined in the late thirties to underline the need for protection of the tribes against exploitation, and the preservation of the three freedoms for them: freedom from fear, freedom from want and freedom from interference. The fact of the exploitation of tribals by money-lenders, corrupt and rapacious officials and oppressive landlords could not be denied. He admitted later that when he spoke in terms of preserving tribal culture, he thought a little statically.

Later he thought in a less static way and spoke about the unity of the hills and plains as essential to the general national interest. The concept of integration subsumed the need for maintaining "cultural identity" of tribals in the wider context of national unity, territorial integrity and socialistic goals. Elwin edged closer to the nationalist school in the sense: "The special care and protection given to the tribesmen must not cast shadow on the unity of India. They must be educated to feel that they are full citizens of the Republic, with real rights and still more urgent duties".

Before independence, through his writings, he made the "dominant social groups conscious of the tribal problem in the national perspective". In this sense he was a guru—as Jawaharlal Nehru called him—to him and others. After independence, he contributed to the development of integrated tribal policy, for all its drawbacks.

In the Gandhian conspectus, the tribal problem occupied a very small space. The extracts quoted above are about all that Gandhiji had to say about the tribes and the issues that bore upon them. For a long time the harijan problem, for social and political reasons, put the tribal issue in the shade; later when the facts came to be known the two were equated. This in itself was a development of great significance. The inclusion of tribal welfare in the reconstruction programme implied recognition of the primacy of putting the tribal problem in perspective for solution.

A queer result of Gandhiji's impact was the emphasis that the "archaic" bhagat element in tribal social movements received; but his influence also helped to add new and wide perspectives to them, and bring a section of the tribes into the mainstream of national life. Also interesting was the interaction of different standpoints on tribals, and the emergence of a perspective and philosophy of tribal reconstruction with its nationalist, secular and integrated orientation.

The tribal welfare programme, which projected his image and message, did not attempt a basic restructuring of tribal agrarian economy to provide the base for economic development. The significance of Gandhiji's later-day radicalism in agrarian matters was missed by the architects of the nationalist or assimilationist approach to tribal issues.

REFERENCES

1. A.V. Thakkar, *Aboriginals' Cry in the Wilderness.*
2. C. Winslow Jack and Verrier Elwin, The *Dawn* of *India's Freedom.*
3. Elwin, *The Foreign Missionary Danger.*
4. *Harijan* 18-1-42, p. 5; quoted in the *Selected Works of Mahatma Gandhi,* chap. 80 vol. six from the *Voice of Truth.* p. *538.*
5. Hiralal Shukla, *Bastar ke Van Vasi Geeton men Gandhi.* The, *Adibasi,* Ranchi.
6. M.K. Gandhi, *Christian Missions: Their Place in India,* p. 78.
7. Pradhan *et al* (ed.), *Anthropology and Archaeology, Essays in Commemoration of Verrier Elwin.* (quoted from *A.A.S.*, vol. 1, No. 2, 1966: 162).
8. Pyarelal, "Bapa of Bapu", pp. 81-82 (quoted). Ibid.
9. S.G. Vaze, "Thakkar Bapa, a tribute", p. 87. Ibid.
10. S.L. Kalia, "The Raj Mohini Devi Movement in Surguja".
11. Suresh Singh, "The Haribaba Movement in Chotanagpur 1931-32".
12. Tendulkar D.G., *Mahatma,* vol. 8, p. 28.

13. Thakkar Bapa, "Aborigines of Orissa,,' *Modern Review*, Sept. 1938; quoted in the footnote of the *Commemoration Volume*, p. 78.
14. "The Problem of Aborigines in India", Gokhale Institute of Politics and Economics, R.R. Kale Memorial Lecture, 1941.
15. T.N. Jagdisan and Shyam Lal (eds), *Thakkar Bapa, Eightieth Birthday Commemoration Volume.*

6

Gandhian Scheme of Education

> "My code of life conduct is simply this: Work hard, play to the allowable limit; disregard equally the good and bad opionions of others; never do a friend a dirty trick; never grow indignant over anything; live the moment to the utmost of its possibilities; with oneself."
>
> **— George Jean Nathan**

Primarily a politician, statesman and social reformer, Mahatma Gandhi has made no less a substantial and solid contribution to the educational thought and practice in India. His life and career is so rich that volumes will be required to give a complete and full idea of his life's mission.

After studying law for 4 years in England, Gandhi sailed back home in 1891 and started his practice in Bombay but failed. Soon he received an offer from an Indian firm, having a branch in South Africa, to go to that country to help them in an important case. In April, 1893, he sailed for Durban. Although his case was over, he continued to stay in Africa for 20 years. It was there that he saw a series of insulting events of disgracing Indians and Black populace and his political feelings were awakened. He founded the Natal Indian Congress in 1894.

In 1903 he shifted to Transvaal. Like Pestalozzi at Yverdon and Burgdorf, Mahatma Gandhi had educational experiences on the Tolstoy Farm. On the Farm he undertook the responsibility of educating his own sons and other children. Like Rousseau and Pestalozzi he came to believe that, "true education could be imparted by the parents, and that there should be the minimum outside help".

Tolstoy Farm was just like a family, where Gandhiji occupied the place of the father. He helped the children in all round development. Training of heart and building of character received his first attention. These pupils had to devote 8 hours a day for vocational training and only 22 hours to book learning. The vocations taught were digging, cooking, scavenging, sandal-making, simple carpentary and messenger work. Since there were no servants on the farm all work was done by the inmates. Besides teaching them the dignity of labour, they were helped to build their physique through manual work and no further games or exercise for that were required. The ages of the children ranged from 6 to 16. They were very happy in learning by doing and in learning by co-operation. English was taught but the medium of instruction in other subjects was mother tongue. Their curriculum included Hindi, Tamil, Gujarati, Urdu, a little of Sanskrit, elementary History, Geography and Arithmetic. Mahatma Gandhi never used any text books. He taught them by word of mouth. That was more interesting and kept the children active as they were stimulated to put questions. Character building was inculcated by example of the virtuous life of the teacher rather than by precept from the teacher. No corporal punishment was given to them even in cases of misconduct.

The creed of non-violence, thus, was put into actual practice. Gandhiji was convinced that, "if good children are taught together with bad ones and thrown into their company, they will lose nothing, provided all of them were put under the watchful care of their parents and guardians".

Gandhiji returned to India in Jan. 1915, and the educational experiments tried in Africa were further continued for a short time at Shantiniketan and then at Sabarmati and Sewagram, where Gandhiji established his own Ashrams successively. At Shantiniketan he taught the inmates the great lesson of 'self help' by asking them to dispense with the cooks and do the cooking themselves. His stay, however, was very short. In May,

1915, he founded the Sabarmati Ashram. Beginning with 20 inmates, it grew into a patriarchal family, which had grown up around its spiritual father—Bapu. There were women and children among the inmates. A school for children and illiterate adults was attached to the Ashram. There were gardens to till and beasts to tend, while every one performed his obligatory task at the spinning wheel. Every work of daily routine was done by the inmates. It was a village which prayed and worked and ate in common. The Ashram was retreat to which men came for inspiration, spending a formative time under Gandhiji's guidance, that they might go out, fired with his spirit, to work for India. In the evening the inmates of the Ashram assembled for prayer. Discussions were held about the content, curricula and method of education in the school there. Gandhiji wanted to make that school a model for others to follow. Wardha scheme or better known as Basic education which came two decades later was the outcome of the experiments at Tolstoy Farm, Sabarmati Ashram and Sewagram.

The inmates of the Sabarmati Ashram had to observe many vows, for example: (1) Truth speaking; (2) Non-violence or Ahimsa; (3) Celibacy; (4) Control of palate; (5) Non-thieving; (6) Non-attachment or non-possession; and (7) Poverty. Then there were certain rules to be observed. For example, only swadeshi articles could be used. Every one had to wear khaddar which was home-spun and home woven. A spirit of fearlessness was inculcated among the inmates. Gandhiji, believed that Indians were in the grip of paralysing fear. They feared their neighbours, their caste, their social superiors and their officials. This Gandhiji, wanted them to rid of. Every Ashramite had to take a vow to end untouchability.

Learning of as many vernaculars as possible was the rule of the Ashram.

Gandhiji founded the Sewagram Ashram, near Wardha in April, 1935. This new settlement was developed from scratch and for the next decade Gandhiji fought his battle for freedom of India from this place. It was here that he conceived the idea of his new system of education. Not only did he expound the Wardha Scheme or the Basic education, a practical shape was also given to the scheme in 1937.

Mahatma Gandhi, the great thinker and experimenter, formulated his own views about everything in the world. Although he expressed his ideas on everything from God to birth-control, for our purposes his belief in God, Truth, *Ahimsa* and dignity of labour are most important. On the bases of these Gandhiji wanted to recreate an ideal spiritual society. He had a profound faith in one God and believed in the unity of man. All that moves in the world, according to him is due to God. Like Froebel he believed God as the Ultimate Reality "behind the universe which is always in a state of flux". While all other things, he said, are subject to change, God is "changeless, that holds all together, that creates, dissolves and recreate".

God is benevolent as Gandhiji saw "that in the midst of death, life persists, in the midst of untruth, truth persists, in the midst of darkness light persists". To him God was "Life, Truth, Light and Love". Not only did he believe in the absolute oneness of God, he also believed in the oneness of humanity.

He remarked, "what though we have different bodies? We have but one soul. The rays of the sun are many through refraction. But they have the same source. I cannot, therefore detach myself from the wickedest soul, nor may I be denied identity with the most virtuous....if we are the sons of the same God and part-take of the same divine essence, we must part-take of the sin of every person, whether he belongs to us or another race".

According to Gandhi God is "indefinable, mysterious power that pervades everything. His (God's) presence is proved not by extraneous evidence but in the transformed conduct and character of those who have felt the real presence of God within"". He, therefore advised to "have a living faith in a living God who is the ultimate arbiter of our fate". His will is supreme. Gandhiji said "all life in its essence is one, and that men are working consciously or un-consciously towards the realization of that identity".

Remarkably, until 1931 he said, "God is Truth". But thence he said, "Truth is God". For, he remarked, "denial of God we have known. Denial of Truth we have not known. The most ignorant among men have some truth in them. We are sparks of truth. The sum total of those sparks is indescribable, as yet-unknown Truth". Truth is an inner voice. It is the cell of conscience. His advice was to realise the "Truth in life". Not only he wanted to realise Truth himself, he wanted everyone to be a seeker of Truth.

It was not scientific Truth that Gandhiji valued so highly, but social truth in all our dealings with our neighbours. He insisted on complete frankness in daily intercourse and condemned the insincerities practised in the name of politeness.

Gandhiji said that we must say "Yes" only when we mean 'yes', and we must say 'no' when we mean 'no', regardless of the consequences. There should be harmony, he held, between thought, word and action.

To think one thing, to speak another and do a third is untruth. "To mean 'no' and say 'yes', to give word and not to keep it, to nurse ill-will in the mind and utter honied words to flatter a man to his face and malign him behind his back, to be fasting outwardly and think all the while of prospective rich fare, to consider a thing to be reprehensible and yet do it, are all examples of disharmony in thought, word and deed and therefore of untruth.

This disharmony breaks up man's personality and leaves him no peace of mind or happiness". He repeatedly advised people to appear as they are. The naturalness was, in his view, a part of truthfulness. Devotion to truth at all costs was a passion with him throughout his life.

Gandhiji staunchly believed that means to attain the goal of Truth is *Ahimsa* or non-violence. To him "*Ahimsa* and Truth are so intertwined that it is practically impossible to disentangle and separate them. They are the two sides of a coin, or rather a smooth metalic disk", where it is not possible to say "which is the obverse and which is the reverse?" It was, therefore, advised that "Truth being our goal, *Ahimsa* should be our supreme duty to achieve the goal. *Ahimsa* enjoins first of all, charity towards those who consider themselves our enemies. A person believing in *Ahimsa* or love must rise above attachment and hatred, fear and vanity. Patience, forbearance, humility, charity and readiness for compromise are also covered by the term non-violence.

A non-violent person must live a life of Tapsaya or austere living. Such a life would purify the spirit. The importance of spiritualism and mortality should be recognised. All evils will be overcome through non-violence. This Ahimsa, Gandhiji declared, should be practised by individuals, groups, communities and nations. This is a great power which must be accepted as the law of life, must pervade the whole being and not be applied to isolated acts" only. Instead of being a "negative attitude, it is a 'positive and dynamic' quality".

Gandhiji believed in the spiritual origin and destiny of man. This destiny, he showed, should be worked out by every one in a moral society, where the inner and the external life of an individual is guided by non-violence, truth and justice. 'That this may be so, it is necessary that in social, political and economic relations the means must be as pure as the ends. If it does not benefit a man to loose his soul to gain the whole world, it does not like-wise benefit a nation to gain the whole world and lose its soul". To attain moral society he wanted democracy and socialism-but no socialism of the Marxian type "where over-centralization and the divorce of moral principles crush the individual".

He advocated decentralizations and higher values of life. For him the principle of decent realization is a moral principle, as it gives freedom to the individual to make a free choice in a variety of fields, Gandhiji refused to be tricked by the rosy socialistic picture of plenty of material goods equally divided.

Gandhian Social Order

Like Rousseau, Mahatma Gandhi wanted to recreate the society and aimed at universal brotherhood, freedom, justice and equality for all. Exploitation of any kind and on any score was alien to him. Emphasis should be on service rather than on exploitation, on co-operation rather than on competition. Establishment of classless society was his greatest dream. Artificial barriers of caste, creed, colour, wealth and power were hated by him. It was a classless society, which according to him could realise the Absolute (God). He agreed with Tagore that individual development could take place in a spiritual society. The chief characteristic of such a society should be love, non-violence, truth and justice.

"Moral force and moral sanction" would be the guiding factors of such a society. In order to avoid the accumulation of wealth in a few hands, he proposed an economic and social structure which should be built upon the decentralisation of industrial agriculture. The decentralisation; he said is possible if we encourage cottage and village industry. He, however, conceded the right to every one to keep as much for himself as was "necessary for a refined, civilized and moral life".

In this society, service to God and community was the greatest creed of Mahatma Gandhi. According to him, "man's ultimate aim is the realisation of God". All the activities—social political, religious—of man, therefore, should be motivated by this one aim. We love and serve God when we love and serve His creatures. Service of all, therefore, should be the first fundamental of every human being. God, said Gandhiji, instead of being in the temple, church and mosque; is to be found in the "temple of humanity" and remarked that "man becomes great exactly in the degree in which he works for the welfare of his fellow men". In a society where the ideal is 'service unto all', there cannot be domination and exploitation of any kind. Moral and equitable principle would help that society to realise God. Who is Truth. *Ahimsa* or love would be the means of achieving such a goal.

The regeneration of Indian society, he believed, could take place only if the villages could be resuscitated. Villages were being exploited by the cities. They depended on the sufferance of cities. He wanted to build a healthy and moral relationship between the two.

Although Gandhiji never thought hypothetically, he gave his conception of future India, "I shall work for an India in which the poorest shall feel that it is their country, in whose making they have an effective voice, an India in which all communities shall live in perfect harmony.... There can be no room in such an India for the curse of untouchability or the curse of intoxicating drinks and drugs....Women will enjoy the same rights as men....This is the India of my dream".

Determining Factors

First it will be pertinent to know the background of his educational philosophy. There were several factors that determined his educational philosophy:

1. His educational experiments at Tolstoy Farm, Sabarmati and Sewagram Ashrams. These have been referred to under our first sub head.
2. His dissatisfaction with the prevailing system of education. System of education introduced by the English did not suit the country. English medium for all the branches of higher learning, in his view, was the greatest handicap. This had created a permanent bar between the highly educated few and the uneducated many. It had prevent knowledge from percolating to the masses. Teeming millions of Indian were wrought in ignorance, superstitions, inertia and illiteracy. Whatever education was given to a small fraction of children was waste as it was given in a passive manner. The child was a mere listener. Some smattering information was pumped into the child, without his realizing the value of the knowledge given to him. Education was not the value of the

knowledge give to him. Education was not related to life. No training was given in power of observation. Practical work was conspicuous by its absence. No sense of citizenship was developed. Gandhiji was convinced that the prevailing system of primary education was not only wasteful but positively harmful. He remarked, "most of the boys are lost to the parents and to the occupation to which they are born. They pick up evil habits and affect urban ways". Such education was neither. "Responsive to the realistic elements of the present situation, nor inspired by any life giving and creative ideal".

3. His philosophy of life. Education being the dynamic side of philosophy, Gandhiji's philosophy of life determined his philosophy of education. He saw the realisation and means of his ideal of life in education.
4. Another factor that determined his educational philosophy was the conviction that social, moral, political and economic regeneration of India depended on education. He wanted to create a social order in which the conditions should be such that each man should be able to realise the highest aims of his life. He should not only adopt a policy of non-interference in others' way of pursuing the same ideal, but he should actually help and co-operate with other fellow workers in their search after truth. Gandhiji believed that such a social order, based on Truth and non-violence, would exclude every type of exploitation,—economic, social, political or even religious.

Thus, keeping in view the aforementioned factors Gandhiji evolved absolutely a new philosophy of education. By education he meant, "an all round drawing out of the best in child and man—body, mind and spirit". He said that literacy should never be the end of education nor even the beginning. "It is only one of the means whereby man and woman can be educated".

True education, according to Gandhiji is that which draws out and stimulates the intellectual and physical faculties of the children. He attached greater importance to the personality of the educated than to the tools and the subjects. A sound education, he believed, should produce useful citizens whole men and whole women—of boys and girls. A whole man or woman is considered one, who has harmonious development of all four aspects of the human personality—body, heart, mind and spirit. Any scheme of education, emphasising only one of these aspects of the personality is a lopsided education.

This was the defect that he found in the prevailing system of education. No effort was being made to adjust the child intelligently and actively to his environment. Education, he took, "not in a parochial sense of a classroom process, but in its broad and true sense of a life long process which begins with the beginning and ends with the end of life going on constantly and unceasingly.

Chief Tenets of his New Educational Philosophy

(1) that there should be free and compulsory primary education;

(2) that the education should be craft centred; (3) that it should be self-supporting;

(4) that it should be given in the mother tongue;

(5) that it should be based on non-violence.

1. Free and Compulsory Education: Mahatma Gandhi wanted that within the ages 7 and 14 there should be free, compulsory; universal primary education. His conception of primary education, was up to matriculation minus the English. In other words he wanted to combine the present primary and secondary education, into one—called the English-less-Matriculation. For, he was convinced that children get nothing more in the high school than a half-baked knowledge of English besides a superficial knowledge of mathematics and history and geography. If English is cut from the curriculum altogether, without cutting out the other subjects, the children in his opinion, can go through the whole course in 7 years instead of 10 or 11. Besides this, manual work can be added, whereby they can make a fair return to the state.

He wanted that the state should also finances permit them to do the same. By this, he never meant that pre-primary or higher education should be neglected altogether. In his own words, "primary education, extending over a period of 7 years or longer, and covering all the subjects up to the Matriculation standard, except English, plus a vocation used as the vehicle for drawing out the mind of boys and girls in all departments of knowledge should take the place of what passes today under the name of primary, middle and high school education".

2. Craft-Centred Education: Gandhiji believed that the highest development of mind the soul was possible only through handicraft. He wanted to begin education of the child, "by teaching it is a useful handicraft and enabling it to produce from the moment it begins its training. Thus every school can be made self-supporting, the condition being that the State takes over the manufactures of those schools". He did not want to teach the handicraft as only one of the subjects of instruction. It was his wish that the "whole process of education should be imparted through some handicraft or industry".

At the same time he said, that the handicraft should not be taught mechanically but scientifically. That is, the child should know the why and wherefore of every process. For example, by teaching Takli-spinning knowledge of the various varieties of cotton, the different soils in different provinces of India, the history of the decay of handicraft, the political reasons for this, including the history of British rule in India, a knowledge of Arithmetic and so on should be imparted.

The craft should not be taught, merely for production work but for developing the intellect of pupils. The manual training should not consists in producing articles for a school museum or toys, which have no value. It should produce marketable articles. The children should not do all this under compulsion or under whip as was done in the early days of factories. They should do it because it interests them and stimulates their intellect.

Gandhiji never believed that the vocational bias will make education dull or cramp the child's mind. Children are sure to be bright and joyful if they receive vocational instruction under competent teachers. Just as Pestalozzi tried his methods on his own son, Mahatma Gandhi tried his methods on his grand-son. He found that his grand-son scarcely felt that he was being taught, because all the time he played and laughed and sang.

By teaching craft, his object was not to produce craftsmen but he wanted to exploit the craft for educative purposes. He wanted that, "stress should be laid on the principles of cooperative activity, planning, accuracy, initiative and individual responsibility in learning". He wanted that the craft should be learnt systematically and scientifically to serve as a means for intellectual work and economic self-sufficiency. The teaching of all subjects, Gandhiji said, should be inspired by the craft.

Besides wanting to do away with the machine, which had killed all sense of art and hand work, Gandhiji wanted such a craft which should have rich educative possibilities. "It should find natural points of correlation with important human activities and interests and should extend to the whole content of the school curriculum".

3. *Self-Supporting Element:* Gandhiji saw that as a nation Indians were so backward in education that they could not be educated if the programme was to depend on money. Crores of children could not wait until the Government found the necessary finances. He, therefore, suggested that education should be self-supporting. It was his belief that handicraft, besides developing the personality of the child, would make education self-supporting.

The critics argued that when people should spend money on primary education Gandhiji was advocating the exploitation of children. They also feared that there would be enormous waste of craft-material at the hands of small children. To this Gandhiji replied, "as for exploiting or burdening the children, I would ask whether we burden the child when we save him from disaster? The tukli is enough good toy to play with and it is a productive play. Even today children help their parents to certain extent.

The Segaon children know the details of agriculture better than I, for they have worked with their parents on the field. Whilst the child will be encouraged to spin and help his parents with agriculture jobs, he will also be made to feel that he belongs not only to his parents but also to the village and to the country, and that he must make some return to them. The children will become self-confident and brave". He believed that, "without the use of hands and feet, the brain would be atrophied, and even if it worked, it would be the home of Satan". There was yet another cause for making his education self-supporting.

He said that free studentship, "lies and should be like, a load upon a conscientious lad's mind throughout his life". Economic calculation in connection with education may be sordid but India's circumstances demand economic calculation. Money is scarce. Colossal illiteracy has to be broken. Mahatma Gandhi was conscious of it. According to him self-supporting education was the only alternative.

By education through handicraft should be self-supporting, he meant that it should be self-supporting during the sum total of 7 years, the period which he prescribed for the primary education. He was conscious of the partial loss during the first years and wished that it should be made up in the following years. In this self-supporting aspect, again, he wanted the State to provide expenses for school buildings, furniture, books and all the apparatus and tools required for craft work. By advocating the self-supporting aspect, he never wanted the craft to be made the be-all and end-all of instruction, thus sacrificing the executive and cultural objectives of education.

He believed that right kind of teachers would teach the children the dignity of labour and those children would regard the craft as an integral part and means of their intellectual growth.

4. *Stress on Mother-tongue:* Gandhiji emphasised mother-tongue both as a subject of study and as a medium of instruction. He found that the greatest handicap of the prevailing system of education was that learning was being imparted through the medium of English. This hindered the development of understanding and precision of thought or clarity of ideas. Mother-tongue, he believed, would enable the children not only to understand clearly the rich heritage of people's idea, emotions and aspirations but would also enable the children to express themselves effectively, clearly and lucidly.

5. *His Creed of Non-violence:* A unique feature of Gandhiji's educational philosophy was the, "application of the law of non-violence in the training of the child as a prospective citizen of the world". Gandhiji was sick of communal and inter-national strife and he wanted to create a generation which should believe in non-violence.

This, he thought, to be the panacea for all evils. He said, "where the whole atmosphere is redolent with the pure fragrance of ahimsa, boys and girls studying together will live like brothers and sisters in freedom and yet in self-imposed restraint, the students will be bound to the teachers in ties of filial love; mutual respect and mutual trust".

Every act of students, he said, should be accomplished by love. His scheme of education wanted to bring an age from which "class and communal hatred is eliminated and exploitation is eschewed". Gandhiji emphatically remarked, "we cannot, will not think of exploitation, and we have no alternative but this plan of education which is based on non-violence".

Naturalism, Idealism and Pragmatism

It is significant to note that Gandhiji synthesized all these three philosophies into his philosophy of education. He was a naturalist, idealist and pragmatist. When he advocates that children should be taught "in an atmosphere free from super-imposed restriction and interference". He is a naturalist. But his ' freedom' is not a 'licence', which may mean that the individual should be allowed to follow his own inclination, whims and caprices. Gandhiji emphasized 'discipline', regulated and well directed self-discipline among children and considered that time and money spent on education wasted if the children did not learn discipline in their school.

Discipline, he believed, should not be imposed from without. There should be an inner urge of the individual to obey the laws and regulations prescribed by the group, community of society. It is in this conception of discipline that he synthesizes naturalism and idealism. He wanted the children to have sufficient freedom so that they may develop and grow. But they must accept discipline and training if they want to develop their powers to the fullest. He believed in the inherent goodness of the child's nature and recognized that activity was the essential aspect of child's nature. He hated verbalism and wanted the child to lead a life of simplicity and naturalness rather than artificially.

No doubt Gandhiji was an idealist. He had a profound faith in God or the Universal Spirit, which permeates in everything He, therefore, wanted man not only to aim at 'self realisation' but also to realize God and be one with Him. Spiritual Realisation, in his view, should be the prime goal of life. Self-realisation, according to him, could be attained by self-abnegation and penance.

Spiritual Realisation, he held, can be achieved by seeking after the Truth, practising Non-violence and doing service to the creatures of God. He considered spiritual realization as essential part of the training of the young.

He said, "to develop the spirit is to build character and to enable one to work towards a knowledge of God and self-realisation....Training without culture of the spirit was of no use, and might be even harmful". His emphasis on harmonious development of personality included spiritual, intellectual, moral and physical development. These factors label him as an idealist.

Obviously, it appears that since Gandhiji believed in self-realisation and absolute truth-the creed of an idealist—he could not be pragmatist, but this is not true. He was a pragmatist in the same degree as an idealist and naturalist. He reconcilled the practical and the spiritual values. It was through grappling with real situations of life that the child realized himself. Learning by experience was the chief motive behind his craft-centred education.

Like Dewey he deems that as true which can be experimentally verified. Like him again, Gandhiji wanted his school to be a doing and a thinking school, instead of listening school. He wanted that all teaching should be carried on through concrete life situations relating to industry or to social and physical environment, so that whatever the child learns becomes assimilated into his growing activity. His was a school which was a place of work, experimentation and discovery instead of being a place of passive absorption of information imparted through books. His was an activity-curriculum like that of Dewey. Through activity the child acquires knowledge and utilizes it for the understanding and control of his social environment. This enabled the child to inculcate social responsibilities, which is the crying need of democratic India.

His craft-centred education is an ample testimony that Gandhiji was a pragmatist. Relating education with real life situation, providing social experience to the child, emphasizing learning by self activity, minimizing verbalism and bookishness, co-ordinating and correlating of the subjects of study are some of the features of Gandhian education which go to prove beyond any doubt that he was a pragmatist.

Aims of Education

Being an idealist and a realist Gandhiji kept main aim and immediate aims of education before him. Knowledge of God, self-realisation, spiritualism and oneness with God was the ultimate aim of education according to him. He laid great stress on 'the spirit' and declared that we should realize the spirit-force or soul-force instead of our being enthusiastic for 'evanescent, transitory and material force'. "True education should result not in the material power, but in spiritual-force".

That is why he laid great stress on religious education, which he thought, should teach the children fundamental virtues of truth, love, justice and non-violence. "Life without religion" Gandhiji held "is life without principle, and life without principle is like a ship without a rudder; and just as a ship without a rudder will be tossed about from place to place and never reach a destination, so a man without religious backing....be also tossed about on this stormy ocean of the world, without reaching the destined goal". God, according to him, could be achieved not by retiring into jungles, but by living in a society and serving it. He preferred to call a student *'brahmachari'* a searcher after God. The means to achieve the knowledge of God and self-realisation are self-control, abstinence and character. Society, consisting of persons having such virtues will be a spiritual society, believing in non-exploitation, non-violence, truth, justice and equality for all. In such society religion would pervade every action-political, economic, educational or social.

Gandhi's immediate aims include : (1) the utilitarian aim; (2) the cultural aim; (3) harmonious development of one's personality; (4) preparation for complete living; (5) character building; (6) sociological aim or training for citizenship.

1. The Utilitarian Aim: Considering the basic needs of man's life as food, shelter and clothes, he advocated the self-supporting education. This self-supporting aspect was meant in two different senses, namely: (*a*) education that will help one to be self-supporting in later life, (*b*) education which meets its own way. According to the first sense Gandhiji wanted the child at the age of 14, that is after finishing a seven years course, to be an earning unit. This was in consonance with the circumstances, obtained in India. Poor peoples' children cannot afford to depend too much on their parents after this age. With this object he emphasized craft. By this he did not want to turn the chills into a base mechanic; but a self-respecting citizen, who would not be a drag on the society. By the second sense of 'self-supporting education' Gandhiji wanted that teachers' salaries should be met out of the productive work of the children, provided that the State takes over such manufacture.

2. Cultural Aim : Cultural aim of education was not neglected by Gandhiji. Culture refines personality. Mere acquisition of knowledge is not enough for a man. He should have the quality of mind, which may be reflected in his daily conduct. Gandhiji attached greater importance to the cultural aspect of education than to the literary. He said, "it should show itself in smallest detail of your conduct and personal behaviour, how you sit, how you walk, how you dress etc.

Inner culture must be reflected in your speech, the way in which you treat visitors and guests, and behave towards one another and your teachers and elders". According to him culture is not the product of intellectual work, but the quality of the soul, permeating all aspects of human behaviour. It is, therefore, an important function of education that children must be taught to have winsome conduct and the career.

3. Harmonious Development of One's Personality: Gandhiji meant by education, "an all round drawing out of the best in child and mind-body, mind and spirit". Harmonious development of all powers-innate-and acquired was the chief goal of Gandhian education. "True education," he said, "must stimulate the spiritual intellectual and physical faculties of the children". This all-round education, he believed could be given through craft.

His emphasis was more on 3 H's (hand, heart and head) than on 3R's (reading, writing and arithmetic). In order to draw the best out of the child and to create real interest in him, physical drill, handi-crafts, drawing and music should go side by side. He was painfully conscious of the fact that prevailing system of education was unbalanced as it exercised only the training of the mind.

Mental training, to him, appeared, nothing if it was "not accompanied by a true training of the heart. It is the harmoniously developed person that adjusts to his life and environments.

4. Preparation for Complete Living: Realizing the complexity of modern life. Gandhiji formulated the scheme of education which would fit the child in later life. Coming into grip with problems and difficulties prepared the child to face the problems of life. A child was considered prepared for complete living if he could adjust himself to self, his occupation and his society.

5. Character Building: Gandhiji made character-building the central purpose of education, and everything else was subordinate to this one purpose. By character Gandhiji did not mean merely a collection of certain skills, habits and principles of conduct. He regarded character as the expression of "the whole personality including its ethical and spiritual aspect". Again he did not conceive character as an unrelated phenomenon, "something self-contained and self-sufficient, independent, of its environment."

He viewed it as a dynamic force proceeding towards a definite direction. An individual lives his own life, the life of the society or the nation he belongs to as well as the life of Universal Man. Therefore he must play his role in this drama of life well. He should conserve within himself the wisdom of the past, making full use of his national heritage. He should try to solve the problems which beset humanity.

He must subordinate his own interests to the greater interests of society. Instead of working for personal gain he must co-operate and collaborate with his fellow beings for bringing about a new social order. If he can do this he is really a man of character.

6. Training for Citizenship: While he advocated self-supporting education, he aimed at producing useful citizens. This is the primary need of democratic India. The future citizens should understand their problems, rights and duties. They should know the co-operative institutions like Panchayats, Municipalities and District Boards which work for the good of all. Contented and happy humanity was the ideal of his plan of education.

'Educate your masters' is the first slogan of democracy and Gandhiji advocated universal education. His aim was to create a classless society. Sociologically the introduction of craft in education "would break down the existing barriers of prejudices between manual and intellectual workers". Craft would produce the dignity of labour in the men. Instead of being parasites or drags on society every person would play his role worthily. Education, therefore, should foster a keen sense of personal worth, desire for self-improvement and social service in cooperative community".

Thus he wanted to create a society based upon love, truth, justice, equality, brotherhood, cooperation and national solidarity. *Sarvodaya Samaj* was the cherished dream of Mahatma Gandhi. The aim of such a *Samaj* should be the uplift of all, regardless of caste, creed and colour. Every member of this Samaj should have the spirit of courage, industry and self-sacrifice.

Again, an educational aim is social when the needs and the requirements of the society are uppermost. All that is taught and inculcated is conducive to the good of the society. Individual's aptitudes and inclinations are subordinated to this highest good. An educational aim is individual when education helps to make the life of individual better, richer and happier. The function of education, in that case, is to secure, "the conditions under which individuality is most completely developed" and personality is exalted. Like Dewey, Gandhiji wants the synthesis of the two. He does not want to destroy the individuality, "which lies at the root of all progress-material and spiritual".

This, he said, because he believed that no two persons are identical. They differ in nature, ability and temperament. But like Froebel he wanted unity in diversity – the individual to develop "for the good of the whole without losing his individual character". He wanted the care of the individual and believed that the society will take care of itself. Here he resembles Rousseau in assigning the prime place to individual in a society. But unlike Rousseau he wants the individual to inculcate a spirit of service and sacrifice for the good of the society or state. He valued individual freedom but did not forget that man is essentially a social being. "Man", he said, "has risen to his present status by learning to adjust his individualism to the requirements of social progress.

Unrestricted individualism is the law of the beast of the jungle". He, therefore, wanted to "strike the mean between individual freedom and social restraint, as he believed that "willing submission to social restraint, for the sake of the well being of the whole society, enriches both the individual and the society." To him individual development and social progress are not contradictory. They are complementary.

He remarked, "if one man gains spiritually, the whole world gains with him....if one man falls, the whole world falls to that extent." Mahatma Gandhi echoes John Dewey when he says, "a nation cannot advance without the units of which it is composed, advancing, and conversely, no individual can advance without the nation of which it is a part, also advancing." Gandhiji held, "that the individual must work out his perfection in a spiritual society".

But Gandhiji did not agree with Rousseau that the individual can develop in a social vacuum. Self-realisation and social service must go hand in hand. Individual, according to him, "can make the best of himself in a state and the state can achieve its highest development only on the condition that each of its citizen gives the best that is in him". The individual develops in a social atmosphere. It is there that it can have common interest and can engage himself in common activities.

Like John Dewey, Gandhiji wanted to transform the schools into communities where individuals get abundant opportunities of social contact and co-operation. Gandhiji synthesized the individual and the social aims of education. He proved it by example and precept that 'self-realisation' and 'social service' were not contradictory. A fusion of the two in a man made the man complete.

An Analytic Assessment

As early as 1906 the Indian National Congress emphasized the importance of national education. During the non-cooperation period in the twenties of the last century many national educational institutions were started. It was realized that all national progress depended upon mass education. The leaders were convinced that the prevailing system of primary education had failed to make the vast majority of people literate.

In 1921 Mahatma Gandhi said, that "the existing system of education is defective in three most important matters:

1. It is based upon foreign culture to the almost entire exclusion of indigenous culture;
2. It ignores the culture of the heart and the hand, and is confined simply to the head; and
3. Real education is impossible through a foreign medium".

It was also in this year that he conceived the idea of self-supporting education and remarked, "We have only touched the fringe of an ocean of children. The vast mass of them remain without education, not for want of will but of ability and knowledge on the part of the parents. There is something radically wrong, especially for a nation so poor as ours, when parents have to support so many grown-up children and give them a highly expensive education, without the children making any immediate return. I can see nothing wrong in the children, from the very threshold of their education, paying for it in work. The simplest handicraft suitable for all, required for the whole of India, is undoubtedly spinning along with the previous processes. If we introduced this in our educational institutions, we should fulfill three purposes, make education self-supporting and train the bodies of the children as well as their minds. Children, thus equipped, will become self-reliant and independent. Under my scheme, no child is entitled to education, who does not spin a minimum quantity of yarn. This scheme does not exclude a liberal education, but on the contrary brings it within easy reach of every boy or girl, and restores literary training to its original dignity by making it primarily a means of mental and moral culture and only secondarily and indirectly a means of livelihood."

Sixteen years later Mahatma Gandhi got the opportunity of influencing Ministers in seven provinces, who had been fellow-workers and fellow-sufferers in the struggle for independence of India. He initiated in 1937, discussions in the columns of *'Harijan'* on a scheme of national education. The chief burden of his theme was that:

(a) course of primary education should have seven years' duration, should be English-less matriculation, including a substantial vocation;

(b) all round development of children should be acquired through profit-yielding vocations;

(c) primary education, besides training the mind, should produce bread-earners from the vocation learnt in school, the state purchasing the manufactures of children;

(d) primary education should be self-supporting;

(e) higher education, instead of being a state obligation, should be left to private enterprise.

Consequently, an All-India National Education Conference was convened at Wardha in October under the Presidentship of Mahatma Gandhi. It was also attended by Education Ministers of 7 provinces where Congress was in power. A scheme called the Basic Education Scheme was drawn up and all ideas of Gandhiji were embodied in it.

To give further thought to the scheme a Committee was appointed under the chairmanship of Dr. Zakir Hussain. This Committee did not wholly support the self-supporting view of

Mahatma Gandhi. They observed that even if it could not become self-supporting it was acceptable "as a matter of sound educational policy and as an urgent measure of national reconstruction. This good education will incidentally cover the major portion of its running expenses".

The committee also took cognizance of one danger that "in the working of this scheme the economic aspect may be stressed at the sacrifice of the cultural and educational objective. Teachers may devote most of their attention and energy to extracting the maximum amount of labour from children, whilst neglecting the intellectual, social and moral implications and possibilities of craft training," and accordingly they desired that such an attitude on the part of the teacher should be avoided.

The Committee also laid down the detailed syllabus and made suggestions about several aspects like the training of teachers, supervision, examination and administration. The Indian National Congress at its Haripura Session in 1938 accepted the principles of basic National Education and authorized the formation of an all-India board to work out a practical programme for the furtherance of the objective. Accordingly the Board, under the name of Hindustani Talimi Sangh was formed under the advice and guidance of Mahatma Gandhi.

Latest Conceptual Development

Since its very inception, Basic education has been misunderstood and misinterpreted in variety of ways. In order to remove mis-understanding and to highlight its significant features, the Government of India has issued an authoritative statement in the following words:

1. Basic education, as conceived and explained by Mahatma Gandhi, is essentially an education for life and an education through life. It aims at creating a social order free from exploitation and violence. That is why productive, creative and socially useful work in which all boys and girls may participate, irrespective of any distinction of caste, creed or class, is placed at the very centre of Basic education.

2. The effective teaching of a basic craft, is an essential part of education at this stage. It makes the acquisition of much related knowledge more concrete and realistic. It makes a powerful contribution to the development of personality and character and instills respect and love for all socially useful work. The sale of products of craftwork is expected to contribute towards a part of the expenditure on running the school or the products may be used by the school children for getting a mid-day meal or a school uniform or may help to provide some of the school furniture and equipment.

3. The fundamental objective of Basic education is the development of the child's total efficiency as well. In order to ensure that the teaching of the basic craft is efficient and its educative possibilities are fully realized, we must insist that the articles made should be of good quality, as good as children at that stage of their development can make them socially useful and, if necessary, saleable. The acquisition of skills and the love for good craftsmanship have deeper educative significance than merely playing with the tools and raw materials. The productive aspect should in no case be relegated to the background. Directly as well as indirectly, efficiency in the craft contributes to the all-round development of the child; but the productive aspect should not be allowed to take precedence over the educational aspect. It sets up before children high standards of achievement and gives them the right kind of training in useful habits and attitudes like purposeful application, concentration, persistence and thoughtful planning. While the teacher should endeavour to explore its economic possibilities fully, in any way, but they should not conflict with the educational aims and objectives. However, in the upper classes of Junior Basic schools and in the Senior Basic schools, it should not be difficult to lay down certain minimum targets of production in the light of carefully assessed experiences.

4. In the choice of basic crafts a liberal approach should be adopted. Only such crafts may be taken up which : (*a*) have significance from the point of view of intellectual

content and (*b*) Provide scope for progressive development of knowledge and practical efficiency. The basic craft must be such as will fit into the natural and social environment of the school and hold within it the maximum of educational possibilities. The idea that has been wrongly created in the minds of some people that the mere introduction of a craft in a school, *e.g.*, spinning, can make it a Basic school does grave injustice to the concept of Basic education.

5. In Basic education, as indeed, in any good scheme of education, knowledge must be related to activity, practical experience and observation. To ensure this, Basic education rightly postulates that the study of the curricular content should be intelligently related to three main centres of correlation *viz.*, craft work, the natural environment and the social environment. The well-trained and understanding teacher should be able to integrate most of the knowledge that he wishes to impart one or two other of these centres of correlation, which form the important and natural foci of interest for the growing child. There may be certain items in the syllabus which cannot be easily correlated directly with any of the three above centres. In such cases, which should occur only infrequently, there should be no objection to these being taught according to the methods of teaching adopted in any good school. In such lessons, the principle of interest and motivation and the value of expression-work should be utilized. In any case, forced and mechanical 'associates' which pass for correlation in many schools should be carefully avoided.

6. The emphasis on productive work and crafts in Basic schools should not be taken to mean that the study of books can be ignored. The Basic scheme does postulate that the book is not the only or the main avenue to knowledge and culture and that, at this age, properly organized productive work can in many ways contribute more richly both to the acquisition of knowledge and the development of personality. But the value of the book, both as a source of additional systematized knowledge and of pleasure cannot be denied.

7. The basic scheme envisages a close integration between the schools and the community so as to make education as well as the children more social-minded and co-operative. It endeavours to achieve this, firstly, by organising the school itself as a living and functioning community-with its social and cultural programmes and other activities—secondly, by encouraging students to participate in life around the school and in organising various types of social service to the local community. Student self-government is another important feature in Basic education which should be envisaged as a continuous programme of training in responsibility and in the democratic way of living. In this way, the Basic school not only helps in cultivating qualities of self-reliance, co-operation and respect for dignity of labour, but also becomes a vital factor in the creation of a dynamic social order.

8. Basic education should no longer be regarded as meant exclusively for the rural areas. It should be introduced in urban areas as well both because of its intrinsic suitability and also to remove the impression that it is some inferior kind of education designed only for the village children. For this purpose, necessary modifications may be made in the choice of basic crafts for urban schools and even in the syllabus but the general ideals and methods should remain the same.

The Curriculum

In fact, in order to acquire "the essential modicum of social and civic training" Gandhiji wanted a syllabus which should enable the child to adjust himself intelligently and actively to his physical and social environment and to craft work "which is their natural meeting point since it utilises the resources of the former (physical) for the purpose of the latter (social)". His attempt, therefore; was to plan an activity curriculum which should transform the schools into, "places of work, experimentation and discovery".

In his curriculum Gandhiji included the following subjects:

(1) Basic craft which may be agriculture or spinning and weaving or card board, wood and metal work.

(2) Mother tongue

(3) Mathematics. In this more emphasis is to be laid on numerical and geometrical problems connected with craft and community life. He wished that children should learn four simple rules by actually working out the problems arising out of craft work and gardening. They should deal with figures which may throw light on the economic and social facts of their village, town or country. This practical measuring and field work and calculations of expenditure and of rural indebtedness would make the learning of mathematics an active process. This would enable the learner to interpret and understand the social environments. An acquaintance with business practice and book-keeping is also essential.

(4) Social studies, which should give to the students an understanding and appreciation of the cultural contribution made through various ages and should explain to man his environment— social, economic, governmental and physical.

(5) General science in which should be included nature study, Zoology, Physiology, Hygiene, Physical culture, Chemistry and knowledge of stars.

(6) Drawing and Music were included to create in boys and girls a real interest in education. Primary education, he said, must include the elementary principles of sanitation, hygiene, nutrition, doing their own work, helping parents at home etc. Realising the physical difficulties of the present generation he prescribed compulsory physical training through musical drill.

Up to the fifth grade of the school the curriculum was to be the same for both girls and boys. In the later stages general science and craft were to be replaced by domestic science in case of girls.

No. exaggeration, Mahatma Gandhiji was a practical psychologist. The theory of education that he formulated after long thought and experience was not without psychological insight. Like Ruosseau he restored the child to his rightful place and made education child-centric. For becoming a real teacher, he said, the hearts of the children should be touched. Their joys and sorrows should be shared and they must be helped to solve their own problems.

Their 'surging aspiration' must be directed to the right channel. Conscious of child's natural instincts, Gandhiji made a full use of them by introducing the takli. The use of takli satisfied the child's instinct of play. But it was a play which was purposeful rather than frivolous. Similarly, the instincts of pugnacity and self-assertion were satisfied by competition of take spinning among the children. 'Curiosity' was satisfied by knowing the why and wherefore of the cotton.

Acquisitive instinct got its outlet when the children prepared some articles and considered them as their own. Love and trust between the teacher and the taught was the cardinal principle of Gandhiji's teachings. Through love, he said, the right type of teacher would be able to "draw forth the best that is in the child through understanding, sympathy, and appreciation of each child's precious individuality. Sweet compulsion of love should be the rule in education".

This would "put the child on its own resources" and would also eliminate punishment. Once when two of the inmates of Tolstoy Farm showed moral fall, Gandhiji was shocked. He handled the situation wisely like a psychologist, instead of resorting to "negative repression, reprimands, moralising and the 'don't method' " he brought about their change of heart by love, sympathy and understanding. In order to make them realise their fault, he observed a fast. This proved very efficacious in bringing the change.

Gandhiji hated verbalism and the use of books. He wanted to depend upon the ears, eyes and hands. His emphasis, like Dewey, was on activities and occupations of real life. To him, the school was a projected home "with the same surrounding, same problems and same occupations". Handicrafts, according to him, would teach the child how to see, think and work when in grip with difficulties. This creates in the child self-reliance and self-confidence.

His plan of education was paedo-centric. His scheme based on activity and the study of the child, could not be otherwise than child-centred. Activity and interest was the core of his scheme of education. But he wanted a purposeful activity like handicraft and manual work. His was a productive, remunerative and educative activity. His activity was a "prime means of intellectual training". It also strengthened the muscles of children and made them physically supple.

Thus the activity coordinated the hand, the eyes and the ears. He remarked, "the hand will handle tools before it draws or traces the writing, the eyes will read the pictures of letters and words as they will know other things in life, the ears will catch the same meanings of things and sentences". By putting into use the child's sense, he develops the power of observation and imagination.

Correlation with craft and with environment and co-ordination with subjects is another psychological factor which received the greatest attention of Gandhiji. He made the handicraft as the pivot, round which the teaching of other subjects like mathematics, history, geography, nature-study should revolve. He wanted an effective and natural correlation between the craft and other subjects and the co-ordination of various subjects.

Gandhi's educational plan is psychological because it, "relieves the child from the tyranny of purely academic and theoretical instruction against which its active instincts always make a healthy protest. It balances the intellectual and practical elements of experience it and may be made an instrument of educating the body and the mind in co-ordination. The child acquires not the superficial literacy—a capacity to read the printed page—but the far more important capacity of using hand and intelligence for some constructive purpose". This enables him to grow better, to gain confidence and to manifest his abilities. The child learns more quickly by actually doing the thing and by understanding the relationship of various branches of knowledge. All knowledge proceeds from the concrete to the abstract, from practical to theoretical.

Activity and movement is the natural urge of the child. Muscles work and then senses understand. In the words of Dewey the active skill precedes the passive in the develop-ment of child nature; expression comes before conscious impression, the muscular development precedes the sensory, Professor Nun said, "For education it is of the highest importance to realise that cognition and action always occur in an organic unity from which neither can be separated without destruction to the other. No mental process or act is excessively knowing, feeling or doing but a harmonious integration of all the three".

Knowledge, therefore, cannot be divorced from action. Practical activity is the best means of instruction in all subjects. Basic craft provides enough scope for satisfaction of child's instincts of curiosity and construction. It develops the spirit of investigation, explora-tion, manipulation and experimentation in him. All these psychological foundations of Gandhiji's plan of education aimed at "literacy of the whole personality".

Sociological Aspects

No exaggeration, while Basic education aims at giving the future citizen a keen sense of personal worth, dignity and efficiency, it inculcates in him the desire for social service in a cooperative community. On account of its being craft-centred it prevents a person from becoming a drag or a parasite on the society. It breaks down artificial social barriers and brings down all the classes to the level of dignity of labour. It trains the individual for citizenship by actually making him share its obligations by repaying atleast a part of his debt to to State.

Basic education wants to create an individual who would look upon himself an integral part of society. He should be able to share the joys and sorrows of the rest of his countrymen. He must have a sense of oneness, of unity, of comradeship first with his country and then with the world. He must realise that he can make his distinctive contribution to the world not by self-centred activity but through co-operative work.

Education Through Work

As popular 'Life is work and work is worship'—this is the dominant feature of Basic education. In fact this should be the dominant feature of every progressive system of education. Recognising the importance of education through work. Mahatma Gandhi says, "The brain must be educated through the hand. If I were a poet. I could write poetry on the possibilities of the five fingers. Why should you think that mind is everything and the hands and feet nothing? Those who do not train their hands and go through the ordinary test of education lack music in their life". In the words of Zakir Hussain Committee report "Modern educational thought is practically unanimous in commending the idea of educating children through some suitable form of productive work.

This method is considered to be the most effective approach to the problem of providing an integral all-sided education. Every productive work or craft has two functions: Primary and secondary. The primary function of work is the training of eyes, ears and hands. Through these lies the training of intellect.

Work gives not only sensory training but also promotes creativity. It awakens imaginative activity leading to the creation of original forms of craft-work. Work is an expression of one's individuality and manifests thought, character and artistic sense of children. It draws out the full and latent potentialities of the child. Cool judgement, patient and sustained pursuit of an objective, self-reliance, awareness of the relation between merit and achievement are certainly looked into craft-centred education.

Knowledge gained through craft, even if limited, is more

valuable and effective than wider knowledge which is mechanically borrowed from books. The primary function of hand work is to develop the willpower and executive ability of children. It helps a national un-figment of their faculties of understanding. This affords them training in discipline because they have to give finished product of some standard with the material supplied, amount of time fixed and shapes and dimensions prescribed.

Economic value and correlating it with various branches of instruction is the secondary function of work. Economic motive of work should not predominate in any system of education. Overemphasis on the economic aspect of craft in Basic education has been responsible for much of the criticism levelled against Basic education. In fact manual occupations are means, more than other school studies. Of obtaining certain intellectual and moral results which are of great value in training of the young. Manual dexterity reacts favourably upon the intellectual faculties and is an important aid to their development. It has been recognised that the development of higher brain centres is intimately connected with that of the motor centres which control the action of the hand, which in their turn depend upon it for their development. It is by creative work that body, mind and spirit can grow. The moment a person handles any raw material with the object of giving it a serviceable function, he becomes a creator and develops inward strength and self-reliance which spur him to greater fulfilment.

When psychologically considered, work is desirable because it relieves the child from the tyranny of purely academic and theoretical instruction against which child's nature always makes a healthy protest. It balances the intellectual and practical elements of experience and may be made an instrument of educating the body and the mind in co-ordination. The child acquires not the superficial literacy but the far more important capacity of using hand and intelligence for some constructive purpose.

The joy of 'self-doing' and achievement is the greatest joy. Practical work appeals to all children at all levels of intelligence, but more especially, perhaps to the less able children, because they can get more satisfaction from practical work than from bookish studies. Practical work gives them the chance to see where they stand. The results are solid and satisfying. If the children make mistakes they can see them clearly and have a firm idea of what they must do to put them right. Children do not work on the craft because they are asked to do it under any compulsion, but because they love to move their hands.

There is improvement in the general attitude of children. Valentine reminds us that when handicraft was first introd-uced there was a decided drop in the need for corporal punishment. Success in work so influences a child's self-respect that he can attack other sides of his school work with greater success.

Abstract thought is hardest to attain but concrete thought has a place of growing importance in this technological age. Work brings in the concreteness of thought; children are not bored with school-work because of practical work. Activity taps the child to the maximum. Interest is aroused. Learning is quicker. What is learnt is more lasting. His hands work to the benefit of his mind. Virtues like planning, accuracy, initiative and individual responsibility are the directs results of productive work. In the words of Henry Ford "true education consists in learning to do by doing, learning to help by helping and learning to earn by earning".

On sociological consideration, work in education tends to break down the barriers of prejudice between manual and intellectual workers. It inculcates a true sense of dignity of labour and of human solidarity. This is the ethical and moral gain of incalculable significance. Human and social values are created. Co-operative activity gives the children a feeling of kinship. Educative-work prepares for future life and teaches system and order. It is the most potent weapon for bringing social co-hesion and unification. It is the most effective means of transforming a society into community where there is a feeling of relationship.

While from the view-point of education, the craft gives

greater concreteness reality to the knowledge, which is to be acquired by the children. In the words of Dr. Montessori, "the sensory motor activities contain the promise and potency of all human progress and their training through crafts lays the best possible foundations for higher intellectual attainments". Knowledge becomes related to life. It is through craft that knowledge is presented in an integrated manner and not in unrelated fragments.

For this certain criteria for the selection of a suitable craft has to be kept in mind.

1. The productive-work or craft should be selected in conformity with the geographic and economic conditions of the locality.
2. It should have rich educative possibilities, having natural points of correlation with important human activities and interests.

Self-sufficiency

The meaning and scope of self-sufficiency in Basic education has undergone many interpretations. Originally Gandhiji's ideal of self-sufficiency meant "something which would meet the recurring expenses in Basic schools from the income derived from productive work done by boys and girls". He explained, "that recurring expenses meant mainly salaries of teachers." He, however, kept an open mind and later explained "that the idea of depositing proceeds from Craft work in the Government treasury or with the management to cover the amounts spent on the salaries of teachers was somewhat narrow conception of self-sufficiency in Basic education.

Society or the state should provide land, buildings, equipment, raw materials, guidance, supervision etc., and the teachers and the pupils working and learning together will constitute a co-operative family producing and using for themselves what they need for food, clothing and other essential requirements of life". Thus self-sufficiency became the watch-word of Basic education. The orthodox basic educationists stuck to this idea and emphasised that a Basic school should be self-sufficient in meeting its recurring expenditure from the income or the craft. Their main argument is that India is a poor country and can never afford to start schools for the vast mass on the responsibility of Government alone. And then education is not a thing which should be delayed.

Only way, therefore, is to have schools which meet their own way. Undoubtedly the idea is laudable but there are practical difficulties in making the schools completely self-supporting. The greatest danger lies in this that the schools might not be converted into factories. The teachers, in their enthusiasm to show their worth, might not emphasis productivity of craft at the cost of educational values of the craft. It is rather feared that "maximum productivity" might become their slogan at the sacrifice of every other educational interest. On the other hand there is no denying the fact that working efficiently on the craft and producing something marketable will infuse confidence and a sense of self-reliance.

Besides the economic and material side of self-sufficiency, there is an idealistic significance of self-sufficiency. In idealistic sense self-sufficiency should mean learning the use of all faculties properly. There should be self-reliance not only in the economic but also in the social and moral sphere. The children must have desirable sense of responsibility. They should manifest thoroughness and efficiency in work. They should use the time economically and resourcefully. They should be able to pull their own weight in the society and should not be parasites on the society. They should have critical power, power of judgement, power of weighing the right and the wrong, truth, justice and love. This is self-sufficiency in educa-tion.

The Correlation

Correlation should be natural and not forced. In order to make it natural and effective following factors are essential :

1. There should be teachers with originality and enthusiasm. They must have creative genius and illustrative talent. They must be in the habit of thinking out from day to day what they have to teach. They must keep comprehensive records of their day-to-day educational procedures so as to utilize these in correlated teaching.
2. The teacher can succeed in establishing correlation only if they have complete grasp of the various processes of craft and prorogued his mental reserved is full of knowledge about the social and physical environment.
3. Rigidity in time-table hinders the process of correlation. Unless teachers get full time, they cannot do justice to bilateral or multilateral correlation of various subjects with the main centre or point of correlation. Shortage of time results in handling the knowledge and the activity loosely and not with firmness of mind.
4. The teacher should have the freedom to follow his own plan of dealing with the different items of the curriculum. The items of curriculum have to be planned round the activity and not that the activity has to be pegged on to the items of the curriculum.
5. Very frequently all the teachers in a Basic school must meet together to discuss the planning of work on the correlational technique. The exchange of ideas will not only facilitate planning but will also sustain interest in correlated teaching.
6. Since the starting point of correlated teaching is the experience of the child, a record of the constructive experiences of children should be kept. It is not essential that immediate experience may be used. The occasion may demand the use of an experience, which the children had long ago.

With the acceptance of Basic Education in 1938, operations commenced immediately. The first school to train teachers was opened in April, 1938, at Wardha. Three national institutions, Jamia Millia Islamia of Delhi, Andhra Jatiya Kalsala of Masulipatam and Tilak Maharashtra Vidyapith at Pune also started their training centres. The Gujerat Vidhyapith of Ahmedabad and the Government of U.P. followed suit. The Governments of C.P., U.P., Bihar, Bombay and Kashmir State enthusiastically espoused the cause of basic education by opening new basic schools or by converting the existing primary schools to the basic pattern. The Governments of Bengal, Punjab, N.W.F.P. and Sind, however, did not join to try this new experiment. The enthusiasm for translating the new ideology into practice was kept up in the year 1939-40 as well. Many new training centres were opened all over the country, a large number of new basic schools were started and many existing primary schools were partially converted.

The Central Advisory Board of Education appointed, in 1938, a Committee to examine the scheme and the progress of Basic education. Their recommendations amounted more or less to a theoretical acceptance of the principle involved. The Central Advisory Board of Education made it clear that the aim of the scheme is not, as is believed by some people, "the production of craftsmen able to practise some craft mechanically, but rather the exploitation for educative purposes of the resources implicit in craft-work". They, therefore, wanted that the craft or productive work chosen should be rich in educative possibilities. It should find natural points of correlation with important human activities and interests. It was desired by the Board that Basic education should have 8 years' course, divided into two stages—the Junior covering a period of 5 years and the Senior of 3 years. The faith in Basic education was reiterated by the Central Advisory Board of education in 1940, when their second Committee made more recommendations about its organization. It was recommended that in each province there should be established a central agency for the disposal of marketable articles produced in schools. For girls attending the Senior Basic

School, they advocated the introduction of subjects like cookery, laundry work, needle work, home crafts, care of children and first aid. It was with domestic science that other subjects were to be correlated for teaching girls on this new pattern.

In October 1939 first Conference of Basic National Education. Conference adopted a resolution that English should not be taught "till the students have acquired a regular education for 7 years through their mother tongue". They recorded that Basic National Education had made steady and encouraging progress during the previous two years and hoped that "it will, in due course, bring about a revolution in the existing system of education in the country". "In order to meet the enormous capital and other forms of expenditure" to be incurred in making 7 years basic education free, universal and compulsory", the Conference urged the Central Government "to bear its due share of the total expenditure of this most important activity of national reconstruction".

The most significant recommendation of the Conference was that the correlation should not necessarily be forced with the basic-craft only, but it should be extended to child's physical and social environments. Appreciating the success of the scheme the Conference pointed out that, "the children in basic schools are more active, cheerful, self-reliant; their power of self-expression is well developed, they are acquiring habits of co-operative work, and social prejudices are "breaking down". They, therefore, very strongly advocated the continuance of the scheme with vigour.

The resignation of Congress Ministers in 1939 and the commencement of World War II gave a setback to the new scheme. Several of the measures sponsored by the Congress Ministers were abandoned. The C.P. Government closed their training centres and confined the experiment of basic education to only 2 selected areas. Orissa Government closed their basic schools and dissolved the Board of Basic Education in 1941. The national workers, however, decided to continue the work independently and a private body called the Utkal Moulik Siksha

Parishad was formed. The villagers lent their support and thus 7 out of 15 schools continued to function. Bihar and Bombay also continued the experiment. The Hindustani Talimi Sangh had to struggle through rough days during 1942-45 on account of official opposition. Several of their workers were arrested. During all these years some of the non-government institutions, however, kept the torch of basic education burning.

When the Central Advisory Board of Education submitted its well-known Sargent Report, in 1944, they incorporated this system of education in their Post-War Educational Development Plan and accepted it as the foundation of the national scheme of educational recon-struction.

In 1945 a National Educational Conference was convened at Wardha. After reviewing the working of the scheme, it was decided to extend its scope. Mahatma Gandhi said, "it should include the education of everybody at every stage of life. A basic school teacher must consider himself a universal teacher", who should teach every villager cleanliness, remove his ignorance and widen his mental horizen. He wanted the teacher, "to establish a living contact with his (villager's) mind and win his confidence". He wanted to cater for education right from the birth of the children and observed, "now our scope is no longer limited to the child between 7 and 14. Nai Talim or New Education has extended its scope today to the whole span of life from the moment of conception to the hour of death".

Basic education was no longer considered a system of education only, but it was now to be medium of bringing social, economic and psychological change in Indian society. As a result of this orientation the conference discussed the 3 stages of pre-basic, post-basic and adult education.

With the attainment of independence the Government of India accepted Basic education as the only pattern suited to children from 6 to 14 years. A committee of experts was appointed in 1948 to suggest ways and means of putting it into full operation. The Committee recommended that universal, compulsory and free Basic education should be completed in 16 years by two Five-year-plans and one 6 years plan. The Constitution of India also provided that each State should provide free and compulsory education for all children up to the age of 14. During the last 13 years much progress has been made. A very large number of basic schools are rapidly being converted to the basic pattern.

For the success of basic schools adequately trained teachers and liberal provision for equipment of craft work are the first essentials. It is then that the superiority of the system will be established and the faith of the people in this education will be increased.

In order to increase training facilities the Government of India sponsored post-graduate Basic Training Colleges, one in each State. Besides producing the staff for secondary basic schools, they also produce administrative personnel to plan, execute and supervise the scheme. "An efficient and sympathetic supervisory staff is almost as important for the new schools as a well-trained teaching personnel". The Central Government is encouraging in every way—more by offering liberal grants—the switch over from traditional education to basic education. In 1956 the Government of India appointed Assessment Committee on Basic Education "to survey the existing situations regarding Basic education in the various states and to think out ways and means of bringing about effective improvements".

The Committee visited eleven States and they tried to assess Basic education at various levels--State Government level, Administrative level, Teacher Training level, Basic school level and Public level.

Recommendations of the Assessment Committee

1. The Government of India should make it clear that Basic education has their concurrence.
2. The Standing Committee's concept of Basic education (as given under a previous section) should be made clear to the Education Ministers and the Education

Secretaries of the various states so that Basic education may develop on approved lines and may be completed within specific time-limits.

3. Regional district-level conferences of the Basic education should be arranged periodically to discuss difficulties, problems, experiences and solutions.
4. Public opinion should be educated through the films, the radio, the press, publications, exhibitions etc.
5. A central Research Institute of Basic education should be established.
6. A high level small Special Committee be appointed to lay down the criteria to evaluate the achievements and progress of pupils from time to time in Basic institutions.
7. Literature suitable for Basic teachers and school children should be produced.
8. A special brochure dealing with how to convert traditional schools into Basic pattern should be published.
9. The question of providing simpler and cheaper buildings to Basic schools should be taken up.
10. Post-Graduate Basic Training Colleges should be started immediately.
11. Post-Basic education should be recognised and linked with the present reorganization of secondary education.
12. States should declare that Elementary schools will be converted into Basic schools and all teacher-training at this level will become Basic teacher-training within reasonable time-limit.
13. Important aspects of Basic education should be introduced in all Elementary schools.
14. Education officers at all levels should be given short and effective courses of training in Basic education.

15. A Joint or Additional Director of Public Instruction should be appointed for Basic education.
16. State Governments should take steps for the supply of raw-materials, equipment etc. whatever is produced, should, as far as possible, be consumed by the teachers and pupils.
17. Land-gifts should be organised.
18. The integrated course of 8 years of Basic education should be kept in view.
19. Universities should recognise Post-Basic education and affiliate Post-graduate Basic training colleges.
20. Local co-operation should be enlisted to attain the success of Basic education.
21. Examinations should be mainly a continuous assessment of work and progress of pupils and this should be considered more important than written examinations.
22. Productive work should in no case become his excuse for lowering standards of learning.
23. English should be offered as an optional subject from the VI grade onwards.
24. Teacher-training should be made more efficient by intensive training in craft, in correlated technique and in child psychology.
25. One member atleast of Basic Training school should know the technique of educational research.

Most of these recommendations have been imple-mented and there is an evidence of briskness in the spread of Basic education. As soon as the attitude of cynicism and defiles is changed into an attitude of optimism and resolu-teness, the flowering of Basic education is a guarantee.

More than fifty years have gone by since Basic education was introduced in our country. But there is a general feeling that it has not yet caught the imagination of people in general. So far the common man has not been drawn towards it spontaneously. Even since independence this system of education has been accepted as a national pattern for primary education. But judging from the opinions of people in general one can say that Basic education is not yet as popular as it should be. There is no denying the fact that this system of education, conceived and propounded as it is, has sound educational theory based on psychological and sociological principle. It must be then in practice that it has fallen short of theoretical expectations. Some of the factors, which are responsible for its slow progress are:

Emphasis on Economic Aspect: Too much emphasis on economic aspect or the productivity aspect, in some basic schools and by orthodox Basic educationists has been responsible for the unpopularity of Basic education.

This emphasis led the common people to believe that the children are turned into labourers. Teachers are remained too much preoccupied in producing as much of vegetables as possible in the school gardens or with manufacturing as much cloth as they could on the school looms. They lost sight of educational objectives of craft in their enthusiasm for showing more productivity.

Absence of Textbooks: In many basic schools learning is restricted to learning from direct experience and to learning from the teacher. Self-study of text books is almost excluded as no books are prescribed. Common people believe that text books play a significant role in the education of the child. Unless a child has an access to a book, his knowledge cannot be logically organized.

Aesthetic Side Neglected: The artistic and aesthetic side of education has not been attended to in some of the Basic schools. The only art work they do is the drawing of the charkha or rice-plant or charts depicting the technique of correlation. Their songs are limited to songs related to *Takli, Charkha, Plough* or the *Rashtrabhasa* and seldom to "lotus bedecked pools, natural phenomena and the like". If not in theory, at least in practice the appreciation of art or beauty is not to be found there.

There are certain misinformed people who are of conservative reactionary nature. They resist progressive improvements. Such people characterize themselves as 'liberals' and take the plea that India being a land of boundaries opportunities, they should remain free from entangling commitments to any pre-conceived design and refuse to be shackled by any set means. They consider Basic education as 'indoctrination' and refuse to be convinced of its being progressive and practical elements.

Costliness of Basic education : The establishment of a good basic school involves a good deal of initial cost on the purchase of equipment for craft. There is always a recurring expenditure on the successful running of a good craft. The income from the products is not commensurate with the financial outlay. This factor discourages the introduction of Basic education on a mass scale.

Opposition of Traditionalists : Some of the traditionalists are apprehensive that since Basic education aims to produce citizens, capable of analysing the weakness of the present social and economic institutions and practices, the status of these people may not be titled. Such a group of people can tolerate Basic education only as a crack-pot academic scheme. They cannot tolerate it if it begins to have a serious impact. They can tolerate it so long as it can produce men who have learnt to accept meekly their subordination. They cannot tolerate it when it begins to teach the common people that they are sovereign in fact as well as in theory.

*White-Collar Complexion of Basic Education :*The work of Basic education was correctly started in villages, but with the help of teachers who were used to an urban life. Unfortunately such teachers misunderstood the whole spirit behind basic education and divided the curriculum in two sections. One was called the craft-section and the other 'education section.' One was called training in handicraft and the other the training of intellect, if the first had nothing to do with the second. They either did not make craft as the medium of instruction or if they made it, they did it more for show and in a frivolous manner rather than for achievement of some good results. The result was that in villages Basic education could not become village-centric.

Apathy of Administrators : In the words of Assessment Committee on Basic education, "It is at the administrative level today, more than any other, that serious difficulties arise in the development of Basic education. Education Departments are concerned with innumerable problems. Basic education is even now only a small and side item in their programmes of work. In none of the states did we find a Director of Public Instruction to whom Basic education was an issue of utmost importance nor did we find any of them fully conversant with the problems of Basic education in their respective states".

Progressive Features

It has been adequately shown as in a previous discussion that Basic education is based on psychological and sociological factors. A scheme based on such foundations is certainly progressive and dynamic.

True education is an all round development of child's faculties. All round development is realizable through action and activity. It is through action that knowledge and understanding develop. In action problems are confronted. Their solutions are sought by thinking and reasoning. Different sources are consulted. Knowledge, which is not the result of an activity is assimilated quickly. It was with these motives that Gandhiji made 'craft' as the bulwark of his educational system. Sound education must be built on the nucleus of craft or productive work.

The bane of our educational system has been that we learn through books and not through activity. Project Method replaced bookish learning to some extent but projects were not planned with a view to meeting social needs, nor did they have any relation to crafts. The value of craft in education had been accepted before Mahatma Gandhi also but craft was never thought of as the medium of instruction. There is no doubt that craft work does call forth several qualities and mental aptitudes.

Education divorced from life is valueless. It should be preparation for life and this system brings the school nearer to realities of life or life is shaped in the school. It is based on the socio-economic structure. The selection of basic craft is made with reference to the community living in the vicinity of the school. Such a school has to produce leaders and workers of that community. The basic education "envisages the school not as a training ground for certain services and professions meant for a small section of the urban population but as an agency for the practical and social education and hundreds of millions of the rural population in whose life the central and significant factor is work which is made the centre and medium of education, thus The breaking down the artificial walls dividing the schools from life". The physical and social environment of the child is made the starting point of education.

Education should fit the child rather than that the child should fit education, is an educational maxim accepted as early as the days of Communius, Rousseau and Pestalozzi. In spite of the repeated assertion of this principle, in the case of India it found expression only in the basic scheme of education. It is this education which is child-centred. The child works at his own pace and plans and executes in his own way. His curiosities are satisfied. Since children are explained the way and wherefore of everything in a correlated manner, they actually look into facts and causes and thus develop a spirit of enquiry. Their constructive and manipulative instincts get outlet. The child takes delight in the experience of doing and his acquisitive instinct gets satisfaction when he handles articles made by him. It is by working on the handicraft that the teacher knows the interest, aptitudes and capabilities of the children. How the child reacts to the problems presented, how he tackles them successfully, how he is discouraged by the limitations or has the knack to overcome the handicaps, these are things of great importance and give to the teacher great insight into the personality of child. This insight helps the teacher to give guidance and counselling on the future career of the child. Activity is the greatest urge of the child and this is amply provided in basic education, and then the activity is not an end in itself, but means to an end.

The teacher of Basic education has to be more active than the traditional teacher. Instead of being a talker he has to be a planner, does and thinker. He has to correlate the various subjects with craft and there comes his real genius at play. He has to keep a discerning eye upon the all-round development of the child and has to attend to him individually, as a practical art cannot be learnt, except by individual attention. It is the zealous and missionary teacher who can be successful. His outlook and temperament have to be adopted to this new way of teaching-learning process. Unless he has himself mastered the craft and has understood the full import of correlating it with other subjects, he cannot succeed in carrying conviction with learners.

The most distinctive feature of Basic education is correlation. Its concept and technique has been discussed under a previous section.

Its emphasis is on co-operation as against competition. The spirit of co-operation is developed through community activities, which include cultural activities, assemblies and activities like cleaning the surroundings, dining together, craft-works sarvodaya work etc.

In recent years it has been thought that there is regimentation in Basic education. Such a notion is false. On the other hand reverse is true. Basic education has the greatest elasticity and variety. Constantly changing demands of a dynamic society can permit any educational pattern to remain static or regimented, much less the Basic education pattern. The central idea of the system is creativity. How can an education, which is creative and related to community life be rigid. Correlation with physical and social environment shows that it is tied to any one text. Basic education creates new values for new India.

Examinations do not occupy the same place in Basic education as they do in the traditional system. No external and public examinations are prescribed for pupils going out of the Basic schools. The attainments of pupils are to be judged from their day-to-day, week-to-week, month-to-month and term-to-term work done in the school, where appropriate records have to be maintained. The teacher takes into account the personal record written work, the power of planning, intellectual progress, habits, artistic gifts etc. in judging the child's progress. He also takes "cognisance of regular attendance, aptitude to work, self reliance and the develop-ment of the scientific attitude in the pupil and test him in the qualities of citizenship and the ideals of public service". The tests may be there but they "should be long enough to cover the whole range of the curriculum and should lie in a form which makes marking objectives".

Unfortunately Basic education has divided educators into two ranks—too 'pro' and too 'anti'. The latter category of educators believe that there "is more of sentiment than of sound educational philosophy" behind Gandhiji's ideas. They say that since the scheme is connected with the name of the Father of Nation and a Great Saviour of India, therefore it is being advocated and followed, because the ruling party has committed itself to work out the scheme, it is sticking to it "through thick and thin".

Now, even if the feeling of sentiment be true, it is not a bad thing to have sentiment for a good scheme. This sentiment is not based upon any extraneous factor but on inherent merits of the scheme. No one can deny that India had to be regenerated socially, morally, intellectually and politically through education. For this a method suiting to the genius of our traditions and circumstances had to be found. Colossal illiteracy, ignorance and squalor had to be broken. Mahatma Gandhi found these means, and then, his educational ideas in no way violate the psychological and pedagogical principles.

A group of educationists feel that all subjects cannot be correlated with craft. But correlation has now been given wider connotation. Besides correlating the teaching of subjects with craft, it is also desired that education should be related to life environments—physical, social and economic. Since the so-called subjects of instruction are branches of knowledge acquired by men in life processes, they can be easily correlated with men's physical, social and economic environment. "Correlation is the natural way of knowing our enviornment. It arouses greater enthusiasm and interest, because by combining the process of learning with practical experience, education becomes significant for the child. Pupils' curiosity and powers of observation in regard to various natural phenomena such as rain, thunder, lightning, and the behaviour of heavenly bodies can be developed to teach geography and science". Historical monuments and buildings offer a good medium of teaching history. Similar use can be made of various customs, celebrations and festivals. Although the Basic system "consists largely of correlation work it does not indiscriminately reject every other method of teaching".

The introduction of craft in Basic education has provoked following doubts:

1. Craft is introduced at too early an age, thus denying the child carefree childhood, which is necessary for the unobstructed development of his natural faculties.
2. Craft tends to become forced child-labour.
3. Emphasis on craft is likely to neglect academic work.
4. Introduction of craft is putting the clock-back.
5. Craft-training is likely to retard the progress of large industries in our country.

The first doubt pre-supposes that the craft would be taught in a mechanical way with the object of giving vocational training to the child with regard to his other development. This is a wrong notion. "The emphasis is not on his craft itself but on the avenues it opens up for the child's natural curiosities and the outlet it provides for practical activity". Craft is taught as an activity having an element of self-doing and thus enjoying. The child gets an opportunity for self-expression. He develops a sense of responsibility.

In a Basic school craft-work is not forced. It is not the product which is more emphasised but it is the process which is utilized for educative purposes.

It is wrong to say that craft-work tends to neglect academic work. Craft in Basic education is made the means of academic work. In it "the hand will handle tools before it draws or traces the writing, the eyes will read the pictures of letters and words as they will know other things in life, the ears will catch the names and meanings of things and sentences' through craft-work.

Craft instead of being mechanical practice, involves oral work and drawing. Gandhiji said that with the disc of a talk he could teach a child everything about a circle without once mentioning the name of Euclid. Crafts promote active and experimental learning.

Why should craft-training in schools stand in the way of development of large-scale industries? On the other hand "education imparted through practical and manual work will produce more efficient and skilled workers than the educa-tion, which is predominantly bookish....Well coordinated training in the use of the hand and the mind, in practical skill, observation and creative work will certainly be a better preparation even for later industrial training than passive education", which prejudices students against manual work.

Craft-work does not put the clock back. India is a land of villages, where 75 percent of the population lives. A larger sector of small-scale industry is, therefore, essential to utilize the limited capital resources of people living in rural areas. Development of small-case industry is also desirable in view of over-populated and under-developed country like India.

Some critics object that the Basic system has neglected physical education by providing a few minutes of physical training in the time-table. But why do they forget that the whole system is based upon play-way spirit. At the same time no one can deny the building up of muscles in doing any craft.

Some people deplore the absence of religious education in the system. It is for them to note that Gandhiji wanted 'godliness' rather than God. He advocated practical religion, rather than a religion of 'rosary beads'. His was the religion of self-help, religion of 'love the creature of God' and he believed in 'he prayeth best who loves best'. He preached the greatest gospel of 'love and human fellowship'. To him the creation of a classless society was the divine message. God has created all alike and it is God's will that all should enjoy material world and spiritual bliss equally with no distinction of caste, colour or creed. This was his great philosophy of religion and life. He wanted the hymns from all religions to be sung.

About Waste in Basic Education : It is argued by some critics that the bulk of what is produced in basic schools is not saleable. Basic education, therefore, is uneconomic and wasteful. It is true that some waste is bound to happen because the children are at a learning stage. Their products cannot be compared with the machine-made articles as regards quality and finish. In the first two years of Basic schools much financial gain is not possible but the loss can be made up in the next two or three years. Then why sell the articles in the market? Why should they not be purchased at reasonable prices by children, teachers and parents?

Basic education on the other hand, instead of being a waste, avoids waste. In the traditional system men are not trained for purposeful life. The children after receiving that education feel lost. They are lost to themselves and lost to the community because what they learn is of not much use to them in life. They become a social burden. In Basic education they learn as well as increase their productive capacity. "Thus basic education is a safe-guard against both waste of money and the even more tragic waste of human personality". And then Basic education is "primarily a scheme of education and not one of production". Why should its productivity be taken into consideration.

The main objectives of Gandhian educational plan may be summed up in his own words: "My plan to impart primary education through the medium of village handicrafts....is thus conceived as the spearhead of a silent revolution-fraught with the most far-reaching consequences. It will provide a healthy and moral basis of relationship between the city and the village and thus go a long way towards eradicating some of the worst evils of the present social insecurity and poisoned relationship between the classes. It will check the progressive decay of our villages, and lay the foundation of juster social order in which there is no unnatural division between the haves and havenots and every body is assured of a living wage and the right to freedom. And all this would be accomplished without the horrors of a bloody class war or a colossal capital expenditure such as would be involved in the mechanisation of India. It would place the destiny of the masses in their own hands".

Mahatma Gandhi revolutioned the whole concept of education. Basic scheme is the most practical and unique contribution of Gandhiji. It is a constructive and human system integrated with the needs and ideals of national life. His Basic education is not an imposition and not imported from west, but a spontaneous outgrowth of the Indian soil. At the same time it is in keeping with the progressive educational thought of the modern age. In it there are certain elements of universal validity.

In the words of B.G. Kher it would produce, "socially more alert and intelligent and more co-operative" citizens having "a keener consciousness of their relationship to the community. He was the first educaionist to advocate the large scale use of handicraft, not only as a productive work but as a pivot round which the teaching of all subjects should be undertaken. He put forward a system which is inexpensive and also in consonance with the needs of our vast rural population. In no other way could primary education be made free, compulsory and effective.

A new social order—known as the Sarvodaya Samaj was his great dream. Such society would be classless. Individual will be conscious of spiritual reality. They will lead a life of simplicity, service and sacrifice. There would be no exploitation but equality and justice. The chief means of achieving this new social order, according to Gandhiji, is education. Education centred round handicraft would produce generation which instead of being drones on the society would be its useful and earnings members.

Mahatma Gandhi's thoughts are in line with the best educational thoughts both in the East and in the West. His objectives of education—both immediate and ultimate—are suited to the genius of Indian culture and heritage. Basic education has now come out of experimental stage and is being tried on a very large scale. Given the proper type of missionary teachers, its success is a guarantee. Earnest effort on the part of the Government and the co-operative spirit on the part of the public will go a long way in making the scheme efficacious. For its successful working Gandhiji made a clarion call to the educationists who have no axes to grind. He never wanted persons who wrangle at loaves and fishes. If the educationists work out the scheme without preconceived notions, there is no reason why the colossal problem of educating the masses should not be solved. "Only they must have a living faith in it. Such faith can only grow from within, it can not be acquired vicariously".

Like many other educators, recognition and appreciation of his theories and experiments came to him during his life time. Although recognised and accepted in India, Gandhiji's philosophy of education has not yet accepted universal recognition. But that time is not far off, when his philosophy will be accepted by all nations as the only way to world peace and progress. There is reason to believe that educational practice all over the world may be influenced by his teachings. His dream of world full of love, fellow-feeling and free from greed and exploitation can be realised if his philosophy is followed. He proved it by his example and precept that inherently human heart is good. Only conditions and opportunities have to be created to develop that goodness. This is the only way to have one world "knit together by bonds of affection and brotherhood".

A great guide, teacher and benefactor of mankind was born in India and sacrificed his life and all for regeneration—political, social, educational and economic of India.

Like Rousseau, Gandhiji restored the child to his legitimate place in the scheme of education. His education was child-centred. Both of them were against verbalism and wanted the child to work with his own hand for the development of his mind. As referred earlier, Rousseau believed in negative education. He wanted the child to learn by error. But Gandhiji's approach was positive and he wanted to make efforts that the child should not commit any error.

Coming to Pestalozzi we can say that if Pestalozzi was called 'Father Pestalozzi', Gandhiji was called the 'Father of Nation'. Both of them stood for the harmonious development of human personality. Pestalozzi advocated education for all. So was the ideal of Gandhiji. Both of them had agriculture and spinning and weaving as the main crafts which must be taught to the child. However, Pestalozzi did not lay much emphasis upon the correlation of craft with the teaching of other subjects, while with Gandhiji this was the main emphasis.

Froebel and Gandhiji agree on many points. The former said that the innate propensities of the child must not be allowed to lie dormant. They must be aroused. Gandhiji also said that the function of education is to arouse the natural powers to their fullest development. Both of them saw spiritual meanings behind every activity. With both, self activity was the chief principle of learning. The importance of social environment was recognised by both. Gandhiji and Froebel are in complete accord as far as the divine unity or God is concerned. Both of them believed that God pervades in everything and that the knowledge about him is the ultimate aim of education.

The two great 'activists'—Mahatma Gandhi and John Dewey— have many common features of educational philosophy. Both of them are realists and pragmatists. They believe in doing and not listening and talking in education. Their ideals of relating the school with society are identical. Their children learn in Co-opertaive Community and Social experience. Intellectual education is advocated by them through crafts and occupations and both of them agree that education should be self-supporting. 'Construction, expression and activity' are the cardinal principles of their teaching methods. Both of them stood for the democratic order of society,. The sustenance of which should be love, equality and justice.

Comparing Tagore with Gandhiji we can see that both of them make their educational system the vehicle of their philosophy of life. Gandhiji's truth and non-violence are akin to Tagore's message of love and universal brothehood. Towards life, however, they have distinct attitudes. Gandhiji evolves a philosophy of action, or a Karam Yog philosophy, suited to the needs and abilities of each and every man. Tagore centred his philosophy on the eternal Anand, although he does not exclude action. Gandhiji's emphasis was on abiding values of life and on social purpose. Tagore's emphasis was on abiding values only.

Both of them make life as the centre of education. They want a curriculum which should provide opportunities for the expression of individual and community life. In their view a school should have the environment and programme in such a manner as to capture the spirit of life. Both Tagore's ideal of education and basic education give a very prominent place to hand work or crafts. While the former emphasises the creative and artistic aspect of hand work, the later emphasises the soil and economic aspect besides the creative. The basic scheme envisages that properly organised craft centred education would break social barriers, teach the dignity of labour, increase the productive capacity and would give concreteness and reality to the knowledge. Tagore gives this concreteness to knowledge in expressional forms like art, music and dramatics. Principle of activity, however, is recognised by both of them, although basic education has gone into greater details in actual practice. The emphasis of both is the child centric education. Education should be joyous to the child. The important role that Nature plays in the education of the child is more obvious in Tagore's system, while such a thing is only implied in basic education.

In conclusion it may be said that Basic education embraces all educational aims and ideals expounded by classical educationists of all ages. It is natural, scientific and psychological and meets the social needs and the economic standards of our country. Taking into account all the pedagogical principles and maxims, it attends to the discipline of the hand and the heart as that of the head. Children are not imitative but have initiative.

Basic Education has ushered in a new epoch in the history of Indian education. For the regeneration of rural India, basic education is the only medium. No education will have appeal to rural masses unless it is related to their life and activities. Since their basic needs are food, shelter and clothing, their education will have to be correlated to these basic needs. It is basic education which is suited to their genius. It is creatively conceived system and it should be boldly executed. It is an activity-centred system where children as well as teachers remain alert and active. Neither the ones are sleepy and passive listeners nor the others are unmindful talkers.

For liquidating illiteracy from poor India, this is the only practical scheme. It is the only system which can keep the rural population tied to their environments with contentment and happiness, instead of running to towns for odd jobs. A new social order is possible through this.

Gandhian scheme is most relevant in the present day context. After over a half century of Independence, illiteracy and other related social evils are as such. To sum up, from the angle of social work, Gandhi's Scheme of Basic Education has much scope of sincere implementation.

7

Gandhian Thought on Social Problems

> "The wisest man may be wiser today than he was yesterday, and tomorrow than he is today. Total freedom from change would imply total freedom from error, but this is the prerogative of omniscience alone."
>
> **—Charles C. Colton**

There are no two opinions but that the prevailing state of affairs in India and elsewhere in the world is far from satisfactory. There is turmoil, discontent, cynicism and decline of values which were considered essential for decent society till a few decades in our country. There is violence in the air and narrowness of outlook which seems to have made many lose the capacity to envisage the futility of seeking individual good at the cost of the nation.

There was a great deal of darkness in the pre-independence era also and there was a great deal of selfishness and psychophancy among upper and middle class Indians. They cringed before the British rulers for small benefits. So called staunch Hindus did not hesitate to earn money by exporting beef and even our girls were trafficked to satisfy the lust of soldiers.

It was the anguished cry of men like Keshab Chandra Sen and others that focused attention on the evil of immoral traffic of the flesh. Sages and patriots like Ramkrishna Paramhansh and Swami Vivekananda, Swami Dayanand Saraswati, Dadabhai Naoroji, Gokhale and Tilak Kindled the spirit of nationalism and made Indians rise above narrow self-interest. They made Indian youth conscious of the fact that they need not feel ashamed of being Indians, that they had a rich heritage in their religion, philosophy and culture which was, if anything, superior to what the foreign rulers had to offer, that these foreign rulers were explioters and India had to break her chains of slavery and become free. The ideal of independence caught the imagination of the Indian youth. The revolutionaries in Bengal, Punjab and elsewhere were fired with patriotic fervour and many a brilliant young man went to the gallows or spent his youth in dungeons or in exile facing agonizing hardships.

Things changed rapidly with the advent of Mahatma Gandhi on the national scene. He gave a new message of hope and self confidence to the people when he presented to them the technique of non violent resistance. "You have to be prepared to lay down your lives when you pursue the path of violent resistance", he said. "If you are ready to lay down your lives in resisting injustice and oppression through non-violent resistance, you will find that this method works far more effectively than the method of violent resistance".

Gandhiji believed that there is spirit of God in every human being. Man is a strange mixture of the divine and the brute. The divine in man can be made dominant and the brute in him put down if we make a determined effort in the right manner. To be able to do so, we must free ourselves from the traits which we wish to see removed in our opponents, as, for instance, narrow self interest or desire to exploit the weak in any shape or form.

A non-violent resistor tries to rouse the conscience of the opponent so as to make him think and revise his opinions and attitudes. This cannot be done by the use of force. It can only be done by self suffering and love. There should be no desire to hurt or humiliate the opponent. The only object should be to make him think and understand the point of view which the Satyagrahi is pleading for.

Gandhiji told the British that their rule over India was bad for India and bad for the British. The British had persuaded themselves that by ruling over India, they were serving India and that the British rule was a blessing for India. They were shocked when Gandhiji bluntly told them that their rule had led to the economic, moral, spiritual and political ruin of India. They used the might of the state to put down the rebels, but non-violent movement grew in strength instead of being suppressed.

Bapu told the Indian people that the British could not rule over India without the co-operation of Indians. Thus non-violation, non-cooperation, civil disobedience and non-violent resistance (*Satyagraha*), became the sheet anchor of India's freedom movement. All classes of people, rich and poor, men and women, young and old, highly educated and illiterate joined the movement. Non-violent struggle for freedom required strength of the soul and not physical prowess. Therefore, women could take an equal part in it as also the old and the infirm. The British were non-plussed.

The British could not but have respect for the *Satyagrahis* who always polite and dignified, did not hit back, nor were cowed down by use of brute force. Ultimately public opinion in their own country forced them to withdraw, not only from India, as rulers, but also from other colonies such as Burma, Ceylon and some African countries where no resistance movement had been organized.

Gandhiji insisted on purity of the means. Freedom won through violence would not be real freedom, he said. He insisted on purity of the heart and development of character on the part of the satyagrahis through the practice of truth, non-violence, non-stealing, celibacy or self-control, non-possession, physical labour, control of the palate, fearlessness, equal respect for all religions, use of *swadeshi* items and eradication of untouchability. Ashram life, which meant an earnest effort to practice the above mentioned eleven vows and constructive programmes which could give some economic relief to the poor, and forge a bond of love and trust between them and the workers, constituted the training for '*Satyagraha*'.

Remarkably, 'Constructive programme' of Gandhiji's conception was a revolutionary programme for the development of non-violent mass strength and non-violent orgainisation of the people. It was not a means for mere unemployment relief that the *Khadi* and *Gramodyog* institutions have become in most cases. In Gandhiji's time there was emphasis on the observance of truthfulness in all our activities. He did not tolerate any hiatus or contradiction between what we said and what we practiced. But today the employees of *Khadi Bhandars* and members of their families, can be seen in nylons without any sense of embarrassment on their part.

Gandhiji attached the greatest importance to the development of character. There was a constant endeavour to make all constructive activities a means of education for the attainment of higher level of thought and action by the individual workers. It was also a means of his identification with the people whom the worker was trying to serve.

Workers led a simple life. Gandhiji always reminded us that true civilization consists in voluntary reduction of one's wants and not in constant desire to have more and more. "Poverty imposed on one is a degrading thing", he said. "But voluntary poverty, voluntary reduction of one's wants, is an ennobling and liberating force". Emphasis on character building was always uppermost in his mind.

Kaka Saheb Kalelkar has quoted Gandhiji on this subject in the following words:

> "India was once a golden land, because Indians then had a heart of gold. The land is still the same. But it is a desert because we are corrupt. It can become a land of gold again if the base metal of our present national character is transmuted into gold". He endeavored to bring about the transmutation. We rose to great moral heights under the inspiring leadership of Mahatma Gandhi and as a result the whole world came to have a new respect for India. The world was impressed by the Indian experiment of non-violence. When we gave up the Gandhian path after the attainment of freedom, they

> were disappointed and so is India today. It has had to pay a heavy price for it.

Sixty one years after Independence where are we? We have no doubt made progress in science and technology. The average expectancy of life has gone up from 39 in mid forties to almost 60 years. The infant and maternal mortality and birth rate and death rate have declined, though not as much as we would have liked. We have more roads and many industries. There are many more universities, medical and engineering colleges, schools and hospitals, but are our people happy? Do they feel free? Have they more self-confidence? No.

We have given up the Gandhian path, the path of simple living and high thinking which was shown to us by Gandhiji and have become lost in the pursuit of mere material progress. The fact that man is the measure of all things, the central factor, and his all-round development is the secret of even material progress, has been lost sight of. So we see corruption, inefficiency, dereliction of duty and a mad rush to make as much money as possible, and in whatever manner it may be possible. The spectre of black money is haunting us and is making a mockery of our efforts at controlling inflation and stabilizing our economy.

There was a time before Gandhi's advent when man in India believed that end justifies the means and, in order to win freedom for India they were prepared to use any means that might be available. But they failed to achieve success.

When, these who believed in the dictum that for the freedom of the country one could commit any sin failed to deliver the goods, Gandhiji demonstrated to the nation that true service to our sacred mother land could not be rendered at the cost of character. The biggest and the mightiest constructive force is the force of character. It is unfortunate that we have neglected the building up of character in the post Independence era. Unless and until we can make up for this grave deficiency, we will not be able to solve the problems that face us and threaten to overwhelm us, whether it be in the economic sphere, social reconstruction, bridging the gulf between the rich and the poor or providing work for each person whom God has given one mouth to feed, and two hands to work.

Corruption is rampant. The more the centralization and controls the more the corruption. In a country where a Chief Minister can sit in his office, use the official stationery, the official files and state machinery to indulge in black marketing of cement, land and many other scarce commodities and claim that he is doing it for the benefit of the poor, who can fight corruption?

Politicians and buraucrats have absoluted corrupted in India. Democracy has be come a mockery. State governments are topped with money power.

Even Indian Parliament is not untouched from it. We have so many scams. Many gangsters are MP. Recent 'Cash for Vote' scandal (2008) is proof our corrupt politicians.

Laws were changed to give income tax exemption for donations given for a consideration and the action was defended on the floor of Parliament. Can we then blame lesser men and women, if they accept these favours as approval by the highest of corruption, black marketing and the like and try to line their own pockets?

Power, said Gandhiji, was a means for the service of the people. If those in power fail to put an end to exploitation, poverty and hunger, it does not help the hungry and the unemployed to know that those who exploit them now are not foreigners, but their own countrymen. We have raised the expectations of the people and have miserably failed to improve their condition. Power seems to have become an end in itself, instead of being means to an end, the end being amelioration of the condition of our poverty strike masses.

Gandhiji told us that the only way of serving the poor was to identify ourselves with them and to deny ourselves what they cannot get. Can you imagine what enthusiasm and energy can be released for productive purposes, if the people can see and feel that their leaders are there to share with them their privations and hardships. I am sure they would grudge their leaders their minimum needs and may even insist on their having better food and other things that they themselves cannot have. In fact, there will be enough to meet the needs of all if the leaders identify themselves with the common man, as it will put an end to thieving and stealing, bribery and corruption, hoarding and black marketing, to a large extent, if not altogether.

But the leaders may not do it. They need money for their party and their elections, so that they can remain in power or can capture power. Those who can give them money are the rich. The rich give donations and make sure that they can make several times more than what they give. So the vicious circle of corruption and exploitation continues. Gandhiji told us that country comes before the party and the family. Now-a-days self-interest, family interest and the party interest come before country. The result is the sorry state of affairs that we see. Prohibition is sacrificed, even though it is enshrined in the Directive Principles of our constitution and everyone who knows that so long as liquor contractors can rob the workers, who become their willing victims under the effect of alcohol, the level of living of the common man can never rise. But liquor contractors can give large donations for election purposes and so they have to be kept in business. Similarly, businessmen in other lines have to be given opportunities of making up for the donations that they might have given. And this can only be done at the cost of common man.

The Election Commission has made valuable suggestions for electoral reforms to curb the power of black money and check the influence of moneyed men on the elected representatives as well as to prevent bogus voting. But no serious thought has been given to these recommendations. The Chief Election Commissioner has suggested:

1. The voters list be prepared every year, not every five years.

2. A copy of the voters list must be displayed at each polling booth, not merely at Parliamentary or Assembly Constituency.
3. Each voter must be issued an identity card with a photograph.
4. A law should be passed requiring a MLA or MP to resign and reseek election if he changes the symbol on which he was elected.
5. Recognition and symbols should be granted to only those parties which are :
   (a) Registered Organisations
   (b) Have a democratic constitution and show that they have elected their office bearers properly as per their constitution;
   (c) Submit their audited accounts to the Election Commission.
6. To eliminate the role of black money and corruption, the Government should pay for the election expenses of the candidates sponsored by recognized parties. No private expenditure should be allowed on the elections.

Government has not yet taken any decision on these important recommendations of the Election Commission. It is for the people to press the Government to accept these suggestions forthwith. If these recommendations are accepted, people will be able to exercise their votes and make their elected representatives more responsive to their demand for securing adequate powers for the Village Panchayats and thus enable them to have a better control and supervision over the local administration.

Decentralisation of political and economic power is an essential prerequisite for real freedom—Swaraj, that will make the people feel free. We have to see things in the villages to believe how the villagers are being treated by the officials. Despite delegation of statutory powers to grassroot level village panchayats the elected members are under the control of bureaucrats, who have the final say in many matters. In connivance with corrupt official system *Pradhans* of village Panchayats have become more corrupt.

It might be said that the Panchayat people will indulge in favouritism and unjust practices if powers are passed on to them. But do not such things happen at higher levels? Panchayat or the *Gaon Sabha* is the only place where people can directly participate in decision making and manage their own affairs. At all other levels they have to function through their representatives without being able to exercise any effective control. At the village level it is possible for all the villagers to understand and express their opinion on various problems and programmes and know how each person functions so that they can throw out an unscrupulous Panch or Sarpanch at the next election.

It is impossible for any central or state government, even if they were honest and efficient, which they are not, to provide good Government. It is necessary that the people themselves be involved in the work for their own betterment, through the democratic process by giving necessary powers to the *Gaon Sabhas* so that the villagers can plan and implement the scheme for the betterment of their villages. The Primary Unit of Democracy and Government must be the village *Panchayat* or *Gaon Sabha*.

Centralization is not the answer for our problems. We have all seen how the educational system is functioning at the village level after the state has taken control of Primary education.

In order to make our democratic setup really effective, the *Gaon Sabha* must constitute the basic unit of Government, followed by Block Samities and *Zila Parishads*. Simultaneously the functions and powers of the District Collector and other officials must be drastically changed.

There was a time when the village in India functioned as a big family. When a wedding party came from another village, they called on any girl from their village who might have been married to a young man in the village that the Barat had come to, in order to give her a present, because any daughter of the village was their daughter.

The villagers also looked after such widows and orphans or old people as did not have their own family members to do so. It was a kind of community social security. But alas, all that has broken down and there is nothing to take its place. Vinobaji tried to revive the community spirit through his "gramdan" movement and some of the villages where powers were transferred to the *gaon sabha* under the *Gramdan Act*, have done a far better job than other villages within the same district, with regard to development and general improvement. They have no doubt made mistakes in some cases, but on the whole they have done well.

No doubt, given the responsibility, along with authority and necessary guidance and advice, the *gaon sabha* can ensure the success of many economic and social programmes, which have remained mainly on paper so far, as for instance, installation of *Gobar Gas Plants* for energy, social forestry for fuel, water conservation, fruits and fodder, feeding programme for the vulnerable groups, timely supply of seed, manure and water for the crops, preventing wastage of water resulting from unauthorized cutting of irrigation connections, better storage of foodgrains, more equitable distribution of kerosene, gas fuel and sugar etc., and enforcement of social measures such as prohibition, prevention of child marriage and child labour, ban on dowry and adoption of a small family norm.

An efficient and honest co-operative system can help the villages with storage and marketing. The village Panchayat can ensure implementation of immunization and other material and child health and welfare schemes, so that the small family norm will be more readily accepted. Even in a communist country like China, they have used influential local women's social affairs committees to sell the idea of a small family norm. The result is that most babies are being born in that country today, to mothers between 25–29 years of age and there are hardly any premature births.

In the advanced countries 80% of the pediatric care is devoted to low birth weight and premature babies. In China, where there is hardly any low weight or premature birth, all the time and energy of the pediatricians is available to look after the normal babies. The infant mortality has rapidly gone down. Many couples are coming forward to get one child certificates, which gives them certain advantages. Incentives no doubt do help, but basically it is the educational effort of the women's social affairs committees which has provided effective motivation for the adoption of a small family norm by the young couples. Some may have a second baby and lose some of the benefits. A third baby is extremely rare and a fourth baby is just not heard of.

What is necessary for us in India today is to find a way to fire the imagination and enthusiasm of our youth, and the common man, so that he feels he is a partner in development. This can only happen if we bring about decentralization, at all levels on the one hand and the leadership once again identifies itself with the people whom they are there to serve. In other words, we have to once again return to the Gandhian Path of simple living and high thinking . Our people will be then willing and eager to make sacrifices for a better future, and the dark clouds of corruption born of mistaken narrow self-interest, will disappear and give place to honesty and idealism. If Indians could rise to great moral heights under Mahatma Gandhi, we can do it again by making a sincere effort to understand the Mahatma's message and put it into practice to the best of our ability.

A large number of voluntary and non-government organizations (NGOs) are working in various fields in different regions. In fact, there is seen a mushroom growth of these organisations.

But well-trained and dedicated social workers if take these

activities in their hands working on Gandhian line of social work, a lot of success can be achieved. India, a vast country largely inhabited by rural mass in delapidated conditions, mostly illiterate and poverty-stricken offer ample opportunity for social service and social work. If the social workers are honest, dedicated and dutiful, they can eradicate all social evils by action and uplift the socioeconomic standard of people.

Here's the only way—follow the path of Gandhian social work!

8

Gandhi on Women: Lesson for Social Workers

Gandhi (forget all so called Gandhis—only Mahatma, Bapu, the father of Indian Nation), was deeply concerned with the cause of nation and its people like many social reformers and leaders hailed from different socio-religious sects of India—be they Dadabhai, Sir Syed Ahmed Khan, Tilak, Lala Lajpat Rai, Gokhale, Ranade, Dayanand, Swami Vivekanand or so many enlightened personalities.

The problem of women received the attention of social reformers right from the beginning of the nineteenth century. Some individuals, organised associations, and journal played remarkable role in bestirring the Indian society to focus its attention on this problem and make efforts in the direction of the Indian women's general emancipation. Gandhi gave a new momentum to this movement.

Basically, Gandhi's treatment of the Indian women's problem can be classified under two heads: (1) his general attitude towards women and his views on traditional problems such as child marriage, widow remarriage, *purdah* system, the practice of *nautch* and *devadasis;* and (2) his efforts to involve women in the national movement and the national developmental programmes.

For Gandhi, every social position had equal value and womanhood could be no exception. Addressing the annual gathering of the Bombay Bhagini Samaj, held on February 20,

1918, he said: "Woman is the companion of man gifted with equal mental capacities. She has the right to participate in the minutest detail of the activities of man, and she has the same right of freedom and liberty as he." (MK Gandhi, *Women and Social Injustice,* p. 4).

He attributed the Hindu *Sastras'* bias for male offspring to historical reasons and expressed his view in clear words: "I make no distinction between son and daughter. Such distinction is in my opinion invidious any wrong. The birth of a son or a daughter should be welcomed alike." In a true *advaitin* spirit he viewed that "The soul in both is the same. The two live the same life, have the same feelings" and considered each to be "the complement of the other." Each one of them, according to him, needed the active help of the other. It would be interesting to examine the dilemma which Gandhi was bound to face *vis-a-vis* the Hindu *Sastras* for which he had high regard and, normally, would not like them to be overruled but some of which contained derogatory remarks about women. It should be noted that whilst Gandhi had immense faith in the wisdom of the *Sastras,* he in the spirit of a true rationalist, believed in the application of reason on every issue which an individual or society confronted.

On *purdah* system he had said: "We must test on the anvil of reason everything that is capable of being tested by it, and reject that which does not satisfy it even though it may appear in an ancient garb." Obviously, he wanted the *Sastras* to be read and understood in the right spirit and if they contained contradictory statements on any particular issue, his advice was to follow the ones which were favoured by reason. He pointed to the fact that the *Smritis* contained several passages which showed respect for women and gave them their due place and cautioned that "all that is printed in the name if scriptures need not be taken as the word of God or the inspired word".

He even went to the extent of suggesting by some authoritative body expurgation of the texts in the *Smritis* which were repugnant to the moral sense. There should be made a clear distinction between the fundamentals of religion and morality and historical realities expressed in some of these ancient texts. Gandhi did not allow himself to be a blind believer in the statements of the *Sastras* but rather showed a rare historical sense. He was fully aware of the fact that the writings generally correspond to various social, cultural and environmental demands and necessities of their times and, therefore, in adjudging an ancient author's statements or views the historical context should always be taken into consideration.

Commenting on Hindu Law giver Manu, he said: "The saying attributed to Manu that for women there can be no freedom is not to be sacrosanct. It only shows that probably, at the time when it was promulgated, women were kept in a state of subjection. The epithets used in our literature to describe a wife are *ardhangini,* 'the better half' and *sahadharmini,* `the helpmate'. The husband addressing the wife as *devi* or goddess does not show any disparagement. But, unfortunately, a time came when the woman was divested of many of her rights and privileges and was reduced to a status of inferiority." (*Harijan,* Oct. 12, 1934)

In broad perspective, Gandhi would fall in the category of those reformers whose models were typically Indian and not western. He had a deep sense of application for Indian ideals and wanted a change in Indian society in conformity with them. He has often remarked that the ideals of womanhood for him were Sita and Draupadi. He was totally against the blind imitation of the West by Indian women. He said: "They may not ape the manner of the West which may be suited to its environment. They must apply methods suited to the Indian genius and Indian environment. Their must be the strong, controlling, purifying, steadying hand, conserving what is best in our culture and unhesitatingly rejecting what is base and degrading. This is the work of Sitas, Draupadis, Savitris and Damayantis, not of amazons and prudes." (*Young India,* Oct. 17, 1929)

This, however, does not mean that he was against Indian girls getting modern education or intended to anathematise all the girls who had received English education. In his concept, the emphasis should be on the universal and essential qualities of women and not merely on the character of woman's rights and about Indian ideal of womanhood he felt that "it was a very high concept, not only of Indian womanhood, but of all womanhood irrespective of race, religion or country." He used the term 'modern girl' for the girls who loved adventure just for the sake of it and dressed just to attract attention of the opposite sex. Later, he specified that the term for him had a special meaning and said that "all the girls who receive English education are not modern girls." (K. Kripalani, *op cit.*)

Obviously, Gandhi holds a unique position among the social reformers and it would be very difficult to bracket him with any one of them. He was deep rooted in the Indian tradition and relied on the *Sastras;* yet he was not an indiscriminate revivalist. He realised the wretched condition of the Indian women and wanted them to be uplifted from their present condition of misery and inequality; yet he did not like them to be a mere replica of the western woman. For the remedy and betterment of their condition he sought support from the Hindu *Sastras* and found it there. If and when the ancient texts contradicted themselves or were not clear he looked towards reason as a watch-dog of his conscience; and in his understanding of the scriptures, the touchstone of their validity depended on whether they conformed to the fundamentals of religion and morality. Among the maladies which preyed on the lot of Indian women, the miserable condition of widows was the most vital of them. The issue was closely related with the custom of marrying young girls at such a tender age when they were not even able to know the meaning of marriage.

For ages, the life of a widow had been a story of life-long humiliation and deprivation. The problem was of such social significance and acute that all the social reformers had been moved to take up the issue and make efforts to improve their lot by persuading people to change their attitude towards the widow and by advocating their remarriage. Ishwarchandra Vidyasagar,

Gopal Hari Deshmukh and Pandita Ramabai had made very sincere efforts in this direction. Gandhi, however, had no intention to advocate widow remarriage on a wholesale scale and confined his attention to child-widows whom he named 'suppressed humanity'.

Marriage, according to him, could, be a sacrament only when the girl was fully developed at the time of marriage. On one occasion he wrote: "I detest child marriages. I shudder to see a child-widow and shiver with rage when a husband just widowed, contracts with brutal indifference another marriage. I deplore the criminal indifference of parents who keep them up only for the purpose of marrying them off to some youngmen of means." (*Young India,* 21.7.1921). He appealed to the parents to absolve themselves of the sin of marrying infant daughters by remarrying them if they had been widows. When a correspondent drew his attention to one of his articles in which, on the one hand, he had called marriage a sacrament and had said that "the union is not the union of bodies but the union of souls indissoluble even by the death of either partly" and, on the other hand, in the very same article, had written that "I consider remarriage of virgin widows not only desirable but the bounden duty of all parents who happen to have such widowed daughters" and asked him to reconcile the two views. Gandhi replied to it in the column of *Young India:* "I find no difficulty in reconciling with the two views. In the giving away of a little girl by ignorant or heartless parents without considering the welfare of the child and without her knowledge and consent there is no marriage at all. Certainly, it is not a sacrament, and therefore, remarriage of such a girl becomes a duty. As a matter of fact the 'remarriage' is a misnomer in such cases."

In fact, according to him, both widows and widowers should not marry as a general rule. To quote Gandhi himself: "I should any day subscribe to a reform in Hindu law making sinful the remarriage of a widow or a widower who voluntarily married after maturity." He appreciated the restraint and suffering of widowhood and goes even to the extent of glorifying the Hindu widow whom he considered as "one of the gifts of Hinduism to humanity." (*Young India*, 19.8.1926). Gandhi's crusade was, thus, not against the system of what he called `real widows' but that of child-widows whose existence he considered "a blot upon Hinduism". In a way he is really fighting against child marriage and not advocating widow remarriage.

For checking the evil of child marriage, Gandhi favoured the introduction of a bill raising the age of consent. Child marriage, to him, was "an immoral and inhuman act" which made innocent girls objects of man's just, ruined the health of many a child mother and, on the top of everything, converted tender-aged girls into widows. He advocated mobilisation of strong public opinion and supported agitations by the local people to put a check to such happenings.

For Gandhi, child marriage was not only a moral and social evil; it was an obstacle even in the way of *swaraj*. He tagged this issue with the struggle for freedom and attacked the custom by appealing to the nationalistic feelings of the people. And, further, he invoked women themselves to work for the welfare of their own sex. He contended that it served no purpose to throw all blame on men and said that the enlightened among them should work among girl wives and girl widows and see to it that small girl marriages become an impossibility. On various occasions, Gandhi also expressed his views on evils associated with marriage ceremony and on the marriage ideal. He strongly favoured simplification of the marriage rites and suggested that the religious ceremonials should not cost more than rupees ten. He said that by exercising self-restraint the rich people should lead the poor and thus be helpful in preventing the waste of national resources. Marriage, to him, was not aimed at the satisfaction of lust only but had also a spiritual and social purpose to fulfil.

Laying down the general condition for ideal marriage, he said that spiritual development occupied the foremost place, then came service followed by family considerations and the interest of the social order, and, in the last, came mutual attraction or 'love'. In his opinion, if the first three conditions are not fulfilled, mere attraction or love could not be held as a valid reason for marriage; but, at the same time, a marriage is ruled out in the absence of love also, even if the other conditions are fulfilled. Marriage only for the satisfaction of sexual appetite was termed as *vyabhichara* (debauchery) by him.

Regarding the ideal of husband and wife, he wrote: "My ideal of a wife is Sita and of a husband Rama. But Sita was no slave of Rama, or each was slave of the other. Rama is ever considerate to Sita... Where there is not true love, the bond has never existed..." With regard to measures against the growth of population, Gandhi seems to be opposed to artificial methods; rather, he suggests ten rules for restricting family through inculcation of discipline and self-control.

Gandhi was totally against the dowry system which defiled the pure character of the marriage institution. Its immediate impact was nightmare for the parents who had marriageable daughters, and in the long run it was also the source of discrimination in Indian society against the birth of daughters. Furthermore, not being able to arrange money, the parents were forced to give their daughters in marriage to absolutely unsuitable matches. He condemned the system and said that it was nothing but sale of girls. With regard to the demand of dowry by the young men in position, his contention was that it would demoralise the youth of the country "by creating in them a sense of unwarranted self-satisfaction", and suggested that a strong public opinion needs to be made against it and such young men "who soil their fingers with such ill-gotten gold should be excommunicated from society." His advice to the parents was that they should not hesitate to marry their daughters to good young men coming from other region and other community.

The main reason of women's pitiable condition was their ignorance and lack of education among them. The *purdah* system was at the root of it as it led to the confinement of the fair sex within the walls of homes and restrict their free movements. The tacit argument that *purdah* was helpful for women's purity of character was absolutely unconvincing to Gandhi. In this connection, he said that chastity is not a hot home growth. It cannot be protected by the surrounding wall of the *purdah.* It must grow from within and men and women have to trust each other. According to him, the *purdah* in India was a recent institution and was adopted during the period of Hindu decline. He was sure that abolition of *purdah* would lead to mass education for both men and women.

We have seen above that for the removal of various social evils pervading the Hindu society and affecting women, Gandhi was in favour of mobilising strong public opinion against them. The local people could even take resort to agitation to prevent, for example, a child marriage. He also favoured the introduction of legislative laws by the government to put a check on such evils. But Gandhi was wary of the limitations of such legal measures and resented the idea of being entirely dependent on them. He believed that legal measures were not enough and that if any change in the condition of women were to come it would come through their own enlightenment, their capacity for resistance against injustice and self-confidence. He exhorted girls to develop self-confidence in themselves and be courageous enough to die if attacked by the brute in man. It was the moral responsibility of the enlightened ones among them to contribute to the welfare of their own sex; they should, for example, be prepared to work among girl-wives and girl-widows.

In fact, what Gandhi meant by equality of men and women was that they were complements of each other. None was the slave of the other but rather each had a meaningful role to play in the family and the social system. Gandhi believed in certain basic differences between men and women and accepted the principle of division of labour between them which according to him had existed since the beginning. He considered women embodiment of self-sacrifice and non-violence and, as such, their occupation should be in conformity with their essential nature. He said: "Equality of the sexes does not mean equality of occupations. There may be no legal bar against a woman hunting or wielding a lance. But she instinctively recoils from a function that belongs to man. Nature has created sexes as complements of each other. Their functions are defined as are their forms." The duty of motherhood, or a caretaker and the household work is the basic task of women and these are in no way less significant than the works done by men. He saw absolutely no wisdom in women being called to ride upon a horse or to hold a rifle. By resorting to different works in accordance with their basic nature men and women simply complemented each other and there was no ground for women to suffer from any inferiority complex.

The most important feature of the Gandhian programme vis-a-vis women was his attempt to involve their active participation in the national movement. He often said that women were an embodiment of love and suffering and in a non-violent struggle she could easily play the role of a leader. Significantly, Gandhian ideology of suffering formed the cornerstone of his concept of non-violence and *satyagraha.*

Interestingly, Gandhi's accent on suffering has been, sometimes, explained as his love for the spirit of cross and martydom. To cite one instance: Gandhi, while asking J.B. Kriplani to go to Noakhali for promotion of communal harmony told him: "You should go and die there." Such instances have been explained as Gandhi's desire to stimulate and whip-up sacrificial tendencies in human nature. While it holds true that Gandhi glorified suffering, yet to understand his unique contribution to the paradigm of suffering, it needs to be placed in a much wider perspective. Gandhi's ideology of suffering transcended the domains of spirituality and individual salvation and encompassed the pursuit of justice in the social and political realms. Suffering as a method of protest in Gandhi's non-violent *satyagraha,* against injustices and wrong doing, was intended to leave a deep impact on the adversaries, whether they were the British imperialists, the high-caste Hindus, the liquor traders or the foreign cloth merchants. He did not visualise suffering as an individual activity striving for personal deliverance but he evolved a collective style of suffering for attainment of larger goals—both social and political.

Another interesting dimension of Gandhian paradigm of suffering was Gandhi's deep faith in the natural superiority of women's capacity to endure suffering and, hence, the pivotal role they could play in the non-violent struggle against British imperialists as well as their own struggle against the pervasive power of patriarchy.

Women, to Gandhi, were the embodiment of *ahimsa,* "weak in striking and strong in suffering." It has been considered that Indian women have tremendous capacity to suffer as subordinate members of family. They inflict suffering on themselves through servitude, devotion, self-deprivation, self-denial, self-starvation, patience and endurance. Their suffering within the family, in a way, was a process of empowerment that eventually gave them access to decision-making in the household.

Gandhi built upon this historical experience of women as sufferers. He brought women's suffering from the private realms of family and household to public sphere wherein their capacity to suffer was transformed into a *shakti* for breaking the chains of enslavement to colonial rule as well as their own enslavement as women. Women's status as sufferers in Gandhi's ideology was the embodiment of her superior powers of endurance, courage, strength and fearlessness rather than symbolic of her helplessness and inferior sexuality.

Viewed from a feminist perspective, Gandhi's emphasis on women's natural and inborn capacity to suffer can be constructed as perpetuation of dominant cultural patriarchal ideal of feminine identity.

However, Gandhi's emphasis on gender stereotypes of suffering was motivated by the desire for universalisation of the spirit of sacrifice and suffering for purification of social life at large. He wanted women to initiate this process of purification through suffering.

During the non-violent struggle which he was carrying against the foreign rule, he said, the contribution of women should be much greater than of men, because they were more sacrificing, had greater powers of endurance and greater courage. During the Civil Disobedience Programme, Gandhi sought the help of women mainly in two measures—in prohibition and in the boycott of foreign cloth.

Reiterating the suitability of women for picketing purposes in the light of his earlier experiences, when it had been done by men, he said: "The picketing of liquor shops and foreign cloth shops by men, though it succeeded beyond expectation up to a point for a time in 1921, failed because violence crept in. If a real impression is to be created, picketing must be resumed, if it remains peaceful to the end, it will be the quickest way of educating the people concerned. It must never be a matter of coercion but conversion, moral persuasion. Who can make", he asked, "a more effective appeal to the heart than woman?" Their appeal", he further observed, "to the merchants and buyers of foreign cloth and to the liquor dealers and addicts cannot but melt their hearts." (*Young India,* 14 Apr. 1937). Latter, Gandhi acknowledged with praise the contribution of women in these regards, but lamented the fact that with the withdrawal of the Civil Disobedience Movement their work had slackened. He reminded women that the prohibition programme was not for a definite period only but until prohibition was proclaimed throughout India they should continue to organise the campaign again and again.

Remarkably, *Khadi* and *charkha* were the two very appealing symbols which Gandhi used in his struggle for freedom to arouse among his countrymen the feelings of nationalism and self-dependence. He invoked women to cast off their foreign clothes and wear *khadi sari* which reminded one of "a woman's innate purity". He not only wanted woman to wear *khadi* but also to spin it during their leisure hours. He exhorted women that they should look upon spinning not only as a means of livelihood but as a national duty. "The economic and the moral salvation of India thus rests mainly with you. The future of India lies on your knees for you will nurture the future generation..." (*Young India,* 11 Aug. 1921).

Further, Gandhi's success in mobilising women for the national movement can be measured by the large number in which women of the country, coming both from high families and from among the common masses, participated in the Civil Disobedience Movement launched by him. Women's participation in the Gandhian movements, particularly the Civil Disobedience Movement, should be considered a revolutionary change. During the *Salt Satyagraha,* women carried illicit salt in their *saris.* Under the leadership of Kasturba Gandhi, they picketed before the liquor shops. Dressed in orange *saris,* women volunteers picketed shops of foreign cloth appealing to people not to buy them. The government took stringent measures but they could not be discouraged. Women unhesitatingly going to jail was a common sight during the movement. Besides this, Gandhi had also appealed to the women to work for the eradication of untouchability. He especially desired the women's associations to take up the work of admitting the depressed classes into the temples. The AICC Karachi resolution of 1931 had pleased Gandhi. He remarked that many a disabilities to which women were subjected would now cease as public employments, offices of power and honour would now be open to women also.

It is significant to note that the participation of women in national problems on such a large scale was no doubt a novel and unique phenomenon in the history of the country. During the movement, they did not remain passive onlookers but actively participated in it and made important contributions. Gandhi laid foundations of a new tradition which enabled the Indian women to play a significant role in the social and political life of the country. He was an acknowledged saint and the purity of his character added a magic to his personality. People of the country had reposed great faith in his leadership. "The menfolk knew that the honour of their women was safe in a non-violent struggle guided by Gandhiji. They, therefore, had no hesitation in allowing their women to participate in the freedom fight." Gandhi had great respect for women and was, in return, greatly respected by them. It was only this mutual faith in each other and respect for each other that made possible this active participation of women in the freedom movement at the national level.

No exaggeration, women's participation in the Gandhian movements was a catalytic process that brought forth women from the confines of the *zanana* to the vanguard of nationalist politics. Significantly, Gandhi's emergence on the Indian political scene revolutionised and intensified women's commitment to the freedom struggle. Viewed from the perspective of women's participation, the freedom struggle crystallised into a tremendous confidence building process which altered women's own perception of their self-image. Participation in the larger liberation struggle not only generated amongst them the confidence to lead their own struggle against patriarchal domination but it also, symbolised a significant breakthrough in the entire public/private debate by producing social sanction for new extra-familial roles.

In nutshell, it can be concluded that even though Gandhi's views on women's emancipation were largely based on the Indian tradition in accordance with the *Shastras,* his initiatives towards women's participation in the freedom struggle has a profound impact, both on the national movement as well as on women's situation. By ensuring societal acceptance and legitimacy for more comprehensive roles for women and by transforming women's own self-definition, Gandhi had, in a subtle but significant manner, fashioned a new identity for Indian women.

II

ON WOMEN'S ROLE

"I am firmly of opinion that India's salvation on the sacrifice— and enlightenment of her women.

"*Ahimsa* means infinite love, which again means infinite-capacity for suffering. Who but woman, the mother of man, shows this capacity in the largest measure? She shows it as she carries the infant and feeds it during nine months and derives joy in the suffering involved. What can beat the suffering caused by the pangs of labour? But she forgets them, in the joy of creation. Who again suffers daily so that her babe may wax from day to day? Let her transfer that love to the whole of humanity, let her forget that she ever was or can be the object of man's lust. And she will occupy her proud position by the side of man as his mother, maker and silent leader. It is given to her to teach the art of peace to the warring, world thirsting for that nectar.

"My own opinion is that, just as fundamentally man and women are one, their problem must be one in essence. The soul in both is the same. The two live, the same life, have the same feelings. Each is a complement of the other. The one cannot live without the other's active help.

"But somehow or other man has dominated woman from ages past, and so women has developed an inferiority complex. She has believed in the truth of man's interested teaching that she is inferior to him. But the seers among men have recognized her equal status.

"Nevertheless there is no doubt that at some point there is bifurcation. Whilst both are fundamentally one, it is also equally true that in the form there is a vital difference between the two. Hence the vocations of the two must also be different. The duty of motherhood, which the vast majority of women. will always undertake, requires qualities which man need not possess. She is passive, he is active. She is essentially mistress of the house. He is the bread-winner. She is the keeper and distributor of the bread. She is the care-taker in every sense of the term. The art of bringing up the infants of the race in her special and sole prerogative. Without her care the race must become extent.

"In my opinion it is degrading both for man and woman that woman should be called upon or induced to forsake the hearth and shoulder the rifle for the protection of that hearth. It is a reversion to barbarity and the beginning of the end. In trying to ride the horse that man rides, she brings herself and him down. The sin will be. on man's head for tempting or compelling his companion to desert her special calling. There is as much bravery in keeping one's home in good order and condition as there is in defending it against attack from without.

"If I were born a woman, I would rise in rebellion against any pretension on the part of man that woman is born to be his plaything. I have mentally become a woman in order to steal into her heart. I could not steal into my wife's heart until I decided to treat her different'y than I used to do, and so I restored to her all her rights by dispossessing myself of all my so called rights as her husband.

"Of all the evils for which man has made himself responsible, none is so degrading, so shocking or so brutal as his abuse of the better half of humanity— to me, the female sex, not the weaker sex. It is the nobler of the two, for it is even today the embodiment of sacrifice, silent suffering, humility, faith and knowledge.

"Woman must cease to consider herself the object of man's lust. The remedy is more in her hands than man's.

"Chastity is not a hot-house growth. It cannot be protected by the surrounding wall of the *purdah.* It must grow from within, and to be worth anything it must be capable of withstanding every unsought temptation.

"And why is there all this morbid anxiety about female purity? Have women any say in the matter of male purity? We hear nothing of women's anxiety about man's chastity? Why should men arrogate to themselves the right to regulate female purity? It cannot be superimposed from without. It is a matter of evolution from within and therefore of individual self-effort.

"Woman, I hold, is the personification of self-sacrifice, but unfortunately today she does not realize what a tremendous advantage she has over man. As Tolstoy used to say, they are labouring under the hypnotic influence of man. If they would relize the strength of non-violence they would not consent to be called the weakerser.

"To call woman the weaker sex is a libel, it is man's injustice to women. If by strength is meant brute strength, then, indeed, is woman less brute than man. If by strength is meant moral power, then woman is immeasurably man's superior. Has she not greater intution is she not more self-sacrificing, has she not greater powers of endurance has she not greater courage? Without her man could not be. If non-violence is the law of our being the future is with women..... Who can make a more effective appeal to the heart than women?

"Women are special custodian of all that is pure and religious in life. Coaservative by nature, if they are slow to superstitions habits, they are also slow to give up all that is pare and noble in life.

"I believe in the proper education of women. But I do believe that woman will the make her contribution to the world by mimicking or running a race with men. She can run the race, but she will not rise to the great heights she is capable of by mimicking man. She has to be the complement of man.

"Woman is the companion of man gifted with equal mental capacities. She has the right to participate in the minutest detail of the activities of man, and she has the same right of freedom and liberty as he. She is entitled to a supreme place in her own sphere of activity as man is in his. This ought to be the natural condition of things, and not a result only of learning to read and write. By sheer force of a vicious custom, even the most ignorant and worthless men have been enjoining a superiority over women which they do not deserve and ought not to have.

"If only women will forget that they belong to the weaker sex, I have no doubt that they can do infinitely more then men against war. Answer for yourselves what your great soldiers and generals would do, if their wives and daughters and mothers refused to countenance their participation in militarism in any shape or form.

"A sister who is a good worker, and was anxious to remain celibate in order to serve better the country's cause, has recently married having met the mate of her dreams. But she imagines that in doing so she has done wrong and fallen from the high ideal which she had set before herself. I have tried to rid her mind of this delusion. It is no doubt an excellent thing for girls to remain unmarried for the sake of service, but the fact is that only one in a million is able to do so. Marriage is a natural thing in life and to consider it derogatory in any sense is wholly wrong. When one imaging any act a fall it is difficult, however hard one tries, to raise on self. The ideal is to look upon marriage as a sacrament and therefore to lead a life of self-restraint in the married estate. Marriage in Hinduism is one of the four *ashramas*. In fact the other three are based on it.

"The duty of the above-mentioned and other sisters who think like her is, therefore, not to look down upon marriage but to give it its due place and make of it the sacrament it is. If they exercise the necessary self-restraint, they will find growing within themselves a greater strength for service. She who wishes to serve will naturally choose a partner in life who is of the same mind, and their joint service will be gain.

"Marriage confirms the right of union between two partners to the exclusion of all the others when in their joint opinion they consider such union to be desirable, but it confers no right upon one partner to demand obedience of the other to one's wish for union. What should be done when one partner on moral or other grounds cannot conform to the wishes of the other is a separate question. Personally if divorce was the only alternative, I should not hesitate to accept it, rather than interrupt my moral progress assuming that I want to restrain myself on purely moral grounds.

"It is a tragedy that generally speaking our girls are not

taught the duties of motherhood. But if married life is a religious duty, motherhood must be too. To be an ideal mother is no easy task. The procreation of children has to be undertaken with a full sense of responsibility. The mother should know what is her duty from the moment she conceives right up to the time the child is born. And she who gives intelligent, healthy and well brought up children to the country is surely rendering a service. When the latter grow up they too will be ready to serve. The truth, of the matter is that those who are filled with a living spirit of service will always serve whatever their position in life. They will never adopt a way of life which will interfere with service.

"'Some people oppose a modification of laws relating to the right of a married woman to own property on the ground that economic independence of woman would lead to the spread of immorality among women and disruption of domestic life. What is your attitude on the question?'

"I would answer the question by a counter-question: Has not independendence of man and his holding property led to the spread of immorality among men? If you answer 'yes' then let it be so also with women. And when women have rights of ownership and the rest like men, it will be found that the enjoyment of such rights is not responsible for their vices or their virtues. Morality which depends upon the helplessness of a man or woman has not much to recommend it. Morality is rooted in the purity of our hearts.

"A young man has sent me a letter which can be given here only in substance. It is as under:

> 'I am a married man. I had gone out to a foreign country. I had a friend whom both I and my parents implicity trusted. During my absence he seduced my wife who has now conceived of him. My father now insists that the girl should resort to abortion, otherwise, he says, the family would be disgraced. To me it seems that it would be wrong to do so. The poor women is consumed with remorse. She cares

> neither to eat nor drink, but is always weeping. Will you kindly tell me as to what my duty is in the case?'

"I have published this latter with great hesitation. As everybody knows such cases are by no means infrequent in society. A restrained public, discussion of the question, therefore, does not seem to me to be out of place.

"It seems to me clear as daylight that abortion would be a crime. Countless husbands are guilty of the same lapse as this poor woman , but nobody every question for them. Society not only excuses that but does not even censure them. Then, again, the women cannot conceal her shame while man can successfully hide his sin.

"The woman in question deserves to be pitied. It would be the sacred duty of the husband to bring up the baby with all the love and tenderness that he is capable of and to yield to the counsels of his father. Whether he should continue to live with his wife is a ticklish question. Circumstances may warrant separation from her. In that case he would be bound to provide for her maintenance and to help her to live a pure life. Nor should I see anything wrong in his accepting her repentance if it is sincere and genuine. Nay, further. I can imagine a situation when it would be the sacred duty of the husband to take back an erring wife who has completely expiated for and redeemed her error.

"Passive resistance is regarded as the weapon of the weak, but the resistance for which I had to coin a new name altogether is the weapon of the strongest. I had to coin a new word to signify what I meant. But its matchless beauty lies, in the fact that, though it is the weapon of the strongest it can be wielded by the weak in body, by the aged, and even by the children if they have stout hearts. And since resistance in *Satyagraha* is offered through self-suffering, it is a weapon pre-eminently open to women. We found last year that women in India, in many instances, surpassed their brothers in sufferings and the two played a noble part in the campaign. For, the ideal of self-suffering became contagious and they embarked upon amazing acts of self-denial. Supposing that the women and the children of Europe became fired with the love of humanity, they would take the men by storm and reduce militarism, to nothingness in an incredibly short time. The underlying idea is that women, children and others have the same soul, the same potentiality. The question is one of drawing, out the limitless power of truth.

"When a woman is assaulted, she may not stop to think in terms of *himsa* or *ahimsa.* Her primary duty is self-protection. She is at liberty to employ every method or means that comes to her mind, in order to defend her honour. God has given her nails and teeth. She must use them with all her strength and if need be, die in the effort. The man or woman who has shed all fear of death will be able not only to protect himself or herself but others also through lying down his or her life. In truth, we fear death most, and hence we ultimately submit to superior physical force. Some will bend the knee to the invader, some will resort to bribery, some will crawl on their bellies or submit to other forms of humiliation, and some women will even give their bodies rather than die. I have not written this in a carping spirit. I am only illustrating human nature. Whether we crawl on our bellies or whether a woman yields to the lust of man, is symbolic of that same love of life which makes us stoop to anything. Therefore, only be who loses his life shall save it. To enjoy life one should give up the lure of life. That should be part of our nature.

"For me there can be no preparation for violence. All preparation must be for non-violence if courage of the highest type is to be developed.... If there are women who when assailed by miscreants cannot resist themselves without arms, they do not need to be *advised* to cary arms. They *will* do so. There is something wrong in this constant inquiry as to whether to bear arms or not. People have to learn to be naturally independent. If they will remember the central teaching, namely, that the real, effective resistance lies in nonviolence, they will mould their conduct accordingly. And that is what the world has been doing, although unthinkingly. Since it has not the highest courage, namely courage born of non-violence, it arms itself even unto the atom bomb. Those do not see in it the futility of violence will naturally arm themselves to the best of their ability.

"It is for American women to show what power women can be in the world. But that can only be when yon cease to be the toys of men's idle hours. You have got freedom. You can become a power for pea by refusing to be carried away by the flood-tide of the psendo-science glorifying self-indulgence that is engulfing the West today and apply your minds instead to the science of non-violence; for forgiveness is your nature. By aping men, you neither become men nor can you function as your real selves and develop your special talent that God has given you. God has vouchsafed to women the power of non-violence more than to man. It is all the more effective because it is mute. Women are the natural messengers of the gospel of non-violence if only they will realize their high estate.

"But it is my firm conviction that if the men and women of India cultivate in themselves the courage to face death bravely and non-violently they can laugh to scorn the power of armaments and realize the ideal of unadulterated independence in terms of the masses which would serve as an example to the world. In that women can take the lead for they are a personification of the power of self-suffering."

This has had been an undenying factor that women are central to development. They control most of the non-money economy through bearing and raising children, and providing much of the labour for household maintenance and subsistence agriculture. Women also make an important contribution to the money economy by their work in both the formal and informal sectors.

Everywhere in the world women have two jobs—in the home and outside it. Women's work is generally undervalued and the additional burden development imposes is usually unrecognized. Their health suffers, their children suffer and their work suffers. Development itself is held back. As Third

World countries face new problems women's role becomes increasingly central.

Women and Contemporary Problems of Development

Following Gandhian line of action, women in different countries have led many movements to tackle contemporary social problems. It has been said that the present paradox of development lies in the mistaken assumption that growth of commodity production will improve the satisfaction of basic needs. Yet the expansion of cash-cropping and production for export has not been accompanied by the trickle down of benefits to the poor, especially poor women, while at the same time it has led to water pollution, soil erosion, destruction of firewood resources and loss of genetic diversity of plant and animal stocks. A new impoverishment of women has been brought about by the absorption into the market economy of much of the natural resources of land, water and timber on which family subsistence depended, without offering women a new means of support.

Their responsibility for maintaining the family by providing food, water and firewood for cooking and heating makes women very aware of environmental degradation and determined to do something about it. To achieve sustainable development, with human and natural resources brought into a dynamic equilibrium, the skills and knowledge of the women, who are the primary sustainers of society, must be utilized. Such active resistance to environmental degradation has forced policy makers to rethink the relationship between development and the environment. The Chipko forest conservation movement in India pre-dated the UN Decade for Women. It became identified with women as it was they who led the fight to protect the forest and so preserve sources of fuel and reduce soil erosion. Firewood is the main source of energy in Africa but it is becoming more difficult to obtain as land is cleared for cash-cropping. In Ghana (Africa), for many families the local supply of wood is now inadequate. Women in households in the savanna have to walk further in search of fuel now than 10 years ago, while over half of those in the forested zone are for the first time experiencing problems, with almost 30 per cent coping with an inadequate supply of firewood. Women have adopted two main coping strategies: reducing the number of cooked meals to one every other day as in parts of West Africa and the Andes, resulting in lower family nutrition levels: and supplementing or replacing fuel wood with agricultural residues such as cassava stalks or dried dung. Some 800 million people now rely on there residues for part of their energy needs thus depriving the soil of inputs traditionally used to improve fertility and soil structure.

Many of women's income-earning activities such as fish-smoking, beer-brewing and pottery-making also depend on adequate supplies of fuelwood. In addition, forests supply other raw materials and food products important to women for household consumption, animal fodder and as a source of income. The spread of irrigation, usually associated with green revolution crops, has led to a decline in both quantity and quality of drinking water. In the Indian state of Madhya Pradesh in 1980 out of 70,000 villages, 36,420 reported water shortages; in 1982 this number rose to 50,000 and in 1985 to 64,565. The burden on women is becoming so acute that they are refusing to marry men from water-shortage areas. The Chipko movement is also trying to protect water sources as it is aware of the link between forest and the maintenance of groundwater levels and water purity. It is now recognized that the exclusion of women from the planning of water supply and sanitation schemes is a major cause of their high rate of failure.

Significantly, 'Drought' in Africa has caused enormous problems for rural women. Even in dry years there are marked local variations in rainfall and so men find it advantageous to have several wives who farm widely scattered plots. This spreads the risk of crop failure and ensures that the husband with many wives will have at least one wife with a successful harvest. It does not reduce the risk for the other wives as traditionally each wife is responsible for feeding her own children. In some parts of the Sudan women are forced to leave their land and migrate to wetter regions where they work as sharecroppers for wealthy landowners and are paid with a percentage of the harvest which can be used to feed their children and their husband.

Often many develooping countries have been forced to ask for financial assistance from the International Monetary Fund. In return for this assistance the IMF usually imposes tough financial constraints and demands that the recipient countries restructure their economies. This structural adjustment generally involves an increase in production for export combined with demand-reducing policies such as removal of subsidies on basic foodstuffs, reduction in welfare services, price rises, wage cuts and job losses. It may be argued that the social costs of structural adjustment would have been worse without the IMF intervention but there is little appreciation by international agencies of the gender bias in their impact. In response women have developed new survival strategies. This behaviour has been called 'the invisible adjustment' implying that women make adjustment policies socially possible by increasing their own economic activity, by working harder and by self-abnegation.

Structural adjustment shifts the burden of welfare from the state to individual families and especially women. Wage cuts force more members of the family to seek paid employment and because women are paid less than men it may be easier for them to find employment. The impact of the economic-crisis of the 1980s on female economic activity rates is very mixed. It varies not only from country but within countries, between economic sectors and urban and rural areas and according to age and educational levels. The most widespread effect was a slowdown in the participation of women in the formal workforce which had been growing since 1960. Women have been particularly affected by the industrial brought about as a result of the introduction of new less labour-intensive technology and of decreased foreign direct investment in assembly industries in most of the 40 Third World countries operating export processing zones. Many women have joined the informal economy or have been forced to migrate. In the Philippines the number of women seeking jobs overseas increased by 70 per cent between 1982 and 1987.

Whether women work often depends on the availability of a daughter to take on domestic chores and childcare. In Malaysia it was found that 31 per cent of girls but only 17 per cent of boys did work in the home. Girls may be taken out of school to replace the mother and so lose their chance to be trained for a better job in the future. For example in Bangladesh, when an IMF-supervised adjustment programme was implemented in 1985, the ratio of girls to boys in primary education fell from 77 girls per 100 boys in 1984 to below 67. Other countries experiencing such changes were Brazil, Chile, Colombia, and Jamaica while decreased female enrolment in secondary schools has been documented for Indonesia, Jamaica, Nigeria, the Philippines and the Sudan.

Increased food prices (forget old days, see currently in 2008 in almost all countries, India being most affected) force poor families to reduce both the quantity and quality of their food intake and women and children are usually most affected. In a slum in Guayaquil, Ecuador, during the economic crisis of 1987-8, 42 per cent of families gave up drinking milk and 79 per cent of children attending clinics suffered from malnutrition. In a sample of 51 countries studied by UNICEF in 1986 all but two had experienced an increase in child malnutrition between 1980 and 1985 and there is some indication that undernourished children were more likely to be female. Increased infant mortality in the period 1982-85 was reported for Brazil, Ghana, Uruguay and the Philippines and in many areas these changes seem to have affected girls more than boys.

Resultantly men migrate to seek work elsewhere with the result that the number of both extended and female-headed households increases. Women become more powerful in the face of such acute threats to the survival of the family because of their traditional responsibility for reproduction. Both mother and daughters work longer hours and time becomes their scarcest resources. Women seek alternative sources of income to compensate for declines in household income and spend longer shopping for and preparing cheaper types of food. Man feel themselves marginalized and the study in Ecuador showed that adult males responded by increasing their alcohol consumption and their level of violence to women while teenage sons turned to dependence on drugs.

Community Management

The poorest families, often headed by women, bear a disproportionate share of the burden of adjustment and the economic crisis has tended to exacerbate pre-existing gender inequalities. Awareness of the needs of their communities tends to be greater among women than men, since it is normally women who have to cope with problems of housing and access to services. Consequently, women often take the lead in demanding improvements in urban services. They may also work together to change social attitudes. Groups of women in Bombay, India, march silently, carrying placards, around houses in which dowry deaths have occurred, public shame on the perpetrators. This is more effective than government legislation in reducing the number of these tragedies. Women's groups in India have also lobbied for legal restraints on the abortion of female foetuses.

No doubt, women's survival strategies often depend on building up networks of women within the community. The communal kitchens set up in Lima, Peru, help to reduce the time women spend individually cooking for their families and so allow them extra time to earn money. Development agencies often advocate the spread of these grassroots separate women's organizations because they feel that they avoid confrontation with cultural patterns which oppose the mixing of unrelated women and men and prevent a submergence of women's interests and loss of leadership to men. However, these women's groups may provide a focus for the politicization of women's lives around issues of prime importance to their domestic role, such as rising food costs and the disappearance of their children at the hands of repressive regimes. This link between the empowerment of women for household welfare and consequent political action has not been analysed by most development workers.

As governments are forced to cut back on public sector spending, the burden of providing basic needs services to poor communities is falling increasingly on women. Women are having to spend precious time negotiating directly with international agencies and non-governmental organizations in order to get free · assistance for their children, and training or credit for setting up income-earning enterprises. Development projects directed at women are often small, scattered and peripheral to the main aims of development. They usually try to promote greater self-sufficiency rather than development in the sense of expansion and qualitative change. Furthermore, the criteria for success are often less stringent than those for projects specifically for men. On the other hand, when general development projects are planned women may find themselves excluded because of restrictive entry conditions. Female-headed households are numerous in the slums of Third Would cities but eligibility for new housing is commonly based on the premise that there is a male head of household. Female household heads may not have an income which is large enough or secure enough to qualify for housing. In self help projects they may not have the time or skills necessary to build a house and if they employ a man to do it they may be cheated. These problems are now widely recognized and can be overcome through training, membership of a women's group or special eligibility conditions tailored to suit the constrains of women's lives.

All world level, the success of the women who organized the rebuilding of their homes after the earthquake in Mexico City in 1986 is a good example. They learned how to lobby politicians, how good to design apartments which were suitable for their lifestyles and family size and how to prevent contractors cheating them. In doing so they not only rehoused their families but also successfully challenged the patriachal structure of households, trade unions and political parties. In the face of an environmental disaster, grassroots women's groups were instrumental in reviving their communities.

Recent Developments

Since the 1950s, when development planning first came into the international spotlight, a number of approaches, having different effects on women, have been tried. They may be detailed as follows.

Anti-Poverty

The second WID approach, it aimed to increase the productivity of poor women and saw their poverty as a problem of underdevelopment not of subordination.

Equity

This was the original approach of Women in Development (WID) and was utilized during the Decade for Women 1975-85. Women were seen as active participants in the development process.

Welfare

This was the earliest approach. It dominated from 1950 to 1970 and is still widely used. Its main purpose was to enable women to be better mothers which was seen as their main role in society.

Efficiency

This is the most prevalent approach used today. Its aim is to ensure that development is efficient and effective. It is based on an awareness that policies of economic stabilization and adjustment rely on women's contribution to development and aims to make them more efficient managers of poverty.

Empowerment

An approach articulated by Third World feminists since the mid-1980s. It aims to empower women through greater self-reliance and sees women's oppression as stemming not only from male patriarchal attitudes but also from colonial and neocolonial oppression. Effort to grafts an awareness of women's needs onto planning through such political action as the Percy Amendment in the United States, which has been followed by similar policies in the Canadian and British government aid agencies and in the World Bank, have had little effect. It is necessary to challenge planning stereotypes relating to the structure of families and the division of labour within low-income households.

Planners are often unaware of the work burdens of women and of their problems of time as a scarce resource. The kind of integrated project women need, such as making health and training facilities available at a convenient time and place for women with small children and little access to transport, is rarely attempted. It is also necessary to distinguish between the practical and strategic needs of women. Practical needs are those such as food and shelter which are required by all the family and are identified as priorities by women and planners alike.

They serve to preserve and reinforce the gender division of labour. Strategic needs are those which can empower women, challenge the existing gender division of labour and bring about greater equality. They are difficult to meet because poor women often do not have time to reflect on such needs because of their immediate requirement of seeking the satisfaction of their practical needs. Because equity programmes disturb the status quo and demand long-term commitment by governments they are rarely implemented.

However, addressing women's strategic needs is vital if fundamental change is to occur. Unfortunately, the costs of ignoring, the needs of women are many: uncontrolled population growth, high infant and child mortality, a weakened economy, ineffective agriculture, a deteriorating environment, a divided society and a proper life for all. For young girls and for women it means unequal opportunities, a higher level of risk and a life determined by fate and the decisions of others rather than by choice.

Conclusion

Economic crisis in many developing countries; enhanced by their peripheral position in the world economy, has led to reductions in spending on health, education and food subsidies and the impact is heaviest on poor women. When women are able to respond successfully to crises they gain status within the household, either because they have become the chief income earner in the family or because they have gained confidence through learning how to negotiate, successfully with national and international agencies, and to work with other women. This very success may provoke an additional crisis in the internal gender relations of the househould. Women's increased power and independence may result in a male backlash of violence and the expansion of female-headed households. It may also lead to more equality and freedom of choice for both men and women.

Trying to develop without acknowledging the people who do two-thirds of the work is inviting failure. Ways must be found to reduce their burden of work' if women are to realize their potential. Development plans for women, where they exist, tend to assume mistakenly that women have free time to devote to new projects and to ignore the heterogeneity and differentiation of women. Remember women are agents of change, not just victims. The United Nations has realized that the role and status of women are central to changes in population and development. It now argues that development plans must be rethought from the start so that women's abilities, rights and needs are taken into account at every stage. Making investment in women a development priority will require a major change in attitudes to development, not only by governments but also by lending agencies. Investing in women is not a global panacea. It will not put an end to poverty but it will make a critical contribution.

Of late, various steps have been taken by various nation-states in this direction, yet these measures have proved only meagre. If we are really sincere to the cause, we have to adopt the measure of strict following. Implement thoughts to action.

Thus, we see ample scope for Gandhian social work for emancipation and empowerment of women. Gandhian principles can help the social workers a lot in this field of action.

REFERENCES

1. C.Y. Chintamani (ed.), *Indian Social Reform,* Part I, Thompson and Co., Madras, 1901, p. 306.
2. M.K. Gandhi, *Women and Social Injustice,* p. 4.
3. M.K. Gandhi. *Hindu Dharma,* Navajivan Publishing House, Ahmedabad, 1950, p. 24.
4. Har Bilas Sarda, *Life of Dayanand Saraswati* (1946), pp. 446-47.
5. D.S. Sharma, *Renaissance of Hinduism* (1944), pp. 178-79.
6. Brij Mohan Sharma, *Swami Dayanand* (1933), pp. 120-122.
7. Heimsath, *Indian Nationalism and Hindu Social Reform,* Oxford University Press, Bombay, 1964, pp. 21-22.
8. Krishna Kripalani, 'Gandhi and Womanhood' in *India Horizons.* Vol. XXIV, No. 4, 1975, p. 26.
9. J.B. Kripalani, *Gandhi: His Life and Thought* (1970), p. 395.
10. J.L. Nehru, *The Discovery of India,* p. 25.
11. *Collected Works of Mahatma Gandhi,* Publication Division, Delhi, Vol. 52, p. 48, quoting *Amrit Bazar Patrika,* dt. 30.11.1932.
12. Lajpat Rai, "Gandhi and Non-co-operation" in Bianche Watson (ed.), *Gandhi and Non-violent Resistance: the Non-co-operative movement of India* (1923), p. 396.

9

Gandhi and Village Economy

> "Khadi is the sun of the village solar system. The planets are the various industries which can support khadi in return for the heat and the sustenance they derive from it. Without it other industries cannot grow. But during may last tour I discovered that, without the revival of other industries, khadi could not make further progress. For villagers to be able to occupy their spare time profitably, the village must be touched at all points."
>
> *(Harijan, 16-11-1934)*

In popular parlance, *Khadi* also known as Khadar (homespun cotton cloth) and *charkha* (hand-spinning), symbolized for Gandhi the village economy and its self-sufficiency. What is needed is that each village be self-sufficient for its basic needs. Although we may not be able to agree with the details which Gandhi gives here, we can very well agree with his fundamental insight. His vision of the village economy is that of self-sufficient and independent units (of production) where the basic necessities of all the villagers are met conveniently and where the Leavers' life style is fostered.

According to Gandhi it "connotes the beginning of economic freedom and equality of all in the country. . . . It must be taken with all its implications. It means wholesale *swadeshi* mentality, a determination to find all the necessaries of life in India and that, too, through the labor and intellect of the villagers." For Gandhi, *Khadi* mentality means *decentralization of the production* and *distribution of the necessaries of life.* Therefore, the formula so far evolved is, every village to produce all its necessaries and a certain percentage in addition for the requirements of the cities, meaning surplus production.

Further, the "message of the spinning wheel is much wider than its circumference. Its message is one of simplicity, service of humanity, living so as not to hurt others, creating an indissoluble bond between the rich and the poor, capital and labor, the prince and the peasant." The *charkha* restores the villages to their rightful place and abolishes distinctions between high and low.

In fact, Gandhi's propagation of *charkha* can be traced to his actual encounter with the situation of the poor. He discovered that there were many *Harijan* families that subsisted on spinning. Thus *Khadi* is the poor person's *staff of life*. It helps the poorest, including the *Harijans*, who are the most helpless among the poorest. They are so because many occupations which are available to the others are not available to them.

Remarkably, *Charkha* for Gandhi is intimately connected to the village life. Ever since Gandhi entered Indian public life in 1915, he had been pleading for a new deal for the village. The acute pressure on land and the absence of supplementary industries had caused chronic unemployment and underemployment among the peasants whose appalling poverty never ceased to weigh upon Gandhi's mind. His advocacy for the Charkha was derived from its immediate practical value as a palliative. The All-India Spinners' Association, to which he had given a good deal of his time during the years of political quiescence, had in a period of ten years extended its activities to 5,300 villages, and provided employment to 220,000 spinners, 20,000 weavers and 20,000 volunteers and disbursed more than Rs. 20,000,000 in Indian villages. Definitely, figures may not seem impressive today in the context of large scale state-sponsored planning, but they represented solid work on the part of an organization often against heavy odds.

Remarkably, the *swadeshi* cult, which insisted on the use of products made in India and had swayed the country during periods of intense political excitement, received a new twist in the 1930s. It was not enough, argued Gandhi, that an article should be of Indian origin; it was equally important that it should be made in a village. He appealed to town-dwellers to examine each article of daily consumption which was manufactured in India or abroad, and to find a substitute for it from the village. The broom (Jharu) could replace a brush; a tooth-stick of a tree for a tooth brush; hand-pounded rice for factory polished rice; handmade sugar for factory sugar, and handmade paper for the products of the paper mills. Village products might sometimes cost more, but they distributed wages and profits among those whose need was the direst. For nearly 150 years, the cities had drained villages of wealth and talent. "For the city dweller," wrote Gandhi, "the villages have become untouchable. He does not know them; he will not live in them, and if he finds himself in a village he will want to reproduce city life there. This would be tolerable, if we could bring into being cities which would accommodate thirty crores of human beings."

As such unhesitatingly Gandhiji admitted "*Khadi* to me is the symbol of unity of Indian humanity, or the economic freedom and equality and, therefore, . . . in the poetic expression of Nehru, `the livery of India's freedom." Within this background of the poverty of the villages and the possibility opened up by the *Charka*, Gandhi could boldly assert: "The spinning wheel is an attempt to produce something out of nothing."

Definitely, a change of attitude towards the *charkha* is difficult and demanding, which needs a revolutionary change in the mentality and taste of many. Easy though the non-violent way is in many respects, it is very difficult in many others. The revival of the *charkha* cannot take place without an army of selfless dedicated Indians with intelligence and patriotism, working with a single mind in the villages to spread the message of the *charkha* and bring a ray of hope and light into their drab eyes. At the same time, Gandhi is of course realistic enough to know that *charkha* and *khadi* alone are not sufficient. "Now I feel that *khadi* alone cannot revive the villages. Village uplift is possible only when we rejuvenate village life as a whole, revive all village industries and make the entire village industrious."

Since eighty-five per cent of the population of India (which still lives) lived in villages, their economic and social resuscitation was a *sine qua non* for freedom. Gandhi described the exploitation of the village in the interest of the town as a species of violence. The growing gap in economic standards and social amenities between the village and the town had to be bridged. This could best be done by volunteers from the towns who spread themselves in the countryside to revive dead or dying rural industries and to improve standards of nutrition, education and sanitation. Gandhi expected these public-spirited men and women to support themselves on 'a village scale'; if they put on their work, a price which villages could not sustain, village economy would face bankruptcy.

Voluntary work alone could overcome the financial hurdle which made official programs of rural uplift a snail-paced affair. Gandhi felt that the villagers could be educated out of this inertia by bands of selfless workers 'infiltrating' into the villages, helping the villagers to revive village industries, running village schools, improving sanitation and popularizing a balanced diet. Labor and material were available in the village; they had only to be harnessed in its service.

To the question "How to turn waste into wealth," was how Gandhi summed up the objects of the All-India Village Industries Association to Lord Farringdon who visited him. Gandhi explained that his programme did not cover rural indebtedness, because "it requires state effort. I am just now discovering things people can do without state aid. Not that I do not want state aid. But I know I cannot get it on my terms."

Among the things which villagers could do, but often failed to do, was to keep their villages clean. Gandhi attributed this to the complex of untouchability: "to the fear of touching our own dirt and, therefore, of cleaning it." He exhorted everyone to be his own `scavenger', to join in a campaign to keep village tanks, wells and streets clean, and to remove the cause for that reproach of Lionel Curtis that Indian villages were `dung heaps.'

Further, basically nutrition was another problem on which Gandhi wrote and spoke. Nutrition took on a new urgency as a problem of the Indian masses when he realized that apart from their poverty their conventional food habits were responsible for their undernourishment. The deficiency in vitamins was inexcusable, when green leaves were available for the asking. He appealed to the Indian scientists to pursue research into Indian diets in the context of Indian conditions:

> "It is for you to make these biological experiments. Don't say off-hand that Bengalis need half a pound of rice every day and must digest half a pound. Devise a scientifically perfect diet for them. Determine the quantity of starch required for an average human constitution. I would not be satisfied until I have been able to add some milk and fat and greens to the diet of our common village folk. I want chemists who would starve in order to find an ideal diet for their poor countrymen. Unfortunately our doctors have never approached the question from the humanitarian standpoint, at any rate from the poor man's standpoint."
>
> — (BR Nanda, *Mahatma Gandhi: A Biography*)

Naturally, was obvious to Gandhi that rural India could not be transformed without the help of the urban intellectuals. To make the country village-conscious, he advised Congress to hold its annual sessions in villages. The Faizpur Congress was the first to be held in a village; Gandhi noted that the session was free from the scramble and hustle inevitable in big towns, that village hedges could be a better substitute for barbed wire, and exhibitions of village handicrafts could entertain as well as instruct.

Naturally work in the villages was an arduous and slow affair; it was 'plodder's work', as Gandhi put it. It did not earn banner headlines in the press and did not seem to embarrass the Government. Many of Gandhi's colleagues did not see how this innocuous activity could help India in advancing to the real goal of political freedom. Gandhi was accused of side-tracking the main political issue. His answer was: "I do not see how thinking of these necessary problems (of village uplift) and finding a solution for them was of no political significance and how any examination of the financial policy of the Government has necessarily a political bearing. What I am asking the masses to do is such as can be done by millions of people, whereas the work of examining the policy of our rulers will be beyond them. Let those few who are qualified do so. But until these leaders can bring great changes into being why should not millions like me use the gifts that God has given them to the best advantage? Why should they not clean their doors and make of their bodies fitter instruments?"

The image of Gandhi's 'perfect democracy based on individual freedom' could be dismissed as utopian, but to Gandhi it was the only form a non-violent society could take. He did not care what label was applied to his ideas. Indian socialists, who by 1935 were a strong wing within the Congress, sometimes criticized him. Gandhi claimed that he was a socialist long before many Indian socialists had avowed the creed. "But my socialism," he wrote, "was natural to me, and not adopted from any book. It came out of my unshakable belief in non-violence. No man could be actively non-violent and not rise against social injustice wherever it occurred."

Gandhiji, believed his non-violent technique could end social injustice no less than foreign rule. By eschewing force, his socialism did not become a pious futility; in spite of its humanitarian and ostensibly gentle methods, it had revolutionary implications. Unlike capitalists and socialists, he considered property as an evil; he saw the unreality of the debate about ownership of property which had little relevance for millions of people who were no more than at a subsistence level, if not below it. Addressing the women of India, he exhorted them to remember that millions of men have no property to transmit to posterity. "Let them learn from them that it is better for the few to have no ancestral property at all. The real property that a parent can transmit to all equally is his or her character and educational facilities."

No doubt, on economic front tolerated the institution of property, not because he loved it or considered it essential for the progress of humanity, but because he wished to abolish it through a non-violent technique. Gandhi would have vested the ownership of property neither in the individual nor in the state, but in God. Those who possessed property were thus to consider themselves as trustees; but they were not to be its primary, let alone exclusive, beneficiaries. No one was to keep more to himself than he needed; everyone was to work according to his or her capacity and to receive according to his or her real need. This theory of trusteeship might seem a rationalization of the privileged position of the princes, landlords and business magnates. In fact, it was a radical theory which called for voluntary sacrifices from the 'haves' in the interest of the 'have-nots.'

Notably, Gandhi's ideas were evolved in response to the social and economic conditions around him. He had once criticized Indian socialists, but as years passed the latter saw that their ideas were present in the Gandhian programs, though sometimes under a guise which they did not readily recognize. Gandhi was not a theorist, but a practical man, dealing with practical problems. In pre-independent India, he had to function without the help of the Government and often in the face of its opposition. The problems of poverty, disease, ignorance and inertia are too serious a problem to be postponed to a distant date.

It is apt to note here that, primary goal of Gandhi's insistence on the village life was to provide the basic necessaries for all. Such a possibility was ruled out in the Indian cities. Gandhi contends: "I have no historical proof, but I believe that there was a time in India when village economies were organized on the basis of such non-violent occupations, not on the basis of the rights of man but on the duties of man. Those who engaged themselves in such occupations did earn their living, but their labor contributed to the good of the community."

If Gandhi asked for a return to the villages, it is not for any nostalgic reason but for the sole purpose of making them self-supporting, self-sustaining, and self-developing. He did foresee that in the villages some extra materials needed for cities would be produced. But he would never imagine that villages (or even nations) would be totally bought up to produce only items for the cities as in the case of the 'Banana republics.'

Gandhiji imagined a simple life style in the villages. At the same time the villages will be hygienic, clean and healthy. The village *panchayats* will be able to take up the works needed to maintain villages free from dreaded sicknesses. It is to be noted that Gandhi himself practiced this simple life and he could meet the basic necessities of life by himself. He narrates, in his autobiography, the interesting incident of how he learned to shave and cut his own hair himself. Gandhi also learnt cooking as part of his simple and self-supporting life style.

The concept of modern 'global village' originated only recently and reflects: the networking made possible due to the Internet, the cultural homogeneity brought about by satellite TV, the fast speed of transport through advanced technology, the conferencing facilities introduced by "video" telephones, and rapid information transfer made possible by advanced satellite techniques.' Global village rightly symbolizes not just the technological advancement of the modern society, but also the cultural and even religious atmosphere of modern or post-modern humans. The future, represented by the global village, it is claimed, is a 'free, democratic, egalitarian' life where conveniences are shared, means are available to all, and each individual is given every opportunity for his/her personal realization of this all.

Whereas Mahatma Gandhi visualized village communities which are themselves self-sustainable and viable. His villages are different, distinct, and have their own independent identities, characteristics and uniqueness. The global village, on the other hand, focuses on a uniform pattern of living, basing itself mainly on technological advancement. The ecological problems, the possibility of nuclear disasters and dangers from genetic manipulations are the direct and perceptible side effects of globalization. Globalization may point to an insecure and hence non-viable future.

In short, the global village fosters uniformity, unity in thought patterns, and the myth of "uninterrupted, unlimited progress." As opposed to this, the Gandhian vision of villages is based on the needs of individual human beings, on a harmonious relationship between humans and nature, on a concern for the lowly and the rejected, on non-violence and *satyagraha*. Gandhian villages take the individual persons and their needs seriously at the core. Their problems and concerns are respected, and their basic needs are met suitably.

Coming to the notion of 'Takers' vs. 'Leavers,' introduced by Daniel Quinn in his world famous novel *Ishmael*, to understand the dynamics operational in the two world views. The 'Takers' are the winners in the power game while the 'Leavers' are the losers in our civilization, who are still present in small pockets of tribal regions and non-developed areas. We shall then show the Leavers' way of living to be best represented by the village life advocated by Gandhi.

Coming to the question of viability, we take the arguments of Quinn that the Leavers have continued to exist in our world for about three million years, and so theirs is obviously a viable way of life. On the other hand, the Takers, in their brief existence of 3,000 years, have brought us to a catastrophic situation, and so their way of life is non-viable.

Gandhi's option for the *Harijans* all through his life indicates that he is a Leaver and his life vision is one where the marginalized are seriously taken care of. At the same time, his opposition to the oppressive system (of the Takers) does not make him opposed to the individual persons! This is another characteristic of the

Leavers' civilization B when they oppose the system they do not oppose the persons who belong to the system. His vehement criticism of industrialized society is based on his concern for individual human beings. Gandhi's critique of the current Takers' civilization, symbolized aptly by his common salt struggle, is uniquely a feature of the Leavers' civilization. Gandhi's own vision of a village economy, exemplified by the spinning wheel, is based on a simple life style where basic necessities are provided for all.

No doubt, many of the ideas of Gandhi are outdated. We cannot imagine a future where we have to return to the romantic village situation of the (imaginary) past. But the concerns and priorities of Gandhi are crucial for the very survival of human society. It is our contention that a viable future can be built only on a model similar to the Gandhian villages and not on the model of the globalized village. We do not advocate that a viable future has to be exactly modelled on the Gandhian understanding of villages. But the concerns of Gandhian villages and Gandhi's priorities are crucial for the viability of our future human existence. This has to be carefully kept in mind when we read the ideas of Gandhi on the future civilization.

The Takers believe that the world is created for them; so they have the right and the commission to rule the world. That they are created to rule the world, to conquer it, improve it and to bring order and harmony into the world, is an unquestioned premise of our society. "You hear this fifty times a day. You can turn on the radio or the television and hear it every hour. Man is conquering the deserts, man is conquering the oceans, man is conquering the atom, man is conquering the elements, man is conquering the outer space." (Ishmail, p. 5). Their law is that of unlimited growth. They assume that unbridled development or economic growth is the panacea for all their problems. This leads to unrestrained production and uncontrolled expansion, needing more conquering. Their way is the only right way; they are convinced that they have found the one right way of living. They expect all others either to follow their way or to lose the very right to exist. They consider it their holy task to police the world, civilize it and set things right in the wild world around them. Such a view on life leads to the impending consequence: destruction of all other cultures, including in the end their own.

Contrary to this, the Leavers believe in the premise that humans are in the world along with other animals and plants. Since the world and humans are God's creation, humans need not feel anxious and need not rule the world. The law followed by the Leavers is that of sustainable growth. It acknowledges that there are many ways and not one right way. Their way is the one found suitable for them and found to work for generations. They, therefore, let the others walk *their* own ways. Their task is to shepherd the earth or to be the pathfinders in the full development of other cultures and peoples.

Unfortunately, the Taker civilization, with their holy zeal of propagating their 'right' way, has destroyed other cultures and led the universe to the ecological and atomic catastrophe in which we find ourselves. Obviously theirs is not a viable civilization. So the task for the future of humanity is to rediscover the Leavers' tradition in our culture B a culture that has enabled us to exist for three million years! Quinn does not advocate going back to the primitive, tribal life style. What he pleads for is to change our attitude and live the Leavers' values in our contemporary society.

At the risk of generalization and over-simplification, we can identify the Leavers with the colonized Indians and the Takers with the British colonizers. Though there will not be an exact match we see similar patterns between the dominating, 'civilized' British and the subjugated, 'uncivilized' Indians. It may be noted that some of the Indians may belong to the Takers category,[6] for ours is only a rough approximation, but this approximation does not affect the conclusions of the paper.

Gandhi would identify himself totally with the dispossessed, the losers, the Leavers. In this section we shall see how Gandhi opted consciously for the *Harijans* (obviously the least of the

Leavers) and stood fearlessly against the system of the British (Takers) without opposing the individuals that constituted the Takers' world.

Gandhi identified himself totally with the dispossessed and disadvantaged, the losers of the modern society. How strongly he felt on the subject of untouchability, the paradigm example of losers, was revealed in his speech at the meeting of the Minorities' Committee on November 13, 1931: "I claim myself in my own person to represent the vast mass of the untouchables. Here I speak not merely on behalf of the Congress, but I speak on my own behalf, and I claim that I would get, if there was a referendum of the untouchables, their vote and that I would top the poll."

In keeping with his commitment to the untouchables, he pleaded for the opening of temples to *Harijans*: "Temples are for sinners, not for saints; but who is to judge where no man is without sin?" He ridiculed the superstition that anybody could be unclean by birth, or the shadow or touch of one human being could defile another human being. Bathing was all very well, he told a village audience, but even buffaloes had long daily baths. `I am a *Harijan* worker, my time is precious,' he scolded a palmist who offered to read his hand. `Is there a cure for untouchability?' he asked a village doctor. In another village a woman barber was brought in to shave him. As she set about her job in a businesslike way, Gandhi noticed she was loaded with gold and silver ornaments. "What are these wretched things?" he said, "They don't make you beautiful. Indeed they are ugly and harbor dirt." The poor woman was visibly disappointed. "I borrowed them especially for this occasion," she replied, "I could not come before you without good ornament." Before leaving she had contributed her wages to the *Harijan* Fund.

Summing up his impressions of the *Harijan* tour, Gandhi declared early in August 1934, that untouchability was on its last legs. He had quickened the conscience of the upper class people to the wrongs they were inflicting on the *Harijans*, and he had roused the *Harijans* to the consciousness of their rights. But the battle was by no means over.

On many occasions Gandhi had undertaken fasts for *Harijan's* causes. C. F. Andrews even wrote to him (March 12, 1933) from Birmingham: "I hardly think you realize how very strong here is the moral repulsion against fasting unto death. I confess as a Christian I should do it and it is only with the greatest difficulty that I find myself able to justify it under any circumstances" (for the *Harijans* and against untouchability). The Hindu Leaders' Conference met at Bombay. The leaders, who included Madan Mohan Malaviya, Tej Bahadur Sapru, M.R. Jaykar, Rajagopalachari, N.C. Kelkar and Rajendra Prasad were anxious for a quick solution. They had, however, to carry with them the leaders of the depressed classes, particularly Ambedkar, who was not only a stubborn advocate of separate electorates but fully conscious of his pivotal position. No solution to which he did not agree was likely to commend itself to the Government. Gandhi was the last person to allow the conference to be stampeded into a wrong decision. He sent a message to the assembled leaders through his son Devadas that he (Devadas) "as his father's son was prepared to forfeit his father's life rather than see any injury being done to the suppressed classes in mad haste." The conference considered a number of proposals; some of its members paid visits to Pune to discuss them with the Mahatma. The meeting had some commendable results.

It is obvious that Gandhi was totally against the corrupt and exploitative system perpetuated by the British. But his opposition was not directed against the individuals in the system, and he could really love the persons in the system: a characteristic Leavers' feature.

"I must not be misunderstood. Though I hold the British rule in India to be a curse, I do not, therefore, consider Englishmen in general to be worse than any other people on earth. I have the privilege of claiming many Englishmen as dearest friends. Indeed, much that I have learnt of the evil of British rule is due to the writings of frank and courageous Englishmen who have not hesitated to tell the unpalatable truth about that rule." In other words, Gandhi believed in conversion and not compulsion, so that the opponents of today might become the reformers of tomorrow.

So far, we have identified some of the cherished concerns of Gandhi for the Leavers as: identification with the "least, lost and lowest," interest for the individual's needs, priority to the basic needs of the people and respecting the persons in the system even when opposing the system.

In view of protecting sustainable village economy, Gandhi had very harsh words against industrialism and machinery. He is categorical in maintaining that "it is machinery that has impoverished India." For him, machinery is the chief symbol of modern (Takers') civilization; it represents a great sin.

Mahatmaji is clear in his affirmation: "My own view is that the evils are inherent in industrialism and no amount of socialism can eradicate them." But he adds his customary caution: "What I object to, is the craze for machinery not machinery as such. The craze is for what they call labour-saving machinery. Men go on `saving labour' till thousands are without work and thrown on the open streets to die of starvation." This reminds us that his criticism is not for its own sake but for the sake of those "thrown on the open streets to die of starvation." Further he is consistent when he asserts: "I am not against machinery as such, but I am totally opposed to it when it masters us."

Gandhi would categorically state his conviction that the mania for mass production is responsible for the world crisis. Granting for the moment that machinery may supply all the needs of humanity, still, it would concentrate production in particular areas, so that you would have to proceed in a round-about way to regulate distribution; whereas, if there is production and distribution both in the respective areas where things are required, it is automatically regulated, and there is less chance for fraud, none for speculation. The reason for his vehement criticism is also given by Gandhi himself. "Industrialization on a mass scale will necessarily lead to passive or active exploitation of the villagers as the problems of competition and marketing come in. Therefore, we have to concentrate on the village being self-contained, manufacturing mainly for use."

Gandhiji is of firm conviction, "Industrialism is, I am afraid, going to be a curse for mankind. Exploitation of one nation by another cannot go on for all time. Industrialism depends entirely on your capacity to exploit, on foreign markets being open to you, and on the absence of competition." Elsewhere he states explicitly. "I want the dumb millions of our land to be healthy and happy and I want them to grow spiritually. As yet for this purpose we do not need the machine." Therefore he affirms: "My fundamental objection to machinery rests on the fact that it is machinery that has enabled these nations to exploit others. In itself it is a wooden thing and can be turned to good purpose or bad."

He further stated, "At the same time I believe that some key industries are necessary. I do not believe in armchair or armed socialism. I believe in action according to my belief, without waiting for wholesale conversion." Further, he affirms: "I refuse to be dazzled by the seeming triumph of machinery. I am uncompromisingly against all destructive machinery. But simple tools and instruments . . . save individual labor and lighten the burden of millions of cottages, I should welcome."

Gandhi as realistic always concedes that machinery has its place; machines have in fact come to stay. But they must not be allowed to displace human labour. He would welcome every improvement in the cottage machine, but he knows that it is criminal to displace hand labor by the introduction of power-driven spindles. He is aware that persons cannot live without industry. "Therefore, I cannot be opposed to industrialization. But I have a great concern about introducing machine industry." "That use of machinery is lawful which subserves the interest of all."

Remarkably, a serious criticism against Gandhi's village

work was that he was turning his back on science and industry and advocating a primitive economy which would perpetuate poverty. In *Hind Swaraj*, Gandhi had criticized machinery, mills and industrial civilization, but during the next forty years of his life he further elaborated his ideas on machinery, relating them to his fundamental doctrine of non-violence. His principal objection to mechanization was that it tended to concentrate the production of wealth in a few hands (which is the grim reality). In a country where the hands were too many and the work too little, machinery could add to unemployment and poverty. "I would favour," he had written in 1921, "the use of the most elaborate machinery if thereby India's pauperism and resulting idleness could be avoided." There was a distinction in his mind, however, between `*mass production*' and `*production for the masses;*' the former under free enterprise often made the rich richer and the poor poorer. He was not opposed to machinery as such. Even his beloved spinning-wheel was machinery, but it was `machinery reduced to the terms of the masses.' He welcomed simple tools and instruments which `lightened the burden of the millions of cottages' without atrophying the limbs of persons. He also recognized that some of these comparatively simple machines, such as sewing machines required factories for their manufacture. "I am socialist enough to say," he added, "that such factories should be nationalized or state-controlled. They ought only to be working under the most attractive and ideal conditions, not for profit but for the benefit of humanity, love taking the place of greed as motive."

II

Despite tall talks, in the wake of new millennium, most third world nations are confronted by increasing poverty, illiteracy, population, environmental degradation, crime, corruption and social unrest. Liberalisation of economies and globalisation are often being projected as the panacea for all these problems. But this is sheer lie.

The unbridled growth in industrial activity in the developed nations has led to disturbing consequences such as unprecedented movement of materials, damage to the environment, and global warming. This is giving a false sense of prosperity but the basic problems of poverty, illiteracy, population, environmental degradation and social unrest continue to plague all developing nations.

Most third world countries on attaining independence, retained the centralised, non-transparent and bureaucratised exploitative colonial institutions. As a result, the national and state governments control most resources and decision-making whereas local governments are weak, ineffective and helpless.

On these, they superimposed Soviet type centralised planning and a controlled economy thus creating a mixed economy in a mixed-up polity. In such centralised systems, bureaucratic overheads, misuse of authority, wastage of resources and corruption are excessive and leave very little resources for the benefit of the society.

Many developing nations also adopted the British Westminster parliamentary system. With a mixed-up executive and legislature, every legislator is a potential minister. This fosters jockeying for power, abuse of authority, instability, jumbo cabinets, and bribing legislators. Legislators, who are expected to be watchdogs over the executive, often become mad or wild dogs of democracy!

While some other nations switched to the presidential system. However, since most power remained centralised with the national government and was not shared with local governments, the presidents often assumed dictatorial tendencies. Pakistan is the example where Army ruled the country in the name popular democracy.

Gandhi found the industrial revolution in the West under which large populations were moving from rural areas to congested cities, disturbing. Democracy, by definition, can neither be socialist nor capitalist. It can only be egalitarian, that is, all have equal political and social rights. Gandhi's search was for an alternative economic model that nurtured a humane society based on decentralised production systems, rooted in villages that acquire urban quality. Most essential goods that people need should be locally produced and consumed thus reducing pressure on transportation and energy consumption. He was not opposed to high science and technology but wanted it serve human needs with a human face, and not destroy human values.

Within local governance, Gandhi laid great emphasis on village governance since being at the grassroots level it constitutes direct democracy whereas all others are representative democracy. According to Indian scriptures, the village parliament consisting of all adult men and women control all village resources, officials and decision-making. Women have thus been franchised in India for 4000 years whereas they got enfranchised in the West only in this century. The village parliament elects the village head and councillors for day to day work usually for a year, and can remove them any time for misconduct. Counsellors are held in high esteem but if the community finds that any one of them has abused authority, he can be summarily removed through simple majority.

The village government gives land and other environmental resources on village lease for specific use. The community thus prevents misuse of land and protects the interests of the weak. Such grassroots empowerment regenerates the spiritual energies of the people for self-development as they are involved in day to day decisions about the community and the environment.

Remarkably, Nation-states all around the world are often created through wars and mergers whereas district or counties are generic. They generally form a mini-catchment in which people have cultural links and can traverse within a reasonable time. They constitute the highest level of local governance. They provide professional support to and coordinate village governments. An intermediate level government is often provided as a link between district and village governments. Large cities have autonomous city governments.

Most social and environmental matters are in the exclusive jurisdiction of local governments. Social or environmental conflict at the grassroots level should be mediated at the intermediate and finally at the district or city level. The state and national governments should have no jurisdiction over such issues. History has shown that communities have lived in harmony with each other at the local level, and that it is higher level politics, priesthood and feudal interests that have divided them. Gandhi was convinced that once control over local resources and decision-making is restored at the local level, most social and environmental issues and all social ills and discords will gradually give way to social harmony and economic self-reliance.

Importance of Regional Planning

Primarily most developing countries adopted Soviet type centralised planning. Under it, the national and state governments controlling most resources, allocate funds for various social, environmental and economic programmes, including social and physical infrastructure, and allocate them to local governments in the from of schemes with preconceived conditions and stipulators often not suiting local needs. This leads to wastage, heavy overheads and application of resources often not suiting local requirements. Centralised planning is linked with development economics. Development economics is a fake discipline that imposes programmes and schemes on local communities thus aliniating them from the decision-making processes. The only scientific method of planning is regional planning. Regional planning takes the available resources into consideration to prepare plans covering socio-economic, infrastructure and environmental issues, expressed in analytical, quantitative and special plans. These plans are reiteratively coordinated at the local, state and national levels. Satellite imagery and geographic information systems now facilitate such planning.

This type of planning was practised by many traditional societies. India has such a full-fledged such scientific planning discipline called vastu shastra. Colonial rule disrupted India from it traditional knowledge base and, in the name of modernity, insensitive leadership continued to pursue centralised systems.

Development economics, based on centralised planning, is a fake discipline. What we need is housewife economics — local governments handle housekeeping while state and national governments provide higher level infrastructure and coordination, but cannot interfere in housekeeping. Effective transparency mechanisms covering the sovereign rights of the people to information, consultation, participation and referendums prevents wasteful bureaucratic overheads, abuse of authority, corruption and wastage.

It is only through such true democracy that local communities can educate themselves, use the environment in a sustainable manner, and ensure adequate health-care to contain the population. It can also generate adequate resources to enable the state and national governments to provide higher level infrastructure including transportation. Needless to say, resource management should be through scientific regional planning, now facilitated though satellite imagery and geographic information systems.

[*Courtesy:* Kuruvilla Pandikattu. For subscribing views, we owe a deep sense of gratitude to the learned scholar.]

REFERENCES

1. Daniel Quinn, *Ishmael* (New York: A Bantam Book, 1995), pp. 38ff.
2. Kuruvilla Pandikattu, "Beyond the Colonial Past: A New Story-ing," *Jnanadeepa*, 1/2 (July 1998), pp. 23-33.
3. B.R. Nanda, *Mahatma Gandhi: A Biography*.
4. Shriman Narayan (ed.), *The Selected Works of Mahatma Gandhi* (Ahmedabad: Navajivan Publishing House, 1968), VI, p. 188.
5. M.K. Gandhi, *India of My Dreams* (Ahmedabad: Navajivan Publishing House, 1992), pp. 20-30.

Glossary

Advaita: Hindu philosophy of Monism or Non-dualism

Agiari: Zoroastrian fire-temple .

Ahimsa - Not harming living things. Philosophy of revering all life and refraining from harm to any living thing. Gandhi compared ahimsa to Christian charity to fellow people. In addition to this, Gandhi also developed the definition of this term to also include accepting bad treatment, humiliation and beatings from fellow humans without retaliating. Gandhi also found this principle in the Bible. If someone strikes you across your right cheek, offer him the left cheek too Non-violence; in its positive aspect-love for all living things.

Allah: Muslim name of God

Amanitvam: humility

Aparigraha: non-possession

Ardhangini: wife; the 'better half'.

Ashram - spiritual community: a commune or communal house whose members share spiritual goals and practices.

Asoka: Indian monarch of 3rd century B.C. famed for his renunciation of empire and conquest and for his rock-edicts embodying Buddhist *dharma.*

Atishudra: One lower than the *shudra,* the fourth caste at the bottom of Hindu social hierarchy; 'untouchable'.

Atman: soul

Avatar: literally, a 'descent'; incarnation of a deity, especially of Vishnu in the Hindu Trinity.

Bansi: bamboo flute as of the divine cowherd, Sri Krishna.

Bardoli: Gujarat village, connected with the Civil Disobedience Movement Bardoli Satyagraha.

Bhagwadgita: (see 'The Gita')

Bhakti: devotion.

Bhangi: *scavenger; sweeper.*

Bharat Mata: Mother India.

Bhogabhumi: Land of enjoyment

Bibhishan: brother of Ravana, in the *Ramayana,*known for his wise counsel.

Boers (War) - Descendents of white settlers that arrived in South Africa in 1653 mostly from Holland and Germany. The Boers always regarded themselves as the rightful rulers of South Africa. War broke out with the British between 1899-1902 who had arrived later in South African and also made a claim to the land. Britain wanted to take over the Boer states of *Transvaal* and *Orange Free State* because of their rich mineral deposits. The British won the war, but returned self-administration to the states a short time afterwards. Many Boers were large landowners and supported the apartheid regime.

Brahma: Hindu name of God the Creator,one of the Trinity.

Brahmachari: A celibate; one who observes Brahmacharya.

Brahmacharya: celibacy; code of conduct involving strict observance of chastity or continence in the pursuit of learning, philosophy and God.

Brahman, Brahmin: member of the first of the four castes, whose chief duty is the study and teaching of the Vedas and the performance of sacrifices and other religious rituals.

Buddha: a. founder of Buddhism, b. about 563, d. about 483 B.C; also known as Gautama, Siddhartha, Sakyamuni, etc.

Caste system - The caste system comes from *Hinduism* and separates the population into four classes: Brahmans/priests, Kshatrigas/warriors, Vaishiy/farmers and merchants and Shudras/laborers. Depending on the state, these four classes are sub-divided into over 1000 castes. *Parias,* that is, outcasts and untouchables are those who do not belong to a caste. Members of the lower castes were never fully accepted by society and often live in great poverty.

Chaitanya: Bengali religious reformer of the 15th century A.D. who is worshipped by his followers as an incarnation of Sri Krishna.

Chakki: Grinding wheel or mill.

Chapati: thin flat cakes made of flour; unleavened bread.

Charkha: Spinning-wheel.

Damayanti: Princess of Vidarbha and wife of Prince Nala of Naishadha, the constancy of whose devotion to each other forms the theme of a well-known episode in the Puranas.

Dandi March: March undertaken by Gandhiji from March 12 to April 5, 1930, from his Sabarmati Ashram to the coastal village of Dandi, about 100 miles distant, with a view to breaking the Salt Law by picking upnatural salt from the sea-shore. His arrest at Dandi was followed by a countrywide movement of Civil Disobedience famous as the Salt Satyagraha.

Daridranarayana: God in the form of the poor and the destitute.

Dasharatha: King of Ayodhya, father of Rama, in the *Ramayana.*

Dayanand: Swami Dayanand Saraswati (1824-83), founder of the Arya Samaj.

Dharma: religion; law of one's being; righteousness; Hindu code of religion and morals or religious and moral duty.

Dharmaja: one born from a sense ofduty.

Dharmayuddha: war fought for a righteous end by righteous means and methods.

Dheds: a community in Gujarat traditionally treated as 'untouchable'.

Dhoti - Indian article of clothing; a simple cloth that is worn similar to a loincloth.

Dhurna: 'sit-down' strike; an early andcrude form of Satyagraha.

Dnyandev: boy poet-saint of Maharashtra of the 13th century A.D., author of *Dnyaneshwari,* a Marathi commentary on the Gita; also spelt as Dnyaneshwar or Jnaneshwar.

Draupadi: consort of the Pandava Princes, in the *Mahabharata.*

Dublas: a backward *shudra* community of Gujarat

Duryodhana: Head of the Kaurava Princes, in the *Mahabharata.*

Dyer: British General who fired on an unarmed assembly in Jallianwala Bagh, Amritsar, on April 13, 1919, killing over 400 people.

Ganga: the sacred river Ganges of Northern India.

Ganja: narcotic from the flower of Indian hemp.

Ghani: village oil mill.

Ghee: clarified butter.

Gita, the: The 'Song Celestial'; a Hindu scriptural work in sanskrit verse, composed some centuries before the Christian era, in which Sri Krishna sums up the essence of Hindu religion and philosophy.

Gokhale, Gopal Krishna: Member of the *Indian National Congress* founded in 1885. He was one of the most important political leaders during India's struggle for independence and a friend of Gandhi.

Gopal Krishna Gokhale (1866-1915), Indian politician, member of the Viceroy's Legislative Council and founder of the Servants of India Society, whom Gandhiji acknowledged as his political *guru.*

Goonda: a rowdy or hooligan.

Goondaism: rowdyism

Gopal: cowherd; a name of Sri Krishna.

Goseva: service of the cattle;cow-protection..

Gram Panchayat: village tribune or 'council of five'.

Gram sevak: person employed in village service.

Gramseva: village service.

Gujarati - a member of a people chiefly of Gujarat speaking the Gujarati language.

Gur: jaggery, indigenous form of sugarmolasses

Guru: teacher; preceptor.

Hakim: practitioner of indigenous form of medicine.

Hanuman: The 'Monkey-God' who serves Ramā in the *Ramayana.*

Harijan: a member of the outcaste group in India: untouchables

Hartal: strike, suspension of normal business.

Hinduism - Religion that originated in India and is still practiced by most of its inhabitants, as well as by those whose families have migrated from India to other parts of the world (chiefly East Africa, South Africa, Southeast Asia, the East Indies, and England). The word Hindu is derived from the Sanskrit word sindhu ("river," more specifically, the Indus); the Persians in the 5th century bc called the Hindus by that name, identifying them as the people of the land of the Indus. The Hindus' own definitions of their community are "those who believe in the Vedas" (see Veda) or "those who follow the way (dharma) of the four classes (varnas) and stages of life (ashramas)." Hinduism is a major world religion, not merely by virtue of its many followers (estimated at more than 700 million) but also because of its profound influence on many other religions during its long, unbroken history, beginning about 1500 BC. The corresponding influence of these various religions on Hinduism (it has an extraordinary tendency to absorb foreign elements) has greatly contributed to the religion's syncretism-the wide variety of beliefs and practices that it encompasses. Moreover, the geographic, rather than ideological, basis of the religion (the fact that it consists of whatever all the people of India have believed and done) has given Hinduism the character of a social and doctrinal system that extends to every aspect of human life. The *caste system* stems from Hinduism.

Hooghli: western most branch of the River Ganges on the banks of which Calcutta is situated.

INC (Indian National Congress) - The INC was founded in 1885 to represent the Indian population in the lands occupied by the British. Under the leadership of Gandhi, the INC developed into a mass paty, which has been represented in the Indian parliament almost unbrokenly since Indian independence

Indigo - Indigo is one of the earliest dyes and was previously very important. It is obtained from indigo plants.

Ishopanishad: one of the major Upanishads.

Jainism: ancient Indian religion, one of the cardinal principles of which is non-violence.

Jains: followers of Jainism.

Janak: philosopher-king of Videha,foster-father of Sita, in the *Ramayana*.

Kabir: poet-saint of northern India,who lived in the 15th century A.D. and who, in his devotional songs, dwelt on the essential oneness of the Godhead and the harmony between Hinduism and Islam.

Kamaja: one born of lust.

Karmabhumi: land of duty.

Karmayogi: one who has devoted his life to action in the selfless service of others.

Khaddar, Khadi: hand-spun and hand-woven cloth.

Kisan: peasant.

Koran: Muslim scripture.

Krishna: divine hero and central figure of the epic, *Mahabharata*, who is worshipped by the Hindus as the 8th incarnation of God.

Kshatriya: member of thesecond (warrior) caste among Hindus.

Likud Block - the Likud, a conservative group formed in 1973 by the merger of several organizations, including the Gahal and Free Center parties.

Lila, leela: divine play or sport; the creation is often explained by the Vaishnavas as the *leela* of God, a conception that introduces elements of spontaneity and freedom into the universe.

Lok Sevak Sangh: Society or association for the service of the people.

Mahabharata, the: Hindu epic having for its theme the story of the great war between the Pandavas and the Kauravas, princes of the Lunar race who were cousins, rival claimants to the throne of Hastinapur, (ancient Delhi).

Mahatma: a person to be revered for high-mindedness, wisdom, and selflessness. The name was given to Gandhi by the Indian people.

Mahavir: Vardhamana. 24th Tirthankar or Prophet of Jainism (b. about 540, d. about 468 B.C.) who is popularly regarded as its greatest promulgator, originally named

mantra, Mantram: sacred or magicalincantation.

Manushya: man.

Marriiage laws: The marriage law was introduced into South African in 1913. According to the law only those marriages that were Christian and which had been authorized by a South African registrar were valid. Hindu and Muslim marriages from India were no longer recognized. This meant that Indian women lost their status. From now on they were regarded only as lovers. This, in turn, created immigration problems and trouble with residence permits, since women were only allowed to stay in the country provided they were married. In addition to this, the new law meant that they lost their dignity. The children of such marriages also lost their status. The consequence of this meant that they were regarded as illegitimate and, for example, lost their right to inheritance.

Massacre of Amritsar - Amritsar is a city in the state of Punjab near the boarder to Pakistan. Thousands of Indians gathered in the city's square in 1919 for a peaceful demonstration. The British army sealed off all the entrances to the square and fired indiscriminately into the crowd. The General in charge of the army later admitted that his aim had been to kill all Indians. He was not punished for his actions, but did leave his post following recommendations by the investigating committee. The massacre caused outrage across India.

Maya: illusion; in Hindu philosophy, Maya is the divine power which has created the cosmos.

Mhayajna: the great sacrifice or ritual of propitiation.

Moksha: liberation from earthly bondage.

Muni: sage; ancient seer.

Nai Talim: literally, 'new education',name given to basic or craft education.

Namaz: form of Muslim prayer, worship.

Nanak: Founder of Sikhism (b.1469-d.1538 or 1539 A.D.)

Natal - A province in the east of South Africa that was a British Crown colony until 1910. Durban is situated in Natal.

Nirvana: Salvation, Buddhist equivalent of ' Moksa'

Orange Free state - South African province; it was founded in 1854 as the second "free Boer republic".

Pancha, Panchayat: the five; the communal tribune or 'council of five'

Panchayat Raj: rule of the Panchayat

Pandavas: the five brothers, prices ofthe Lunar Race, who were the victor in the Maharashtra war

Paria - Pariahs are those without a caste they are also called the untouchables. They are at the very bottom of Indian society. They are prevented from entering into many parts of Indian public life. For example they are not permitted to draw water from village wells, because the rest of the residents would be fearful of becoming unclean. Gandhi stood up for the untouchables, calling them God's children.

Pinjrapoles: institutions for looking after old and disabled cattle

Poorna Swaraj: full self-government or complete independence

Prahlad: son of Hiranyakashipu, amythological demon king; Prahlad's worship of Vishnu led to persecution by his father who was ultimately slain by Narasimha, the ' Man-Lion' avatar of Vishnu

Pritam: Pritamdas, Gujarati poet ofthe 16th century A.D. who composed numerous devotional songs

Raj: kingdom, rule, regime

Rajachandra, Raychandbhai: Jain saint and philosopher, contemporary of Gandhiji, whom the latter acknowledged as his spiritual GURU. He died in 1900

Ram, Rama: hero of the epic, RAMAYANA,who is regarded by Hindus as an ideal man and king, and worshipped as the 7 thin carnation of God

Ramakrishna: Bengali saint (1836-86 A.D.) who was the GURU of Swami Vivekananda and who taught the oneness of the Godhead and the basic harmony of all religions. The Ramakrishna Mission is named after him

Ramanuja: Vaishnava scholar of the 12th century, who propounded Dualistic philosophy

Ramayana: Hindu epic narrating the story of the abduction of Sita, wife of Rama, prince of Ayodhya, by Ravana, demon-kingof Lanka and her rescue after the conquest of Lanka by the armies led by Rama and the death of Ravana at Rama's hands.

Ramji Mandir: Rama's temple

Ravana: the demon-king of Lanka, whose abduction of

Sita, led to his destruction at Rama's hands, in the *Ramayana*.

Registration law - in 1907 a registration law was introduced into South Africa. According to the law, all Indians were required to register themselves with a fingerprint under a description of their person. They were then given a registration certificate that had to be carried with them at all times. Non-cooperation would be met with deportation to India.

Rowlett Act - Named after its inventor Judge Rowlett; an emergency decree was imposed over parts of India according to which people suspected of committing political crimes could be sentenced without trial. Fair trials and constitutional law were no longer in force.

Ruskin, John (1819-1900) - English writer, art critic, and reformer, a dominant tastemaker among intellectuals of the Victorian period. His book entitled Unto this Last made a deep impression on Gandhi and affected his thinking on the kind of structure society should strive for. He implemented these ideas on his farms and in Ashram. Other actions, too, such as the Spinning Wheel Campain was derived from this thinking.

Sadavrat: charity

Sahadharmin: wife

Samagra Gramseva: all-round village service

Samskaras: innate tendencies inherited from past life, religious customs

Sanatanist: faithful follower of ancient Vedic religion

Sannyas: abandonment of all worldly ties with a view to fixing the mind on the Supreme Being

Sannyasi: one who has taken to SANYAS

Sarvodaya: welfare of all

Satvika: tending to truth

Satya: truth

Satyagraha - Philosophy of nonviolent protest, or passive resistance. M. Gandhi introduced it in S. Africa (1906) and, from 1917, developed it in India in the period leading up to independence from Britain. Satyagraha seeks to conquer through submission. It involves refusing to submit to or cooperate with anything perceived as wrong, while adhering to the principle of nonviolence in order to maintain the tranquillity of mind required for insight and understanding. The principle played a significant role in the U.S. civil rights movement led by Martin Luther King. The best known Satyagraha campaign was the Salt March in 1930.

Satyagraha: recourse to truth-force or soul-force.

Satygrahi: one who practises Satyagraha.

Savitri: wife of Satyavan who according to legend, reclaimed his life from the God of Death.

Scharon, Ariel - Israeli soldier and right-wing politician. Sharon was born in Kfar Malal. He had a long military career, serving in several positions in the Israeli Defence Forces (IDF). Sharon headed the commando group known as Unit 101, which was set up in 1953 to conduct reprisal operations against Arab marauders, and was Head of Southern Command from 1970 to 1973. Sharon played a central role in the breakthrough to the west bank of the Suez Canal, as a reserve commander, during the Yom Kippur War (1973). He served as defence adviser to the government from 1975 to 1976. In the national unity government formed jointly by Likud and Labour in 1984, Sharon served as Trade and Industry Minister. Sharon is widely seen as a prominent member of the right within Likud. In September 1999 he became the party's leader, replacing the former prime minister Binyamin Netanyahu who resigned after losing the election in May.

Shankara: Hindu philosopher of the 8th century A.D. who was one of the foremost exponents of Non-dualism of the Vedanta school of philosophy.

Shastras: the Hindu scriptures

Shloka: metrical verse or composition

Shudra: member of the fourth or menialcaste among Hindus

Sita: wife of Rama

Smritis: the Codes, based onrecollection of the Shastras

Sthitaprajna: literally, 'one of steadfast mind' ; a soul unaffected by extremes of joy and sorrow

Sudama: the indigent boyhood friend and associate of Shri Krishna, whom the latter hours, in the BHAGAVATA

Surdas: blind Hindi poet of northern India wholived in the 16th century A.D.; his poetical work, Sursagar, narrating thestory of Krishna, is immensely popular with Hindi-speaking Hindus

Swadeshi: belonging to or made in one's own country

Swargarohan Parva: the name of the last of the eighteenth sections of the epic MAHABHARATA which describes how, when Yudhisthira, the eldest of the five Pandava brothers, retired to the Himalayas, towardsthe close of his life, and lost his wife and four brothers one after another, Indraappeared in his chariot to take him in the flesh to his (Indra's) SWARGA, i.e, hisheaven where mortals after death enjoy the results of their good deeds on earth,

Tadgud: Jaggery prepared from the juice of palmyra fruit

Tapascharya: penance

Tilaks: Sandalwood/vermilion caste-marks on the forehead

Transvaal - Founded in 1884 with the amalgamation of several smaller Boer states into a independent Boer republic; rich in minerals such as diamonds, gold, platinum and uranium; capital was Pretoria.

Tukaram: Poet-saint of Maharashtra who lived in the 17th century A. D. and who composed thousands of devotional songs

Tulsidas: Hindi poet of northern India who lived in the 16th century A.D. and who composed, among other works, *Ramacharitamanasa,* (lit. The Holy Pool of the Life of Rama), retelling the epic story of the exploits of Rama. This work is held in the highest veneration by all Hindi-speaking Hindus

Upanishads: ancient Hindu philosophical treatises, appended to the Vedas and regarded as equally authoritative as the Vedas

Vaidas: practitioner of Ayurveda system of indigenous Indian medicine

Vaishyas: members of the third Varna (cultivator and mercantile class) among Hindus

Valmiki: first of Sanskrit poets and author of the Hindu epic, RAMAYANA

Varna: colour; one of the four divisions of Hindu society (i.e., Brahman, Kshatriya, Vaishya and Shudra) based on hereditary occupations

Varnashrama: four-fold division of Hindu society

Vedanta: a system of philosophy springing from the Upanishads

Vedas: most ancient Hindu scriptures,composed of hymns to various deities. There are four collections of these hymns, known as Rigveda, Samaveda, Yajurveda and Atharvaveda

Vidura: the low-born but 'wise one'in the MAHABHARATA honoured by Sri Krishna

Yajna: ritual or religious sacrifice

Yoga: Hindu system of contemplation for effecting union of the human soul with the Supreme Being

Yogi: one who practises yoga

Yudhishthira: Eldest of the Pandava Princes, celebrated for his right conduct

Zamindar: Land holder

Zend Avesta: Zoroastrian scriptures

Zoroaster: Founder of religious system known as Zoroastrianism. He is also known as Zarathustra or Zerdusht. The Parsis of India, who areemigrants from Persia, are followers of this prophet

Zulu rising - In 1906 there was a rising of the Zulus in *Natal,* which led to bloody battles with the British. Inidans were deployed as paramedics on the British side.

Bibliography

Arunachalam, K. , "Sarvodaya Approach to *Social Development Aspect of Social Education* ASSWI pp. 25-26.

Bharati, K.S. (2005), *Encyclopaedia of Gandhian Thought* (6 vols.), Anmol, New Delhi.

Boss, P. (1967), *Social Policy and the Young Delinquent*, Routledge and Kegan Paul, London, p. 30.

Brij Mohan Sharma (1933), *Swami Dayanand*, pp. 120-122.

Charles, K.J. (1983), *Total Development,* New Delhi: Vikas Publishing House Pvt. Ltd., p. 94.

Collected Works of Mahatma Gandhi (1932), Publication Division, Delhi, Vol. 52, p. 48.

Corrigan, P. and P. Leonard (1978), *Social Work Practice Under Capitalism*, Macmillan, London. P. Halmos, *The Personal and the Political* (Hutchison, London, 1978).

D. Donnison *et al.* (1975), *Social Policy and Administration Revisited,* revised edn. Alen and Unwin, London, p. 21.

Daniel Quinn (1995), *Ishmael,* New York: A Bantam Book, pp. 38ff.

Department of Social Welfare (1976), Ministry of Education and Social Welfare, Government of India, *Handbook on Social Welfare Statistics.* New Delhi.

Elwin, *The Foreign Missionary Danger.*

Fletcher, R. (1962), *The Family and Marriage* (Penguin Books, Harmondsworth.

Gandhi 'Question Box', *Harijan* 26 July 1912.

George S.K. and G. Ramachandran (1952), *Economic Peace,* Wardha, p. 148.

Gandhi, Mahatma, *Harijan Sewak,* 15.9.1946.

Gandhi, Mahatma (1949), *The Problem of Education,* Ahmedabad.

Gandhi, Mahatma (1960), *Trusteeship,* Ahmedabad, pp. 3-49.

Gandhi, Mahatma, *Young India,* 6 December 1928.

Gandhi, 'New Year' in *Indian Opinion* 2.1.1909.

Gandhi, 'The Secret of Swaraj', *'Young India'* 19.1.1921.

Gandhi, 23 January 1935 quoted by S. Radhakrishnan, *Contemporary India* (London: Allen and Unwin, 1938), p. 21.

Gandhi, *Harijan* 6 Feb. 1931 quoted by J.D. Sethi, *Gandhi Today* (New Delhi : Vikas Publishing House Pvt. Ltd., 1979), p. 138.

Gandhi, *Hind Swaraj,* 1908.

Gandhi, M.K., *Hindu Dharma,* Navajivan Publishing House, Ahmedabad, 1950, p. 24.

Gandhi, M.K., *India of My Dreams* (Ahmedabad: Navajivan Publishing House, 1992), pp. 20-30.

Gandhi, M.K., *Women and Social Injustice,* p. 4.

Gandhi, Mahatma, *Young India* quoted by Ravindra Nath Mukherjee, *Social Thought* (Mousoorie Saraswati Sadan 1965), p. 369.

Gandhi, quoted by R.N. Mukherjee, *Social Thought,* p. 416.

Gandhi, Yervada Mandir Chapter VI 1930 quoted by Charles, *Total Development.* 1983, p. 95.

Gandhi, *Young India,* 13 Nov. 1924, pp. 85-86.

Greek Dorothy (1974), "An Interview with Paul Samuelson *Spain,* June.

Hancock Nunn, T., *The Minority Report* (National Poor Law Reform Association, undated), p. 10.

Har Bilas Sarda (1946), *Life of Dayanand Saraswati*, pp. 446-47.

Harijan, different issues.

Heimsath, *Indian Nationalism and Hindu Social Reform,* Oxford University Press, Bombay, 1964, pp. 21-22.

Hiralal Shukla, *Bastar ke Van Vasi Geeton men Gandhi.* The, *Adibasi,* Ranchi.

HMSO, *Parliamentary Debates, Standing Committees* (Vol. 11, session 1969-70), Committee B, sitting 1, column 5.

Home Office, *Report of the Committee on Children and Young Persons* (HMSO, London, 1960), Cmnd. 1191.

Jagannadham, V., *Administration and Social Change* (New Delhi: Uppal Publishing House, 1978), p. 162.

Jagdisan, T.N. and Shyam Lal (eds), *Thakkar Bapa, Eightieth Birthday Commemoration Volume.*

Jaggannadham, *Administration and Social Change* (New Delhi: Uppal Publishing House, 1978), p. 161.

Kalia, S.L., "The Raj Mohini Devi Movement in Surguja".

Kripalani, J.B., *Gandhi: His Life and Thought,* Delhi, 1970.

Kriplani, J.B. (1979), *Gandhi—His Life and Thoughts,* New Delhi : Sangram Books, p. 368.

Krishna Kripalani, 'Gandhi and Womanhood' in *India Horizons.* Vol. XXIV, No. 4, 1975, p. 26.

Kuruvilla Pandikattu, "Beyond the Colonial Past: A New Storying," *Jnanadeepa,* 1/2 (July 1998), pp. 23-33.

Lajpat Rai, "Gandhi and Non-co-operation" in Bianche Watson (ed.), *Gandhi and Non-violent Resistance: the Non-co-operative movement of India* (1923), p. 396.

Marshall, *Social Policy,* Chapter 5, especially pp. 74-6.

Mirza Ahmed (1991), "Social Development and Human Rights" *Journal of Social Work* (Lucknow), p. 3.

Nehru, *A Bunch of Old Letters,* 1958, pp. 506-7.

Nehru, *The Discovery of India,* p. 25.

Pani, Susmit et al. (2008), *Reflections on Gandhi: The Forgotten Mahatma*, Zenith Books International, Delhi.

Pradhan *et al* (ed.), *Anthropology and Archaeology, Essays in Commemoration of Verrier Elwin.* (quoted from *A.A.S.*, vol. 1, No. 2, 1966: 162).

Pyare Lal, *Harijan* 25 Nov. 1952.

Pyarelal, "Bapa of Bapu".

Ramchandra Guha, "Guardians of the Gandhian Way," *Indian Express* Magazine Section October, 7, 1990), p. 4.

Rao, V.K.R.V., *The Gandhian Alternative to Western Socialism* (New Delhi: Bhartiya Vidya Bhawan Publication, 1958), pp. 47.

Seed, P. *The Expansion of Social Work in Britain* (Routledge and Kegan Paul, London, 1973).

Sethi, J.D., *Gandhi Today*, p. 139.

Sharma, D.S., *Renaissance of Hinduism* (1944), pp. 178-79.

Shastri, Raja Ram, *Social Work Tradition in India.* Welfare Forum and Research Organisation, Varanasi, 1966, pp. 2-3.

Shriman Narayan (ed.), *The Selected Works of Mahatma Gandhi* (Ahmedabad: Navajivan Publishing House, 1968), VI, p. 188.

Singh, A.B., (1991) "Towards Gandhian Philosophy of Social Development in India" *Journal of Social Work* Vol. VIII (Lucknow: Dept. of Social Work Lucknow University), p. 69.

Sugata Dasgupta, "Local Community and New Economic Order", *Perspectives on Voluntary Action*, pp. 25-26.

Sukhamoy Chakravarty (1987), *Development Planning* (Delhi: Oxford University Press), p. 8.

Suresh Singh, "The Haribaba Movement in Chotanagpur 1931-32".

Tendulkar D.G., *Mahatma*, vol. 8, p. 28.

Thakkar Bapa (1938), "Aborigines of Orissa,' *Modern Review*, Sept. quoted in the footnote of the *Commemoration Volume*, p. 78.

Thakkar, A.V., *Aboriginals' Cry in the Wilderness.*

The Family and the Young Offender (HMSO, London, 1965). Cmnd. 2742.

Townsend, P. (1976), *Sociology and Social Policy*, Penguin Books, Harmondsworth.

Vaze, S.G., "Thakkar Bapa, a tribute".

Victor S. D'Souza (1991), Harnessing Lok Shakti for Development" *Perspectives on Voluntary Action* (New Delhi: NIPCCD Publication), p. 3.

Wadia, A. R. (1961), "Ethical and Spiritual Values in the Practice of Social Work", in A. R. Wadia (ed.), *History and Philosophy of Social Work in India*, Allied Publishers Private Limited, Bombay, p. 15.

Whittaker (1974), J.K., *Social Treatment*, Aldine, Chicago.

Winslow, C., Jack and Verrier Elwin, The *Dawn of India's Freedom.*

Index

G

H

I

K

L

M

N

O

P